The Ultimate Wine Lover's Guide

2005

BARNES & NOBLE BOOKS

NEW YORK

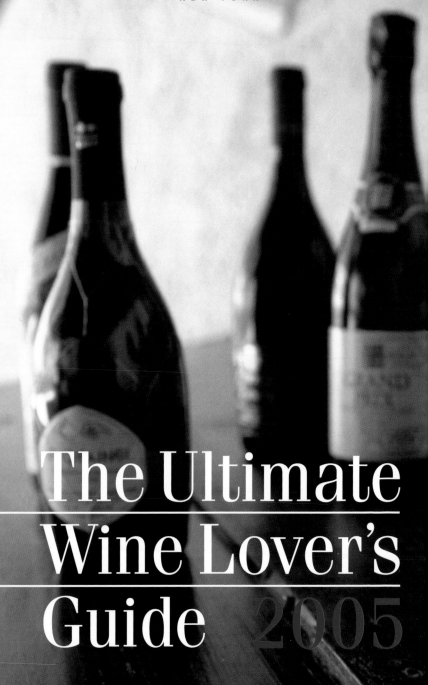

The Ultimate
Wine Lover's
Guide 2005

FRED DuBOSE
EVAN SPINGARN
WITH
NANCY MANISCALCO

The Ultimate Wine Lover's Guide 2005

© 2004 by Barnes & Noble Publishing, Inc.
Photography and illustration credits are found on page 272
and constitute an extension of this copyright page.

FIRST EDITION

2004 Barnes & Noble Books

Barnes & Noble Publishing
122 Fifth Avenue
New York, NY 10011

ISBN 0-7607-5832-0

First Printing

Printed and bound in China

Design: Richard J. Berenson
           BERENSON DESIGN & BOOKS, Ltd.,
           New York, NY

CONTENTS

Welcome!

*G*ETTING TO KNOW WINE is an adventure, and few journeys are more leisurely, interesting, and fun—something you, as a wine lover, probably already know. If you're a beginner just striking out, get set for a wonderful trip. Even the most seasoned connoisseur will find new territory to explore, and this book is a companionable guide.

Wine is typically enjoyed—and is best understood—in the company of food. That has been its traditional role from the feasts of the pharaohs to the banquets of ancient Rome to the modern restaurant wine list. Some people even think of wine as a sort of condiment for food, an endlessly variable "sauce" of sorts that uplifts both the dinner and the one who dines. With this in mind, each description of the 1,000 + wines in *The Ultimate Wine Lover's Guide* includes a food–pairing suggestion.

In 1992 Nancy Maniscalco (pictured at right with Evan Spingarn) opened Nancy's Wines for Food on the Upper West Side of Manhattan, sparking a wine boutique trend that continues to this day. Small, friendly and welcoming, with its wines lined invitingly against the walls and tagged with handwritten cards describing them, the store offers scores of terrific wines, many under $10; unusual finds from all over the world; and a philosophy that personal taste and enjoyment always trump the worship of labels. The shop was, and remains, a place where any wine snobbery should be left in the wet umbrella stand by the front door.

The same philosophy underpins this book. Nancy, her expert staff, and co-author Evan Spingarn (wine educator, writer, and former wine manager of the store), have sifted through twelve years of wine–buying (and many more of tasting!) to recommend their favorites in each price range—and in so doing, expand the consumer's horizons. More than a shopping list, *The Ultimate Wine Lover's Guide* is an introduction to wines you don't want to miss.

Some of these wines are famous, and justly so. Others are bargains, simple and pleasing. But beyond the advertised brands and the flashes-in-the-pan lies another tier, a category of wines that as yet fits no

marketing plan. They are first and foremost food wines. Such wines appear in the carafes and tumblers of bistros as well as the dusty cellars of a chateau. And in both places, we can search them out: the hidden gems, the true originals, the wines that have something to say. When you find them, you come to understand the difference between wines made for the collector or trader or swigger and those made for that luckiest of creatures—the average wine lover.

How the Book Works

In the interest of practicality, the book groups wines by price bracket, from the least expensive to the most. In the Primary Red Grapes and Primary White Grapes chapters, grapes like Cabernet Sauvignon, Merlot, Chardonnay, and Sauvignon Blanc are featured because their wines are what most American wine lovers drink.

♣ Chapters featuring the wines of secondary, or lesser known, grapes—Other Choice Reds and Other Choice Whites—introduce you to some of the best blended and single-grape wines out there, while a chapter on sparkling wines ventures well beyond the borders of

Champagne. Fittingly, the book ends with an eclectic and tempting collection of fortified and dessert wines.

❧ A Country and Region special index enables you to locate at a glance the book's Burgundies, Bordeaux, Sancerres, American wines, Australian and New Zealand wines, and a scattering of those from other parts of the world.

❧ A Food and Wine special index guides you to the wines that pair well with meats, cheeses, pizzas, egg dishes, vegetables, salads, and more.

❧ Separate appendices provide contact information for every domestic winery represented in the book, as well as for the wealth of importers of foreign wines.

Terminology

Wine has a language much its own, meaning you're likely to come across some unfamiliar terms. What's the difference between an appellation (which, depending on the country, can be referred to as AOC or DOC) and a winegrowing region? What's the translation of foreign terms such as *terroir* and *Grand Cru* and *cuvée*, and why is it a good idea for any wine lover to understand what they mean? The Glossary pages 218–223) will help make sense of the standard wine vocabulary, so don't forget to turn to it as necessary.

WINESPEAK

In typical wine writing, the words chosen to describe a wine's flavors and aromas can seem over the top, and often are. How on earth are you to know how "crushed seashells" taste or how "underbrush" smells? Still, one must have a point of reference.

A century ago wine vocabulary was based on social class, with wines described as noble, well bred, or classic. The descriptors later shifted to terms based largely on gender—feminine, delicate, and soft as opposed to manly, muscular, and robust. It wasn't until the 1970s that the comparisons to fruits, vegetables, and minerals came to the fore. There's no question that this newer vocabulary offers more room for comparison—and some wines do indeed taste distinctly of grapefruit or cherries or minerality. Other descriptors merely give us the idea: for fruity wines, orchard fruits, citrus, or berries; for herby wines, lavender or bay leaf; for sweetly scented wines, jasmine, violets, or roses; for minerally wines, wet stones or slate.

Don't let such words intimidate you. They're meant to help, and you'll soon enough be coming up with your own.

Reading the Wine Descriptions

The descriptions of the wines recommended in *The Ultimate Wine Lover's Guide* follow the same format, and the sample entry shown here will familiarize you with it.

Note: While naming the wines also follows a set format, the names may not be exactly as they appear on the wine label. The aim is to give you all the words you or a wine merchant will need to identify the wine, with the key words set in capital letters.

1. Winery/Producer	**Ferngrove**
2. Type of wine	**SHIRAZ**
3. Body and Nutshell description	**Medium-bodied. Plush fruit, modest tannins, and real intensity.**
4. Description and Food suggestion(s)	Made from grapes grown in an unusually cool region in Western Australia, this Shiraz has an impressive density of fruit spiced up with herbs, mint, and loads of black pepper. More Rhône-like than classic Aussie, it's elegant with herbed red meats and cold cuts.
5. Price	$10-12
6. Place of origin	*Frankland River, Western Australia*
7. Importer	*Imported by Bayfield*

1. Winery/Producer

It may be the boldest or the smallest name on the label, but this is the most important piece of information you need to identify a wine. It is the legal title of the estate or co-op or person who created the wine.

2. Type of wine

In Europe, wines are generally named for where they're from, such as Chianti, Bordeaux, or Rioja. In the United States and other countries, wines are most often named for the grape they're made from, such as Cabernet, Chardonnay, or Riesling. (See page 88.)

3. Body and nutshell description

The first boldface notation gives the impression of "weight" in a wine, whether full, medium, light, or somewhere in between. (Remember that a wine can be light-bodied, but still "full" of flavor.) The second boldface notation usually refers to mouthfeel, but mainly serves to make it easier to compare one wine to another within a price bracket.

4. Description and food suggestions

The description of the wine, which also often notes something of interest about the vineyard or winemaker, will vary in length. The food–and–wine suggestions are based on either regional tradition, actual experience with the wines at the table, or both. Please remember that these suggestions are meant to be merely representative of the kinds of foods the wine pairs well with, not by any means the only appropriate choices. Your palate is the final judge.

5. Price

The prices given are ballpark figures. They are based on a standard retail mark–up (generally 50%) from known wholesale prices, confirmed by prices found in actual stores and on the Internet.

6. Place of origin

Where the wine was made. U.S. wines specify a region as well as a state when possible. If no region or town is given, it is because the grapes for the wine came from more than one place. For example, if half a wine's fruit came from Napa and the other half from Monterey, its appellation is simply "California," the common denominator for both appellations.

7. Importer

Foreign wines can have multiple importers on a national level, so although the importer we name is one source for the wine, it may or may not be the source for it in your area. For an explanation of how an importer might help you find a wine, see page 228.

Locating Wines

Your friendly local wine merchant is your best information source when you're unable to locate one of the wines described in *The Ultimate Wine Lover's Guide* (and any other publication, for that matter). As a back–up, all of the U.S. wineries and foreign wine importers are listed, starting on pages 224 and 228 respectively. Also check out the special feature "Find That Wine!" on page 200.

If all your efforts come to naught, there's another tack to take: Describe the elusive wine's characteristics to your wine merchant and see what he or she recommends as a substitute. It's true that no two wines are identical, but you know your taste in wine. The time and effort you put into wine appreciation may reap undreamed–of rewards.

CHAPTER ONE

Primary Red Grapes

The high-flying grapes of red winedom are a multicultural bunch—among them, Cabernet Sauvignon and Merlot from France, Nebbiolo and Sangiovese from Italy, and Zinfandel, an honorary Californian by way of Eastern Europe.

What makes reds red? The inclusion of pigment-rich grape skins during the fermentation process. With rare exceptions, grape flesh is too pale to give wine even the blush of a rosé, much less the blackish red of a Syrah.

Cabernet Franc

This early-maturing black grape has been cultivated in France for more than five centuries. A major component in the wines of Bordeaux, it comes into its own in the Loire.

ABERNET FRANC is the gentle grandfather to Cabernet Sauvignon's red-blooded *bon vivant*, yielding wines with a bit less body and tannin. As a matter of fact, the grapes are indeed close relatives: Recent tests at the University of California at Davis found Cabernet Franc and Sauvignon Blanc to be Cabernet Sauvignon's ancestors—and whether because of cross-breeding or a happy accident of pollination is anyone's guess.

Native to France, Cabernet Franc is frequently blended with Cabernet Sauvignon and Merlot in the wines from the Médoc, Graves, and St. Émilion districts of Bordeaux. In the Loire Valley, however, Cab Franc stands alone, creating fruitier, lighter wines than those of Bordeaux and typically graced with aromas and flavors redolent of raspberries, bell peppers, and herbs.

Cabernet Franc–dominant wines have what is called in wine lingo "lively acidity"—a characteristic that works in their favor at the dinner table. Cab Francs go particularly well with roasted meats, fatty fish like salmon and tuna, and green salads and vegetables. Yet despite their many charms, searching for quality Cabernet Francs from any country or region is no easy task. If a wine store stocks them at all, they are likely to be outnumbered ten to one by Cabernet Sauvignon.

Outside France, Cabernet Franc has long been grown in Italy, espe-

cially in the northeastern region of Friuli. In the United States, it is found in the cool, inland climates in which it thrives—mostly California's Napa and Sonoma valleys, the Pacific Northwest, and New York State, but also in parts of the Southwest and Southeast.

Under $12

Caves des Vignerons de Saumur
SAUMUR-CHAMPIGNY
Light-bodied.
Nicely fruity and juicy.
This "bistro red"—casual, inexpensive, and meant for immediate drinking—comes from a quality-minded cooperative of French growers. Serve it lightly chilled with appetizers or spicy fare. $6–8
Loire, France
Imported by Fruit of the Vine

Jacky et Fabrice Gasnier
CHINON "Les Graves"
Light- to medium-bodied.
Soft yet lively, with a bright finish.
Hints of earthiness and cedar waft from this raspberryish wine, which has surprising length of flavor. It's a fine choice for herbed fish or greens. $10–12
Loire, France
Imported by Sussex

Mionetto
CABERNET FRANC
Medium-bodied. Succulent, fruity, and fairly intense.
The largest Prosecco maker in Italy also turns out some especially food-friendly reds and whites, with this wine a prime example. Herby, berryish, and lively on the palate, it enhances the flavor of classic Mediterranean ingredients like olives, broccoli rabe, peppers, and tomatoes. It's also an excellent red to serve with fish. $10–12
Veneto, Italy
Imported by House of Burgundy

Domaine Saint Vincent
SAUMUR-CHAMPIGNY
"Les Trezelliéres"
Light- to medium-bodied.
Succulent and well balanced.
This Cab Franc is the red wine you imagine you'll sip while sitting in a café in Paris, perusing the newspaper and snacking on a baguette or omelet. $10–12
Loire, France
Imported by Winebow

Domaine du Roncée
CHINON
Light- to medium-bodied.
Vibrant, zesty, and full of fruit.
This reliable bargain Chinon sports red currants and cherries all over. It's all the more delightful with a light chill. Think cold cuts, ham sandwiches, and traditional and veggie pâtés. $10–12
Loire, France
Imported by Langdon Shiverick

$12 to $20

La Tunella
CABERNET FRANC
Medium-bodied. Succulent and meaty on the palate.
Vintner Livio Zorzettig's enticing Cabernet Franc smells of sweet herbs, tastes like ripe berries, and works with food as few other wines can. Vegetables, tomato-based dishes, and  hearty pastas are perfect partners for this darkly sensuous Italian red. Drink it young. $12–14
Friuli, Italy
Imported by Wm. Grant

Frederic Mabileau
ST. NICOLAS DE BOURGUEIL
Light- to medium-bodied.
Delicate and savory,
with great balance for food.
Red wines like this—light, yet with plenty of flavor—are exceedingly hard to come by. Plummy, herbaceous, and downright classy, it's a hit with

vegetables or a salad of goat cheese and fresh tomatoes. $12–14
Loire, France
Imported by Bayfield

Domaine des Roches Neuves
SAUMUR-CHAMPIGNY
Medium-bodied. Rich and elegant, with a long finish.
The reverberating red fruits and earthiness of this wine are propelled forward by mouth-watering acidity. It's one of the most versatile food wines in the world, spanning the culinary map from pork roasts to broiled fish, steak tartar to baked vegetables, roast chicken to chimichangas. The estate's fuller-bodied **"Terres Chaudes"** ($20 +) is an unheralded masterpiece. $12–14
Loire, France
Imported by VOS

Clos Roche Blanche
TOURAINE ROUGE "Cabernet"
Medium- to full-bodied.
Big, dense, and mouthwatering.
Crafted 100% organically and shot through with black fruits and minerals, this is high drama for a Cab Franc. In its first year in bottle, it's a vivid partner for herbed lamb and beef. After that, the wine starts to soften, the berries and jam emerge, and it becomes amazingly versatile with white meats, grilled fish, and vegetables. The 2002 is the best vintage tasted to date. $13–15
Loire, France
Imported by Louis/Dressner

Pellegrini
CABERNET FRANC
Medium- to full-bodied. Abundantly flavorful and finished with oak.
An impressively constructed red whose ample oak is usually matched by enough black cherry and blueberry fruit to back it up. An outstanding vintage like '97 makes it easy to understand why the vineyards of New York's Long Island have attracted so much attention. Good, curranty wine for beef and lamb. $16–18
North Fork of Long Island, New York

Hagafen
CABERNET FRANC
Medium-bodied.
Fruity and firm—and kosher.
Though this kosher wine is loaded with tasty red cherry and cranberry fruit, it shows oak treatment that borders on the excessive in many vintages. Still, it's the best kosher Cab Franc on the market and an elegant partner at the Passover table with brisket and other traditional fare. $17–19
Napa

Charles Joguet
CHINON "Cuvée de la Cure"
Medium- to full-bodied. Rich, powerful, and often tannic.
This wine is an expression of its superbly situated vineyard, the small and essentially organic Clos de la Cure. The winery suggests keeping this violet-scented and raspberryish Chinon for a few years before drinking, and so do we. Pork loin pairs well with it, as do pâtés of duck or goose liver. $17–19
Loire, France
Imported by Kermit Lynch

Pierre Breton
BOURGUEIL "Les Galichets"
Medium-bodied. Vividly juicy and scintillating on the palate.
This completely organic wine is about as pure an expression of *terroir* as you'll find in the middle Loire. It's a serious wine for foodies, with mouth-watering acidity and pronounced fragrances of

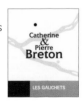

TWO SKY-HIGH ST. ÉMILIONS

The birth of your first child . . . your golden wedding anniversary . . . It takes either a very special occasion or a very fat wallet to enjoy **Château Cheval Blanc,** of the St. Émilion appellation in Bordeaux. The 2000, 1998, 1990, and 1982 vintages of this Cab Franc–dominant wine, blended with Merlot and a bit of Malbec, will set you back anywhere from $150 to $1,000.

Cheval Blanc's costliness is partly due to the fact that its annual production is much smaller than that of other Bordeaux wines, including Haut-Médoc's Château Lafite Rothschild. But it is its potential to age into the most exciting Cabernet Franc in the world that sends the price soaring. Cheval Blanc is good enough to drink right away, with scents of ripe black fruits, exotic Asian spices, minerals, herbs, and a hint of eucalyptus. But with bottle age it becomes a beguiling symphony of scents and flavors—magic in a bottle! At the table, it's a spectacular match with roasted leg of lamb.

Another premium St. Émilion is **Château Ausone,** with new releases costing around $400. Its dense black bramble fruits, barrage of violets and truffles, and cedary high notes are all pleasant, but it's the wine's unmistakable minerality that captivates. The best vintages, including 1996 and 2000, have a cellar potential of up to fifty years. A perfect partner? A stuffed veal roast. *Both wines imported by Diageo*

CHÂTEAU CHEVAL BLANC
1ᵉʳ Grand Cru Classé
1989
St Émilion Grand Cru
APPELLATION SAINT-ÉMILION GRAND CRU CONTROLÉE

Mis en bouteille au Château   13 ¾ BY VOL.
Sᵗᵉ CIVILE DU CHEVAL BLANC, Hᵗⁱᵉʳˢ FOURCAUD-LAUSSAC
PROPRIÉTAIRES A ST-ÉMILION (GIRONDE) FRANCE   750 ml
PRODUCE OF FRANCE

green tea, bell pepper, and raspberries. One of the few reds that can handle asparagus, it's also ideal for bell pepper and eggplant dishes. Pierre Breton makes several other wines, all worth trying. $18–20
Loire, France
Imported by Louis/Dressner

Olga Raffault
CHINON "Les Picasses"
Medium- to full-bodied. Rich, solid, and built for the long term.
For some tasters, the Olga Raffault estate represents the benchmark for Cabernet Franc in the Loire. Complex but tight in its youth, Les Picasses should be softened up either by aging or by being splashed around in a decanter. Try it with lamb chops or aged goat cheeses. Also look for **"La Poplinière,"** a delicate but stunning (and less costly) single-vineyard release in 2002. $18–20
Loire, France
Imported by Louis/Dressner

$20 to $40

Yannik Amirault
BOURGUEIL "Quartiers"
Medium-bodied. Savory, with beautiful concentration.
This wine comes from one of the great producers of the tiny Bourgueil appellation, which lies on the north bank of the Loire in the western part of the Touraine. Its wines are typically more aromatic and tannic than those of nearby Chinon. Pure, fragrant raspberries are the theme of this Bourgueil, with subtle murmurings of sweet herbs, mint, and minerals. At the table, it's sheer elegance with steak *au poivre*. $23–25
Loire, France
Imported by Weygandt/Metzler

Philippe Alliet
CHINON "Vielles Vignes"
Medium- to full-bodied.
Intensely flavored, rich, and deep—and a big finish to boot.
Black fruits and roasted coffee run wild in this well-regarded French interpretation of Cab Franc. Because it's so vintage-sensitive, it isn't released in the U.S. every year. The wine is super with grilled vegetables, meat-and-mushroom dishes, and anything gamey. Ailiet's **"Coteau de Noire"** bottling ($28–32) is denser and benefits from cellaring. $24–26
Loire, France
Imported by Jeroboam

Schneider Vineyards
CABERNET FRANC
Medium- to full-bodied.
Polished and fruity, with a zesty finish.
Bruce Schneider put New York State Cabernet Franc on the map the moment he started making it in 1994. His attractive version, blended with a small percentage of Merlot, is judiciously oaked and loaded with blueberry and sweet cedar flavor. A natural with Long Island duckling. $24–26
North Fork of Long Island, New York

Paumanok
CABERNET FRANC
Medium- to full-bodied.
Big and bold, with lots of oak.
Made in America and more Bordeaux than Loire, this richly put-together Cab Franc is especially tasty in the 2001 vintage. It's pricey for its type, but the quality is evident; anyone who likes good St. Émilion should enjoy this wine. Goes well with red meats, especially lamb. $28–30
North Fork of Long Island, New York

Cabernet Sauvignon

*The best-known grape to millions of wine drinkers
reigned for centuries in the heart of Bordeaux,
then reinvented itself in the vineyards of California.*

ABERNET SAUVIGNON began its storied ascent in the area
called Bordeaux, on the banks of the Gironde and Garonne
rivers in western France. The Romans planted the grape, the
French nurtured a great wine from it, and the English shipped it to every
far-flung port of their empire. But just what is it that makes Cabernet so
perfect for winemaking?

When carefully tended in the right climate on gravelly, well-
drained soil, the Cabernet grape can make wines of impressive body,
dark color, high tannin, and deep flavors—predominantly black currant,
cedar, and bell pepper. Blended with Merlot (which lends softness) and
Cabernet Franc (which offers acidity), Bordeaux wines strike an ideal
balance: They're rich and lengthy; they keep and develop further complexity with age; and they're exceptionally able to reflect the soil and
environment in which they are grown—the quality known as *terroir.*

Until the 1970s, Cabernet Sauvignon's chief interpretation was this
Bordeaux blend, the best examples of which came from the wealthy
estates of the Médoc and Graves growing areas. Then, in California,
winemakers discovered the next great stomping ground for Cabernet
wines: the Napa Valley. Here the grape was vinified on its own, creating
huge, powerhouse reds packed with sweet fruit and aged extensively in
new oak barrels. A few vintners who decided to continue pursuing the
Bordeaux–style blend also found success, coining the term "Meritage"
for their opulent wines; these have since become some of the highest-
priced wines in the world.

Happily, most Cabernet is not of this rarefied sort. Today's wine
lovers find bottlings that cost under $20 (most ready to drink upon
release)—and they come not only from California and France but from
Australia, South America, and elsewhere. The best of these are fruity,
balanced, and show the grape's classic flavors. In a few other cases, the
wines achieve the kind of extraordinary quality and dizzying prices
commanded by the top wines from Napa and Bordeaux, upholding
Cabernet's unparalleled international reputation. For many collectors,
"King Cab" remains the benchmark by which quality wine is judged.

Under $12

Carta Vieja
CABERNET SAUVIGNON
Light- to medium-bodied. Ripe, smooth, and true to the grape.
This Chilean find is an amazingly consistent bargain, and easily mistaken for a $15 red. Berry fruit abounds, with little or no oak in evidence. Pour a bit into whatever you're cooking and drink the rest with dinner. $4–6
Maule, Chile
Imported by F. Wildman

Château Tour de Goupin Rouge
BORDEAUX
Light-bodied. A fruity, buoyant Bordeaux with a good dollop of Merlot.

This organically grown, cherry-scented sipper finishes with a pleasant, minerally tang. It's good company at cocktail parties with light appetizers. $8–10
Bordeaux
Imported by Baron François

Vina La Rosa
CABERNET SAUVIGNON/ MERLOT "La Palma"
Medium-bodied. Dry, elegant, and nicely textured on the tongue.
The style of this 60% Cab and 40% Merlot from Chile is more akin to Bordeaux than the New World. Coffee, earth, and savory dark fruit are its themes. A true bargain that goes well with fun fare like burgers, sandwiches, kebabs, and fajitas. $8–10
Rapel, Chile
Imported by American Wine Distributors

Château de Ribebon
BORDEAUX
Medium-bodied. Savory, with balanced fruit and a good dose of Cabernet Franc.
Wine lovers everywhere should be thankful that there are still wines like this left in Bordeaux. An exercise in elegance, it offers raspberries, herbs, and honest complexity for an affordable price. A great match for stuffed mushrooms, pâté, or cold cuts. $8–10
Bordeaux
Imported by Serge Doré

Château Bastian
BORDEAUX
Medium-bodied. Intricate aromas and the classic taste of Bordeaux.
"Expensive-tasting" wine for the thrifty drinker. Just sip its cherry-like, rose-scented fruit some lazy Sunday afternoon with cheese and crackers, then finish it that evening with a club steak and a side of mashed. $8–10
Bordeaux
Imported by Lauber

R.H. Phillips
CABERNET SAUVIGNON "Barrel Cuvée"
Medium-bodied.
Dry, silky, and easy to sip.
Mild oak and blackberries fuse well in this tremendously popular and consistent California Cab. Phillips's "Toasted Head" line has many fans, but we prefer the regular bottling. Enjoy with burgers, meatloaf, and semi-firm cheeses. $9–11
Dunnigan Hills, California

Castle Rock
CABERNET SAUVIGNON
Medium- to full-bodied.
Rich and polished on the palate.
This increasingly popular Napa Cabernet, dominated by black cherries and pipe tobacco, is

surprisingly gutsy for the price. Useful for burgers but worthy of sirloin steaks. $10–12
Napa

Blackstone
CABERNET SAUVIGNON
Medium-bodied. Easy on the palate, with an oaky finish.
This is probably what most people are looking for in a California Cab. Sourced from vineyards halfway between San Francisco and Santa Barbara, it's a pleasing mix of cherries and milk chocolatey oak. Try it with cheeseburgers, franks, or a meatloaf sandwich. $10–12
Monterey, California

Cartlidge & Browne
CABERNET SAUVIGNON
Medium- to full-bodied. A classic California Cab.
Mocha notes from oak are balanced gracefully with lively, black currant flavor in a Cab that is better (and lower-priced) than many of its western cousins. A terrific steak and grill red. $10–12
California

$12 to $20

Powers
CABERNET SAUVIGNON
Medium-bodied. Well-balanced, smooth, and judiciously oaked.
Washington wines grow in near-desert conditions, which render the reds a bit more curranty and acidic than most California Cabs and Merlots. This example is a tasty partner to any foods with a good char, including grilled burgers and chops. The vineyard's high-end flagship "**Mercer Ranch**" ($18–20) ages well. $12–14
Washington

Monterra
CABERNET SAUVIGNON
Medium-bodied. A particularly ripe, satiny wine that washes over the palate.
It's cherries, cherries, and more cherries in this Cabernet for Merlot drinkers. It needn't be drunk with food to be enjoyed, but simple chicken dishes, chops, and hard cheeses would find it a nice complement. $12–14
Monterey, California

Dalton
CANAAN RED
Medium-bodied. A fruity, lip-smacking blend.
Cabernet Sauvignon, Merlot, and Shiraz form a unique trio in this Israeli kosher wine, a good choice for dishes with sweet or salty flavors—say, cabbage stuffed with raisins or peppery meats. The straight **Cabernet Sauvignon** ($26–28) offers a richer, drier style. $16–18
Galilee, Israel
Imported by Abarbanel

Pagor
CABERNET SAUVIGNON
Medium- to full-bodied. Great taste driven by fruit, not oak.
Exquisitely ripe black cherry and mocha flavors define Ed Pagor's Rolling Hills Vineyard boutique Cab (sometimes hard to find), with fruit sourced from the Temecula Valley. Great with highly seasoned meats. $16–18
South Coast, California

De Loach
CABERNET SAUVIGNON "Estate"
Medium-bodied. Mellow yet mouthfilling, with tannins on the soft side.
Formerly labeled "Los Amigos," this is one of De Loach's most easily enjoyable wines. It's at its best after three or four years, and

the '99 is spicy, cherryish, and still drinking great. The pricier O. F. S. Cab ($34–36) is mostly just oakier. Try the basic estate wine with a skirt steak smothered in garlic and parsley. Yum! $16–18
Russian River, California

Barnwood Vineyards
CABERNET SAUVIGNON
Medium- to full-bodied. Deep, smooth, and modest in oak and alcohol.
This small-production gem, from grapes grown at high elevation in California's Cuyama Valley, is made without chemical treatment in the vineyard and whole-berry fermented for extra fruitiness. The result? A forthright, wonderful, and ready-to-drink Cabernet. All of Barnwood's wines are excellent values, and the high-end blend of Merlot, Syrah, and Cabernet called **Trio** ($24–26) is superb. Try the Cab with sliced duck breast in peppercorn sauce or with anything fresh off the grill. $18–20
Santa Barbara, California

Alexander Valley Vineyards
CABERNET SAUVIGNON
Medium-bodied. Plump and friendly mouthfeel.
One of our favorite affordable Cabernets out of

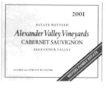

California year after year, this wine features delicious cherry fruit with hints of mint and milk chocolate. For Mom's meatloaf or cheesy casseroles. $18–20
Alexander Valley, California

Cape Mentelle
CABERNET SAUVIGNON/MERLOT
"Trinders"
Medium- to full-bodied. Well-rounded, fruity, and flavorful.
This popular red (60% Cabernet, 40% Merlot) comes from the estate that put Margaret River on the map. Intended for immediate enjoyment, it's a boatload of blackberries dusted with spearmint—a flavor profile typical of the appellation. It sings with minted lamb. $18–20
Margaret River, Western Australia
Imported by Clicquot

Bleasdale
CABERNET SAUVIGNON
"Mulberry Tree"
Medium-bodied.
Sweetly ripe and satiny.
It seems this Down Under winery can't produce anything but fabulously jammy, minty red wines with explosive finishes— which is perfectly all right with us. It's particularly tasty when enjoyed with saucy, spicy fare like barbecue. $18–20
Langhorne Creek, South Australia
Imported by Southern Starz

Domaine Mosse
ANJOU ROUGE
Full-bodied. Dark, densely layered with flavor, and more savory than sweet.
This 100% Cabernet Sauvignon (unusual for a Loire wine) is full of ripe raspberry fruit, with pepper, moist earth, herbs, and licorice serving counterpoint. It's complex stuff—and frankly magnificent. One of the world's most "adult" lamb partners, it's also a good match for pepper steak, hearty stews, and stuffed green peppers. $18–20
Loire, France
Imported by World Wide Wines

Pheasant Ridge
CABERNET SAUVIGNON
Medium-bodied. Smooth, fleshy, and balanced on a dime.
This Cab leads the charge of quality red wines emerging out of the American Southwest. A touch gamey and full of prunes and

PHEASANT RIDGE

cherries, it's a cheeky, oaked New World–style wine that's a terrific pick for barbecue aficionados. Yee haw! $18–20
Lubbock, Texas

Pellegrini
CABERNET SAUVIGNON
Medium- to full-bodied. Dark, dense, and moderately tannic.
A carnivore's wine from Long Island, with black currants, mulberries, and tarry, smoky oak nuances coming through.
A rolled pork roast would excel as a partner, as would a hickory-smoked rack of ribs. $18–20
North Fork of Long Island, New York

$20 to $40

Murphy-Goode
CABERNET SAUVIGNON
Medium- to full-bodied. Pleasant and polished, with a ripe fruit core.
Murphy-Goode has long been one of the region's biggest names, and their winemaking has changed for the better. As of 2001, the oak-alike wines of yore were replaced by those with less time in wood, fabulously ripe fruit of the maraschino cherry variety, and reasonable alcohol levels. Enjoyable young, this Cab brings out the best in duck. $20–22
Alexander Valley, California

Tim Adams
CABERNET SAUVIGNON
Full-bodied. Satiny, plush, and multidimensional.
A limited-production Australian wine (and winemaker) with a following. Aged in a combination of French and American oak, it surges with blackberry, blueberry, and cocoa; in some years, it's distinctly minty as well. Underpriced compared to its peers, and a flashy match for barbecue. $20–22
Clare Valley, South Australia
Imported by Commonwealth

Philippe-Lorraine
CABERNET SAUVIGNON
Medium- to full-bodied. Elegant, subtle in its power, and very dry at the finish.
This extremely small-production Napa Cabernet, with its earthy but understated palate, is about as close as California ever gets to the Médoc. It's often a good bet in years with modest vintages. Uncork, let breathe, and serve with rack of lamb, roasts, and even good old-fashioned Beef Wellington. $20–22
Napa

Devil's Lair
CABERNET/MERLOT
Medium- to full-bodied. Strong and firm, with seductive and mouthfilling fruit.
About three-quarters Cabernet Sauvignon and a quarter Merlot, this strapping wine from the wild country of Western Australia is a fun, fruit-driven Aussie special. It's deeply cut with black currant, black cherry, and cappuccino flavors. Amazing for grilled lamb chops or other meats bound for the barbie. $24–27
Margaret River, Western Australia
Imported by Southcorp

Château de France
GRAVES
Medium- to full-bodied.
Velvety and mouthfilling.
The flavor of this rich, red
Bordeaux is layered with sweet
herbs, currants, and cherries.
Excellent for drinking young,
it's good with mild meats like
brisket or braised short ribs.
The producer's **Le Bec En Sabot**
second label ($12–14) is an
outstanding value. $25–30
Bordeaux
Imported by Bayfield

Les Ormes de Pez
ST. ESTÈPHE
Medium- to full-
bodied. Tannic
and meaty.
This wine—
typical of St.
Estèphe in its
earthiness—
remains one of
the best values
in Bordeaux. It's a treat for
Francophiles and anyone who
likes a hint of turf in a wine. A
hearty companion to charred
steaks and game. $25–30
Bordeaux
Imported by Diageo

Château Les Barraillots
MARGAUX
Medium-bodied. Mouthfilling,
with a clear expression of fruit.
With its savory array of black
fruits, subtle violets in the nose,
and complex earthiness, this is
everything you could wish for in
Margaux—and a natural partner
for filet mignon. Foodies might
like to try it with sautéed wild
mushrooms and a drizzle of
truffle oil. $25–30
Bordeaux
Imported by Bayfield

Best's Wines
CABERNET SAUVIGNON
"Great Western"
Full-bodied.
Multiflavored and firmly textured.
Worthy of long-term cellaring,
this blue-chip collectable Cabernet
from low-lying mountains in
Victoria, Australia, is in the great
old-fashioned style. Its currant
fruit is topped by detectable layers
of berry compote and bittersweet
chocolate. Great for steak and
anything gamey. $30–35
Grampians, Victoria
Imported by Epicurean

Heitz Cellars
CABERNET SAUVIGNON
Medium-bodied.
Ripe-fruited and understated,
yet meaty at the end.
Fans of this legendary estate
mourn the loss of Heitz Cellars
formidable founder Joe Heitz, but
classy Cabs are still made from his
Napa properties. Enjoy the basic
release with lean steaks and chops.
The **"Trailside"** ('97 and '98, at $50
and up), with its endlessly deep
palate and nose like a fresh pot of
coffee, stands up well to crusty,
dry-aged porterhouse. $35–40
Napa

$40 to $60

Château Talbot
ST. JULIEN
Medium- to full-bodied.
A bit oaky when young, but soon
blossoms with sweet fruit and a
soft mouthfeel.
We love this estate for its
extraordinary consistency and the
approachability of its wines.
Cherries, strawberries, milk
chocolate, and roses swirl through
the mouth in practically every
vintage. (For new wine lovers,
this is a great introduction to fine

A BIG, BOLD CAB

Winemaker Rick Small established Woodward Canyon Winery in the Walla Walla Valley in 1981. Today he turns out Cabernets and Merlots to be reckoned with—one of the reasons Woodward Canyon is considered one of the best estates in Washington. The winery's benign-sounding **Woodward Canyon "Artist Series" Cabernet Sauvignon** ($35–40) is not for the faint of heart. It's black in the glass, very full-bodied, and smoky at the finish—a Kodiak bear of a wine that should hibernate well in the cellar. In the meantime, tame its youthful tannins with game or fatty red meats.

Bordeaux.) Superb with short ribs and roasts of pork or veal. $40–45
Bordeaux
Imported by Diageo

Bernardus
MARINUS
Full-bodied. Luxurious and full-flavored, with a smooth finish.
Some vintages are better than others, but overall this proprietary blend of Cabernet and Merlot from California's Central Coast is elegant and delicious. Dense plantings, tiny yields, and Bordeaux-style vinification are the secret of its success. Ready to drink young with leg of lamb and lean cuts of beef. $45–50
Carmel, California

Cosentino
MERITAGE "The Poet"
Full-bodied. Deeply fruited and opulent, especially when young.
In 1986, Mitch Cosentino's "The Poet" became the first so-called Meritage (Bordeaux- style blend) in California. About two-thirds Cabernet, it's formulated like a Bordeaux yet remains distinctively Californian in its in-your-face ripeness and drinkability. Gratifying with double-thick pork chops or steak in rich sauces. Also look for the

winery's less pricey Crystal Valley line, which features a decadent, cassis-like Cabernet. $45–50
Napa

Penley Estate
CABERNET SAUVIGNON
Very full-bodied. Deep berry taste laced with ribbons of caramelly French oak.
Kym Tolley's deservedly famous Aussie Cabernet has taken the word "delicious" to new levels. It's easily the best of its class in Coonawarra, and one of our favorite Cabernets made anywhere. Serve with lamb, beef, or game hens stuffed with porcini mushrooms. $45–50
Coonawarra, South Australia
Imported by Old Bridge Cellars

Forman
CABERNET SAUVIGNON
Full-bodied. Rich and complex, like a fine Graves made on California soil.
Ric Forman, a pioneer Napa vintner, makes monumental Cabernets. They're generally plump and giving, with black currant, blackberries, minerals, and hints of cedar threaded intricately into the mix (shades of St. Émilion Château Haut-Brion). Worthy of a standing rib roast or a late-evening session with some aged farmhouse cheddar. $50–60
Napa

Clos du Marquis
ST. JULIEN
Full-bodied. Velvety on the palate and particularly ripe and expansive.
Crafted by the talented Michel Delon, this hedonistic Bordeaux leaves you smacking your lips from its sweet kirsch finish. You would be hard pressed to find a bad vintage. Glorious with prime rib but versatile with roast pork and poultry as well. $50–60
Bordeaux
Imported by Diageo

Château Pontet–Canet
PAUILLAC
Very full-bodied. Richly tannic, inky, and built to last.

Not a wine for wimps, Pontet-Canet packs in as much black fruit, stone-and-flint aromas, and strong ripe tannin as possible. Hot-weather vintages like '89 and '96 take years to come around, so we advise proceeding as follows: a) Cellar the wine as long as possible; b) decant it and let it breathe for two hours or more; and c) serve it with rare, fat-marbled beef. $45–50
Bordeaux
Imported by Diageo

Château Gruaud Larose
ST. JULIEN
Medium- to full-bodied. A suave wine with a long, perfumed finish.

This luscious Bordeaux has the sweet yet solid character of mountain fruit, a lot of cherry, and a wonderful sense of completeness. An exquisite rare roast-beef partner. $40–60
Bordeaux
Imported by Diageo

Over $60

Duckhorn
CABERNET SAUVIGNON
Medium- to full-bodied. Impressive, penetrating on the palate, and very black.
Founded by Dan and Margaret Duckhorn in 1976, Duckhorn Vineyards is one of California's perennial stars. Though best known for Merlot, the winery also produces an outstanding, mineral-rich Cab, mostly allocated to restaurants. The wine should be cellared—but if you can't wait, let it breathe for two hours and enjoy with a Black Angus steak. $60–70
Napa

A LEBANESE BEAUTY

In 1930, the estate of Château Musar was established just north of Beirut by the brave and irrepressible Gaston Hochar. His son Serge, a winemaker since 1959, continues the tradition. Undaunted by war, border disputes, and Syrian tanks parked in the vineyards, the estate continues to create a unique blend of Cabernet, Cinsault, and Syrah that combines the roastiness of the Rhône with the savor of left–bank Bordeaux. Medium–bodied **Château Musar Red** (around $40, though up to $100 for older vintages) is marvelously supple, subtly tannic, and usually mature at release (current release: '96). A knockout with food, it's a beautiful partner for game birds and aged crumbly cheeses. *Imported by Broadbent*

BEAUJOLAIS NOUVEAU

*W*HETHER YOUR HEART races when you see the posters that go up in wine shops each November trumpeting *"Le Beaujolais Nouveau est arrivé!"* or you merely marvel at the marketing genius of the French, there's no denying that Beaujolais Nouveau is the beloved tipple of millions of wine lovers. Perennially delicious, this fresh and fruity wine is bottled fast, then rushed to markets around the world via airfreight to arrive in wine stores on the third Thursday in November—its official first sale date.

And what leads up to this yearly ritual? Each year in the days immediately following harvest, many wineries in France's Beaujolais region select a portion of their production to undergo a special type of fermentation called carbonic maceration, which captures the freshness, charm, and grapiness of the year's Gamay fruit. And, unlike aged wines, Nouveau is released when only seven to nine weeks old. (Tradition says it was the wine made for the vineyard workers to enjoy at the end of the harvest.)

Because it's an uncomplicated wine meant to be consumed in the first six months after release, Nouveau's appeal is universal. So, come November, plan a visit to your local wine merchant to pick up a few bottles and join the fun.

Price Note: Beaujolais Nouveau that is shipped by air to arrive on the third Thursday in November is typically priced between $8.99 and $9.95 per bottle. A week or two thereafter, boat shipments arrive in retail shops and the bottle price drops to $5.99 to $7.99. The most universally available Beaujolais Nouveau is made by George Duboeuf, but many other fine examples are its equal or better.

Beaujolais. It's a lovely red to serve with hors d'oeuvres, light fish dishes, and sushi. $11–13
Beaujolais
Imported by Weygandt/Metzler

Over $12

Domaine de Peyra
CÔTES D'AUVERGNE
"Vielles Vignes"
Light- to medium-bodied. Rustic and full-flavored yet surprisingly gentle.
Some bottles of this fruity, floral, fascinating wine (100% Gamay grown at the headwaters of the Loire in central France), show a light haze because the wine is organically produced and unfiltered. But don't worry: Lightly chilled, it makes a perfect foil for flavorful fare—everything from Szechuan noodles to pungent cheeses to chicken paprikash. $14–16
Auvergne, France
Imported by World Wide Wines

Domaine du Clos du Fief
JULIÉNAS
Light- to medium-bodied. Fresh-tasting, balanced, and layered with flavor.
Michel Tête's elegant Cru Beaujolais from his small estate in Juliénas is full of fresh apples, berries, and minerals. It's a traditional charcuterie partner but is just as good with poultry and vegetables. Tete's **Beaujolais-Villages** ($16–18) is equally classy and reliable. $14–16
Beaujolais
Imported by Louis/Dressner

Château des Tours
BROUILLY
Medium-bodied. Fat, pungent, and built like good Burgundy.
No candy and bananas here. This sophisticated Beaujolais is an earthy, complex partner for savory food like grilled fish, savory tarts, and herbed roast chicken stuffed with white mushrooms and onions. $14–16
Beaujolais
Imported by Baron François

Château de Pizay
MORGON
Medium-bodied. Concentrated fruit that's bold in the nose and on the palate.
A consistently fine Cru Beaujolais, with black plum and berry fruit packed into its buoyant, balanced frame. The estate's **Régnié** ($13–15) is just as good, and its **Beaujolais** ($9–11) is a bargain. Both the Morgon and Régnié make especially good partners for ham and saucy, salty meats. $13–15
Beaujolais
Imported by M. Scott

André Rampon
RÉGNIÉ
Light-bodied. Fragrant, silky, and exquisitely delicate.
This wine stands above even its Cru Beaujolais contemporaries. With a modest 12% alcohol, it's redolent of fresh cherries, it's true to its *terroir*, and it's about as graceful as red wine ever gets—in a word, perfect. You'd be hard pressed to imagine a better red wine for fish. $16–18
Beaujolais
Imported by D. Bowler

Henry Marionnet
TOURAINE ROUGE
"Premiere Vendange"
Medium-bodied. Intensely aromatic, with amazing depth of flavor and a long, complex finish.
Perhaps the greatest Gamay we've ever tasted. Imagine a Beaujolais reduced to its essence, shot through with the minerals of the Loire Valley soils. Completely organic, less than 12% alcohol, no added sugar or sulfites—just wild blackberry and boysenberry fruit and the "funky" quality that wine drinkers either love or hate. Bring on the sausages, pâtés, and sweetbreads. $18–20
Beaujolais
Imported by Weygandt/Metzler

Grenache

*The primary grape of the wines of Châteauneuf-du-Pape,
Grenache is most often used in blends—the reason
it's one of the most widely planted vines in the world.*

F WINE GRAPES got report cards, Grenache would get an A for "gets along well with others," lending, as it does, strength and sweet fruit to thousands of international blends. But on its own, its grade slips to B– because the wines made from it are frequently overburdened with alcohol. The 100% Grenaches among the wines we've chosen here are the impressive exceptions.

A hot–weather variety, Grenache thrives throughout southern France and Spain (where it is called Garnacha), Morocco, and other sun-struck climes. In France, it is often blended with Syrah, Mourvèdre, and Carignan, a group that wine writers call "the usual suspects." In Spain, it partners with the Tempranillo grape or shines on its own in the formidable red wines of Priorat. Italy joins the growers' club with Guarnaccia on the isle of Ischia and Canonau in Sicily. But Grenache's spiritual home is France's Southern Rhône, where it heads a gang of thirteen grape varieties in the wines Châteauneuf–du–Pape and its neighboring appellations. Whenever you buy a bottle of red Côtes du Rhône, what you're most likely getting is a blended wine based on Grenache.

Other interpretations include the inexpensive jug wines of France's Languedoc and California's Central Valley, tongue–tingling rosés from all over, and some intense, late–harvest dessert wines (see pages 210–213).

Growers in Australia and California have taken a liking to the grape and some produce 100% Grenaches. But without the addition of other varieties for balance, Grenache's alcohol and tannin remain a bit of a problem. As a result, those who want a stand–alone wine will usually do better with a Shiraz/Syrah from either place.

Under $12

Campo de Borja
BORSAO RED
Medium-bodied.
Sweetly ripe and
fun to drink.
Here's a jolt of
blueberry syrup and
spice (70% Grenache,
20% Cabernet

Sauvignon, 10% Tempranillo)
that borders on outright sweetness in warm vintages. It's a great
choice for pizza with the works
or an overstuffed burrito. $6–7
Campo de Borja, Spain
Imported by Tempranillo

Bodegas y Viñedos del Jalon
VIÑA ALARBA
Medium-bodied.
Ripe and mouthfilling.
This 100% old-vines Grenache,
grown south of Rioja, is whole-
berry fermented to accentuate
the fruit. Bursting with roasty red
cherries and sweet coffee flavors,
it's a treat not only with Spanish
rice and beans but also with
pepperoni pizza, burgers, and
spicier Chinese dishes. $6–8
Calatayud, Spain
Imported by Tempranillo

Domaine l'Ameillaud
CAIRANNE
Medium- to full-bodied.
Hearty and satisfying,
with bold, spicy flavor.
This big Côtes du Rhône Villages
smells as if someone tipped the
contents of a whole pepper
shaker into the fermenting vat.
It's consistently one of the best
values on the market. A winner
with meat stews of any sort.
$10–12
Rhône, France
Imported by Jeroboam

Les Vignerons d'Estézargues
CÔTES DU RHÔNE
"Genestas"
Medium- to full-bodied.
Slurpy, velvety, and dark.
Blended from Grenache, Syrah,
Carignan, and Mourvèdre, this
wine is 100% organic, made
from old vines, and piled high
on the palate with smoke-
scented bramble fruits. Enjoy it
with fork-tender meats like
braised short ribs or pot roast.
$10–12
Rhône, France
Imported by World Wine Wines

Domaine des Jougla
SAINT CHINIAN
"Cuvée
Tradition"
Medium- to
full-bodied.
Opulently ripe
and pungent—
a "peasant red."
This meaty blend
of Grenache,

Syrah, and Mourvèdre is a good
choice for wine lovers in the
mood for a red that pulls no
punches. A great partner for
sausages, raw milk cheeses, and
traditional French country fare.
$10–12
Languedoc, France
Imported by Baron François

Vinicola del Priorat
PRIORAT "Ónix"
Medium- to full-bodied.
Thick, sweet, and rustic.
A 100% Grenache that could
almost pass as dessert in most
vintages, this day-glo purple
wine is a big cherry-berry fruit
bomb. It cries out for hearty
fare like fried thick-cut pork
chops and roasted red meats.
$10–12
Priorato, Spain
Imported by Tempranillo

$12 to $20

Château de Pech–Redon
**COTEAUX DE LANGUEDOC
"La Clape"**
**Medium- to full-bodied.
Big, earthy, and opaque.**
Black as Texas crude, this rustic
red is made from 50% Grenache,
30% Syrah, and 20% Cinsault.
The barnyardy aromas so admired
by the French may not be for
everyone, but this wine's the real
deal from southern France—the
kind the locals drink with peppery
meats, country pâté, charcuterie,
and hearty stews. $12–14
*Languedoc, France
Imported by House of Burgundy*

Château du Trignon
CÔTES DU RHÔNE
**Medium-bodied. The
quintessential Côtes du Rhône—
dry, dark, spicy, and satisfying.**
This blend of Grenache, Syrah,
and Mourvèdre
is a super
value in every
single vintage.
Teeming with
black cherries,
licorice, and
black currants—and usually
slightly singed with oak—this is
terrific with barbecued meats or

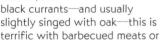

burgers topped with a thick slice
of smoked cheese. $12–14
*Rhône, France
Imported by Kermit Lynch*

Domaine de Fontenille
CÔTES DU LUBERON
**Medium-bodied. Starts gently,
then fills the mouth with
enticing flavors.**
This smoky, dark wine from
Provence (half Grenache, half
Syrah) is redolent of *garrigue,*
the aromatic mix of lavender, turf,
and herbs that perfumes the local
countryside. Try it with sausages
and peppers, chicken Provençal,
or pepper jack cheese. $13–15
*Rhône, France
Imported by Weygandt/Metzler*

Domaine Bressy–Masson
RASTEAU "Cuvée Paul Émile"
**Full-bodied. A concentrated wine
for people who like it "chewy."**
Rasteau, a venerable southern
Rhône appellation, is a haven for
roasty, unapologetic, black wines
like this one—a blend of 70%
Grenache from hundred-year-old
vines, 20% Syrah, and 10%
Mourvèdre. A defiant non-sipper,
it demands the richest and
fattiest of birds, beef, and game.
If you want something gentler
with more fruit, try **La Souco
d'Or** ($20–24) or the estate's

FOUR BARGAIN CÔTES DU RHÔNES

From the Rhône Valley in southern France, **Domaine Les Grands Bois
Côtes du Rhône** ($11–13) is a reasonably priced red that's complex, savory,
dry, and elegant. Its flavor? Roasted fruit accented by earthiness. When
drunk young, it's lovely with roast chicken or picnic foods. Another bargain
Côtes du Rhône from the same estate, **"Cuvée Gabrielle"** ($16–18), is sup-
ple, sweetly ripe, and teeming with strawberries—a great fondue wine. The
estate's deluxe bottlings, **"Cuvée Mireille"** and **"Cuvée Maximilien"**
($18–$22), are superb examples of Rhône *terroir* and outclass many pricier
wines we've tasted; look for 2000 or '01 with these. Both are worthy of your
finest roasts, ragouts, and ribs. *Imported by Weygandt/Metzler*

regular bottling **Rasteau–Villages** ($14–16), impressive in its own right. $20–24
Rhône, France
Imported by Jeroboam

Domaine Chaume–Arnaud
VINOSOBRES
Medium-bodied. Succulent, graceful, and silky-soft on the palate.
There's an elegance and balance in this blend (Grenache, Carignan, Cinsault, Syrah, and Mourvèdre) that recalls Burgundy more than the Rhône. Its soft berry fruit, allspice, and earth flavors work nicely with winter vegetables and white meats. For a great bargain, try nonvintage **"Vin de Pays des Portes de la Mediterranée"** ($8–10), as winsome as they come. $14–16
Rhône, France
Imported by Jeroboam

Buil & Giné
PRIORAT "Giné Giné"
Full-bodied. Rustic and very bold, yet with a distinct impression of sweetness.
This Grenache/Carignan blend tastes like a molasses fruitcake studded with figs and cherries. It's too syrupy for some and a delirious pleasure for others—but whatever your taste, you'll do well to have some sweet glazed ham or barbecue on hand when you open the bottle. $16–18
Catalonia, Spain
Imported by Think Global

Domaine Le Mas de Collines
GIGONDAS
Medium- to full-bodied. Extremely elegant, with deep fruit and great complexity.
This wine is late-released, so current vintages tend to be about four years old (look for '99 now). It's worth the wait: The first blast

out of the glass is ripe plum fruit, followed by an alluring mélange of dried strawberries, sage, and sweet earth. This is a deluxe dinner red at a more-than-fair price. Enjoy it with roasted pork or veal, stuffed or sauced birds, and hard sausages. $18–20
Rhône, France
Imported by Bayfield

Joān d'Anguera
MONTSANT "La Planella"
Full-bodied. Very dark and satiny.
Montsant, formerly part of the Priorat appellation, is home to huge, sun-roasted reds based on Grenache and Carignan. Case in point: this overwhelmingly luscious, barrel-aged, 100% Grenache. Its cassis-syrup finish is irresistible with fruit-sauced roasts of pork or duck. $17–19
Catalonia, Spain
Imported by De Maison

Domaine Alary
CAIRANNE
Medium-bodied. Solid, savory, and lengthy.
This unfiltered blend of 85% Grenache and 15% Syrah boasts the classic Rhône roster of tarry, herby, smoky nuances and packs them snugly into every corner of your palate. It's a surefire partner for Provençal ragouts and smoky cheeses. Also look for this estate's **"La Grange Daniel,"** a super $10–12 *vin de pays,* and **"La Brunote"** ($20+), beautifully crafted and full-blooded. $17–19
Rhône, France
Imported by Weygandt/Metzler

$20 to $40

Alvaro Palacios
PRIORAT "Les Terrasses"
Medium- to full-bodied. Subtle for Priorat—drier, more elegant, and almost Bordeauxlike.
Young Alvaro Palacios has conquered Catalonia with his wines from Priorat, a hotbed of "big reds" eighty-five miles southwest of Barcelona. This isn't his most expensive or famous Priorat, but it is splendidly balanced, subtle, and complex, with soft but lasting tannins and a knockout palate of figs, earth, and tobacco. Enjoy it with slow-cooked meats, a filet mignon wrapped in bacon, or a platter of Spanish cheeses and thinly sliced *jamon Iberico*, the prized cured ham of Spain. $25–30
Catalonia, Spain
Imported by M. Skurnik

Clos du Mont-Olivet
CHÂTEAUNEUF-DU-PAPE
Medium- to full-bodied.
Classic Châteauneuf of fine strength and depth.
Sourced from old vines (75% Grenache), devoid of new oak, and unsparing of tannin, this is about as traditional as Châteauneuf gets. It is fragrant and almost musky, with red fruit, incense, and wood spice notes. Stick to top vintages like '95 (hard to find now) and 2000, then bring out their best with rare roast beef. Try the estate's **Côtes du Rhône "Monteuil La Levade"** ($10+) for everyday sipping. $30–35
Rhône, France
Imported by North Berkeley

Bonny Doon
LE CIGARE VOLANT
Medium-bodied.
Surprisingly light on its feet for such a richly flavored wine.
Randall Grahm, the winemaker-cum-philosopher of Santa Cruz, steals wine lovers' hearts every vintage with his California tribute to Châteauneuf-du-Pape. Poised, welcoming, and elegant, it offers baked earth and spices to spare, a suave fig-and-cherry center, and subtle tannins. Ideally a duck wine, but not bad with a Thanksgiving turkey. For kicks, try Grahm's **Clos de Gilroy** ($12–14) juicy and Grenache-based. $30–35
California

WINE FROM VERY OLD VINES

Châteauneuf-du-Papes bear the mark of distinction, but **Domaine des Peres de l'Eglise "Le Calice de St. Pierre"** stands out among its peers: It consists of 85% Grenache (90+ year-old vines), 3% Syrah, 2% Mourvèdre, and a 10% field blend of over 100-year-old vines. One of the great wines of the Rhône, it's medium-bodied, graceful yet complex, and priced at a surprising $35–40. The 2000 vintage, the first under the estate's current winemaker, was the breakthrough, and '01 was even better. The wine has all the bacon, wood smoke, and roasted fruit you could wish for, couched in a gentle mouthfeel; its long, fruit-driven finish is barely brushed with tannins. Cellar it or serve with pâtés and terrines, delicate game hens, a glazed ham, or even a hearty salad of romaine hearts, walnuts, and blue cheese. *Imported by Weygandt/Metzler*

Domaine le Sang des Cailloux
VACQUEYRAS
Very full-bodied. Thick in the mouth, with layers of flavor and a velvety finish.
Widely accepted as the finest wine of its appellation, this red drinks as forcefully as the domaine's name ("blood of the stones") suggests. Rife with aromas of roasted meats, espresso, and dark, sensuous cassis syrup, it seems almost made-to-order for fatty birds with crispy skin and plenty of hot Dijon mustard. $30–35
Rhône, France
Imported by Kermit Lynch

Laderas de Pinoso
ALICANTE "El Sequé"
Very full-bodied.
Sheer power and class, with an incredibly lengthy finish.
This old-vines Grenache, from an estate owned by the legendary Artadi family of Rioja, is similar to Priorat but seems drier and more Rhônelike. An impressive wine, it sports bacony, leathery, and complex iron-and-mineral aromas. Cellar it or serve it with a rack of lamb or roasted meats of any kind—the more garlicky, the better. Also look for **Laderas de El Sequé** ($12–14), the estate's superb second label. $35–40
Valencia, Spain
Imported by European Cellars

Charles Melton
NINE POPES
Very full-bodied. What Australians do best: huge power wedded to thick, delicious fruit.
A 70% Grenache from ancient vines blended with Shiraz and Mourvèdre and aged fifteen months in French and American oak. The finished wine's nuances of pepper, chocolate, and leather are very attractive, but it's mostly the mouth-flooding fruit you're paying for. You might cellar this wine, but we like drinking it young with delectables like sauce-slathered babyback ribs. $35–40
Barossa Valley, South Australia
Imported by Commonwealth

Over $40

Le Bosquet des Papes
CHÂTEAUNEUF-DU-PAPE
Medium- to full-bodied. A plush, cellarable wine.
This definitive Châteauneuf, from the husband-and-wife winemakers the Boirons, has enormous appeal, with liqueurlike richness and Sunday-breakfast aromas of strong coffee, mixed-berry jam, and sizzling bacon. It begs for such rich foods as grilled and smoked meats, hard cheeses, and good old-fashioned Beef Stroganoff. Some tasters prefer **"Cuvee Grenache"** ($26–28), the 100% Grenache release. $40–45
Rhône, France
Imported by A. Junguenet

Rotllan Torra
PRIORATO "Amadis"
Very full-bodied. Dark and sensuous, and tannic.
This is the flagship cuvée of a young winery housed in an ancient monastery. Winemakers Jordy and Albert Rotllan make wine from 100% Grenache and age it in barrel and bottle for several years. The result is a powerful mingling of raisins, chocolate, coffee, smoked meat, and sensuous black cherries at the finish. It goes best with the richest fare: game birds, sausages, winter stews, or chateaubriand with Bearnaise sauce. Don't overlook their juicy, vigorous second label wine, **Selleccio**— at $15, a true bargain! $50–60
Catalonia, Spain
Imported by De Maison

Merlot

In California, this European blending grape came on like gangbusters in the 1980s. Today it's the basis for the best-selling wine in America.

F AMERICANS were waiting for a red counterpart to Chardonnay—the gentle-natured white of low acidity, soft structure, and responsiveness to oak treatment—they found it in Merlot. "Smooth" is the adjective most often used to encapsulate Merlot's appeal, and a less complex wine such as this has its place as a nice 'n' easy sipper. With food, however, it often falls short because of its low acidity and invariably heavy oak treatment.

Merlot's runaway success has much to do with timing. It came along just as Americans were becoming more interested in red wine, then rapidly became so popular that American producers could barely keep up with the demand.

Across the Atlantic, Merlot is Cabernet Sauvignon's partner in the traditional blends of Bordeaux, where it lends softness and, in some cases, additional fruit (it ripens sooner in the vineyard than Cabernet). Where Cabernet likes rocky soils with good drainage and warm weather, Merlot prefers clay soils and cooler weather—at least in Pomerol and St. Émilion, where many of the world's best Merlot-dominant wines are produced. There's also plenty of Merlot coming from Italy, although some American palates find it a little too earthy and herby. No such reservations are likely to apply to the Merlots of South America—particularly those from Chile, where the damp soils of the Central Valley do the grape proud.

In this country, states north, south, east, and west have joined California in the rush to produce Merlot, with Washington and New York leading the pack. As a result, many valuable old vines of heirloom varieties—Zinfandel chief among them—have been ripped out. If Merlot's popularity wanes, it will be interesting to see what will happen to all these newly planted vines. Will they, too, be replaced? Or will American vintners, faced with economic need, return to Merlot for its original use—as the perfect blending grape?

Note: A second or third wine rarely crops up in the following recommendatons because Merlot makers usually stick to the basic varietal.

Under $12

Reserve St. Martin
MERLOT
Light- to medium-bodied.
A juicy red with a smooth,
easy-sipping character.
This French Merlot has a touch
of spice and lots of fruit—mostly
plums and fresh figs. A fine
cocktail-party wine or picnic
partner. $6–7
Languedoc, France
Imported by Pasternak

Pierre Jean
MERLOT
Light- to medium-bodied.
Simple and fruity.
Berries are the theme of this
pleasing cocktail-style Merlot.
Have a glass when you get home
late from a hard day at the office
and a second glass with the pizza
you order later. $6–7
Languedoc, France
Imported by House of Fine Wines

Aresti
MERLOT "Montemar"
Medium-bodied. Big, bold style.
A surprisingly inexpensive Merlot
from the heart of Chilean wine
country—the Curico Valley in
Maule. Its bargain price, plus the
intriguing flavors of cocoa and
roasted coffee, make this wine a
winner. It's terrific for all things
grilled—especially burgers loaded
with cheese and bacon. $7–8
Maule, Chile
Imported by Broadbent

Domaine de la Patience
MERLOT "Cuvée St. Guilhem"
Medium-bodied. Surprising heft
at a low price.
A rustic, satisfying red table wine
from vineyards on the Gard river
between the French cities of
Nimes and Avignon. Flavors of
black fruits and earth seem
highly concentrated, and the
winemaker goes easy on the oak.
It's rich enough for meats but
good just on its own. $8–10
Languedoc, France
Imported by World Wide Wines

McGuigan Brothers
MERLOT "Black Label"
Medium-bodied. A quaffing wine
with plenty of fruit and no oak.
This Aussie Merlot is the kind of
wine you pray they're pouring by
the glass at your corner bar and
grill. Easy to drink, no hard edges,
and blissfully unoaked—just pure,
honest cherry fruit. A versatile
wine with pub grub, fruity
enough even for spicy Buffalo
chicken wings. $7–9
Hunter Valley, New South Wales
Imported by Winebow

CHILE'S BEST BARGAIN?

How and why the Carta Vieja estate turns out such delicious wines selling
for as little as $4 remains a mystery. Then again, maybe it's because this
winery in Chile's Maule Valley has been owned and operated by the del
Pedregal family for seven generations. A textbook case of practice makes
perfect? Easily the peer of any $10–15 Bordeaux, the medium-bodied **Carta
Vieja Merlot** ($4–5) has cherry liqueur earthy complexity to spare. It's a
Merlot that's plump, smooth, and perfectly balanced—and with terrific
mouthfeel in the bargain. Serve it at your next party, either with the appetizers or as a base for sangria. *Imported by F. Wildman*

Heritage Road
MERLOT
Medium-bodied. Sweetly ripe, flavorful, and smooth.
An Australian wine full of everything Merlot lovers crave: thick plum and malted milk flavors in the smoothest style imaginable. Kick back and sink into a glass of this comforting red while you munch on leftovers from last night's holiday party. $8–10
Hunter Valley, New South Wales
Imported by R. H. Phillips-Hogue

Petit Chapeau
MERLOT
Medium-bodied.
Soft and round in the mouth, with ripe fruit in good vintages.
Selected and "made to spec" for New York's celebrity sommelier Daniel Johnnes. The '02 is fine, but previous vintages have hit the bull's-eye with their spiced red cherry fruit and food-friendly balance. Pour this at your next pizza party or backyard barbecue. $9–10
Languedoc, France
Imported by Jeroboam

Château Les Tuileries
BORDEAUX
Light- to medium-bodied. A zesty, bright-fruited cocktail red.
This Bordeaux hits the shelves early each year and is often gone by the end of summer. Ripe, soft, and easy to drink, it's good served as a pre-dinner apéritif, alongside cold cuts and grilled meats, or with game hens stuffed with herby wild rice. $9–10
Bordeaux
Imported by International Gourmet

Moss Bridge
MERLOT
Medium-bodied. Sweetly ripe fruit that bursts in the mouth.
Winemaker Jim Olsen first marketed this brand in England, where he was told, "Bottle the wines young and fresh. And throw away the oak barrels." That sound advice resulted in a Merlot of astonishing purity that positively glows with cherry and pomegranate flavors. Great with all-American classics like mac 'n' cheese, BLTs, fried chicken, and turkey burgers. $10–11
California

Bogle Vineyards
MERLOT
Medium-bodied.
A good, fleshy style that's smooth and satisfying.
After twenty years in California, the reliable Bogle winery produces one of the smoothest and tastiest Merlots out there. Burgers and fried chicken are pleasant partners, but anybody could enjoy this wine on its own. $10–12
Monterey, California

Guilhem Durand
MERLOT
Medium- to full-bodied.
A gutsy red with smooth balance and concentration.
For fans of big French reds who don't want to pay a big price. Dark chocolate, smoke, and black currant rule the palate in a wine with an emphasis on ripeness and a pleasantly strong aftertaste. Great with lamb couscous, chops, cheeses, cold cuts, and sausage. $10–12
Languedoc, France
Imported by Weygandt/Metzler

CALIFORNIA'S KING OF KOSHER

The Baron Herzog Winery makes some of the most consistently high-quality bargain reds and whites in the world—and kosher in every sense of the word. The fruit for **Baron Herzog Merlot** ($11–13) is sometimes sourced from Bordeaux, sometimes from California. Either way, the finished wine is easy to enjoy, with a lush taste of red fruits and modest hints of sweet tobacco. At the table, it's a classic chicken casserole and pot roast partner.

Headed by master winemaker Peter Stern, the winery combines a forward-looking California attitude with the strict kosher supervision accorded its Merlots, Chardonnays, Cabs, and other California varietals.

Chartron La Fleur
BORDEAUX
Medium-bodied.
Supple in the mouth, elegant, and pleasingly fragrant.
This wine is a joint venture of U.S. importer Eric Solomon and Margaux's Chateau Kirwan. The proportion of Merlot to Cabernet varies year to year, but the dry, spiced cherry flavors of the Merlot always dominate. A fine sipping wine or traditional partner for semi-soft cheeses like Brie and Camembert. $10–12
Bordeaux
Imported by European Cellars

Hahn Estates
MERLOT
Medium-bodied. Supple, fruity, and noticeably oaked.
A cool climate Merlot with a simple, pleasing palate of red berries and wood. It's easy to see why this wine is so popular. Good for sipping or for pairing with fried chicken or spicy catfish fillets. $10–12
Monterey, California

Waterstone
MERLOT
Medium-bodied. Medium fruit, medium tannins, medium price.
This California Merlot is one of the surest red wine values around. Hints of spiciness and malt nicely complement the very

soft core of fruit. Sip it on its own, with takeout chicken, or with simple luncheon fare. $11–13
California

$12 to $20

Cartlidge & Browne
MERLOT
Medium-bodied. Classic California Merlot—only better and bigger than most.
Tony Cartlidge has long been a reliable source for value wines (his Manzanita Canyon line is a hit with supermarket shoppers, and rightly so). We like his premium Merlot, which features figs and cherries and an aftertaste of vanilla oak. It's an honest, no-nonsense red with a burger. $12–14
California

Château Laveau
BORDEAUX SUPÉRIEUR
Medium- to full-bodied.
Dry and meaty, with a long, lush finish.
Inky-colored wine with essences of earth, black currants, and leather. A steak-eater's red for sure, this Bordeaux is also interesting with firm cheeses like cheddar or Jarlsberg. $12–14
Bordeaux
Imported by Wines for Food

Scarbolo
MERLOT
Medium- to full-bodied.
Strong, savory, and dry.
Italy's interpretation of Merlot tends to be earthier and a little edgier than the oaky American version—so while this is an absolutely elegant, well-turned wine from an esteemed estate, it's not for everyone. In any case, it definitely wants food. Think baked pastas, roast chicken, and prosciutto. $12–14
Friuli, Italy
Imported by Domaine Select

Señorio de Sarria
MERLOT "Viñedo No. 4"
Medium-bodied.
Silky-soft and incredibly fruity—an atypical Spanish red.
Cherries, cherries, cherries! The sweetness, succulence, and powerful fruit of this Spanish wine are the perfect foil to salty Smithfield ham and dishes peppered with chilies. $13–15
Navarra, Spain
Imported by Spain Wine Collection

Château Penin
BORDEAUX SUPÉRIEUR
Medium-bodied.
Soft and seductive.
No secret recipe here: just a mouthful of cherryish, satiny-textured Merlot beefed up with a little Cabernet in a perfectly balanced composition. What's not to like? Superb with *steak frites* (garlicky hangar steak with shoestring fries) or a savory mushroom tart. $13–14
Bordeaux
Imported by Bayfield

Château Le Croix de Bert
ST. ÉMILION
Medium-bodied. Understated and classy, with a firm finish.
This St. Émilion—80% Merlot, 10% Cabernet Sauvignon, 10% Cabernet Franc—offers delicious black cherries and what Bordeaux lovers call "dustiness," but it tends to need for a year or two for its tannins to soften. A great choice for collectors who need something to drink while their more expensive selections mature. Excellent with lamb chops flavored with thyme. $13–15
Bordeaux
Imported by Bayfield

Coturri
MERLOT "Workingman's"
Full-bodied. An organic red-cherry mélange.
Crafted by one of California's best winemakers, this rigorously organic, turbo-driven Merlot is halfway to kirsch yet has an almost completely dry finish. It goes well with fall and winter dishes like roast turkey and acorn squash. Occasionally, the estate also releases pricier Merlots from neighboring vineyards—**Maclise** ($25–28) and **Feingold** ($50+), hedonistic wines with Portlike finishes. $16–18
California

Château La Fleur Plaisance
ST. ÉMILION **Grand Cru**
Medium-bodied. A gentle wine that lingers on the palate.
This is an extremely elegant and refined Bordeaux, showing textbook aromatics (think black cherries dusted with cocoa). Early twentieth-century wine writers and the French would call

A WINNER FROM WALLA WALLA

The benchmark Washington red may be **L'Ecole No. 41 Merlot** ($33–35). The family-owned winery that makes this full-bodied, dense, thick-textured (and cellarable) wine is housed in a turn-of-the-century schoolhouse in the village of Frenchtown, in District No. 41.

Deeply extracted, barrel-aged for a year and a half, and sourced from fruit purchased across the Yakima and Columbia valleys, this Merlot is clearly an effort to cram as much black cherry flavor as possible into a bottle. Serve it with grilled red meats or duck in cherry sauce.

it "feminine." Surprisingly, the estate's second label from **Montagne–St. Émilion** ($10–12) is often the heartier wine. Pair both with filet mignon smothered in sautéed mushrooms. $18–20
Bordeaux
Imported by Bayfield

Château Grand Pey Lescours
ST. ÉMILION **Grand Cru**
Medium-bodied.
A traditional Bordeaux—
very dry and succulent.
The aromas of this wine suggest a comforting, congenial gentlemen's club: Cigar box, wood smoke, and soft leather accent a basic palate of sundried cherries. Better still, all of a good wine's building blocks are firmly in place. Enjoy it with a steak with Bordelaise sauce and quietly contemplate the lost pleasures of the Gilded Age. $18–20
Bordeaux
Imported by Bayfield

Clos La Chance
MERLOT
Medium- to full-bodied.
A sleek, graceful style with
multidimensional flavors.
Excellent acidity propels the flavors in this California blend (85% Merlot and a little Cabernet Franc, Petite Sirah, and Cabernet Sauvignon) which range from cherry, mulberry, and plum to a whiff of graham cracker. Our choice for chicken pot pie, double-crème cheeses, and burgers with the works. $18–20
Central Coast, California

Château Lapostolle
MERLOT "Cuvée Alexandre"
Medium- to full-bodied.
A deep, sensuously textured
wine with a powerful finish.
From a Chilean estate renowned both for value and quality. With help from Bordeaux oenologist Michel Rolland and a fine selection of fifty-year-old vines, Lapostolle produces a reserve Merlot that delivers a nice hit of black cherry fruit backed by secondary flavors of coffee and soil that are definitively Chilean. Serve it with marinated flank steaks or broiled portobello mushrooms. $18–21
Colchagua, Chile
Imported by Schieffelin & Somerset

$20 to $40

Montes
MERLOT "Alpha"
Full-bodied. A powerful Chilean
red that responds well to cellaring.
Somewhere between the lean French Merlots and the fat, oaky American ones stands this "gaucho wine," redolent of beef, tar,

$12 to $20

Ferrando
CAVANESE ROSSO
Medium-bodied. A vigorous
Piedmontese cocktail.
Half Nebbiolo and half Barbera,
this quirky wine is hard to stop
sipping—especially with food. We
love its cherry-berry fragrance and
succulent acidity with red sauces,
sundried tomatoes, grilled fare, or
even a whole stuffed fish. $13–14
Piedmont, Italy
Imported by Rosenthal

Rainoldi
ROSSO DI VALTELLINA
Medium-bodied. Vividly fruity
and juicy—almost sweet.
With all that lively blackberry fruit
and the magenta-purple gleam in
the glass, you'd think this wine
was Barbera or Zinfandel, not
Nebbiolo. It's versatile with food,
especially spicy tomato sauces
like Fra Diavola. $14–16
Lombardy, Italy
Imported by Opici

Antichi Vigneti di Cantalupo
COLLINE NOVARESE
"Agamium"
Medium-bodied. Aromatically
complex, with juicy acidity
and a long finish.
From the northernmost vineyards
in the Piedmont, this pretty wine
eschews the hard, vigorous style
of Barolo, focusing instead on
lush red fruits capped by scents
of roses and leather. It's a deluxe
choice for pizza with black olives
or pasta puttanesca. Also try their
single-vineyard **Ghemme** ($40–50),
for which this producer is famed.
$17–20
Piedmont, Italy
Imported by Polaner

$20 to $40

Marziano & Enrico Abbona
NEBBIOLO D'ALBA
Medium- to full-bodied.
Unusually ripe-fruited for
Nebbiolo, with incredibly
forceful aromatics.
Nebbiolo d'Alba is a DOC zone
(*Denominazione di Origine*
Controllata is Italy's version of the
French AOC) near Barolo, and its
wines need less aging and are less
expensive. Yet this wine easily
beats half the Barolos out there
for sheer flavor and enjoyment.
The elusive tar, spices, and dried
flowers of the Nebbiolo grape
come through in spades, but the
chunk of fruit at the core makes it
downright sexy. Hovering around
14% alcohol yet never out of
balance, it's perfect drunk
young with rich polentas, pork
medallions, or a mushroom
risotto. $20–25
Piedmont, Italy
Imported by Polaner

Valdinara
NEBBIOLO D'ALBA
"Sontuoso"
Medium- to full-
bodied. This deep,
sleek wine lives
up to its name—
sumptuous.
Only about 1,600
cases of this

gorgeous wine are made each
year, sourced from the sunniest
part of the Careglio family vineyards in Alba. Sweet for Nebbiolo,
cherryish, leathery in scent, and
deeply satisfying, it outdoes
itself with osso buco and other
slowly braised meats. $20–25
Piedmont, Italy
Imported by J. Given

AN EASYGOING BAROLO

A Barolo we particularly like is **Antario Barolo "Vigneto Castelletto"** ($29–32), easy on the palate and the pocketbook alike. It's a gentler version of the hefty Barolo (in fact, it's about the lightest Barolo we know), and we find it consistently pleasing, with soft black fruit and a clean finish. Floral aromas and berries dominate, with a faint licoricey note in the back. Stick to current vintages and enjoy them with braised meats like chicken and veal, or cannelloni with red sauce. *Imported by F & F Wines*

Antoniolo
NEBBIOLO "Juvenia"
Full-bodied. Plush and velvety with opulent aromas.
What's not to like in this wine? It's fresher tasting than Barolo, cheaper than Barbaresco, and fruitier than Spanna. Serve with steak or lamb. $20–22
Piedmont, Italy
Imported by M. Skurnik

Aurelio Settimo
NEBBIOLO LANGHE
Medium-bodied. Ripe and earthy, with a succulent finish.
Tiziana Settimo, daughter of Aurelio, makes a superb, highly traditional **Rocche Barolo** ($50–55), but she also puts aside a small amount of Nebbiolo juice from Langhe each year for earlier release. Her Nebbiolo Langhe is aged for a year, then bottled for drinking in the near term. This earthy, berryish, super value is perfect for slow-cooked meats or polenta with mushrooms. $21–23
Piedmont, Italy
Imported by Verdoni

$40 to $60

Piero Busso
BARBARESCO "Vigna Borgese"
Medium- to full-bodied. Needs breathing, but comes around with a wallop of fruit.
Barbaresco can sometimes be harsh, but not Busso's. Pure

blackberries dominate the palate, augmented by the classic violety, earthy aromas of Nebbiolo. This suave, "modern" style from organically grown fruit is quite versatile with red meats, baked pastas, grilled kebabs, and roasted winter vegetables. $40-48
Piedmont, Italy
Imported by Vias

Carbone Monchiero
BAROLO "Montanello"
Medium-bodied. Exotically fragrant, forward, and richly layered.
Marco Monchiero makes several exciting Nebbiolos, including a bargain **Roero Superiore** ($20), but the vineyard-designated Montanello is his flagship wine. An hour's breathing time will release its entrancing violet and lavender aromas. Serve with well-marbled beef or lamb—and if you can find truffle-infused olive oil at your market, here's your chance to use it. $40-50
Piedmont, Italy
Imported by Matt Brothers

Roagna
BARBARESCO
Medium- to full-bodied. Seductively fragrant, lasting, and balanced.
Father-and-son winemakers Giovanni and Alfredo Roagna own twelve of the fourteen acres of I Paglieri, one of the Piedmont's blue-chip vineyards. From here they make a wonderful, tar- and violet-

flavored Barbaresco that continuously evolves on the palate. This is a wine worth spending an evening with as you snack on olives, crusty bread, and a chunk of good Parmesan cheese. The Roagnas' more opulent *"Pajé"* ($50) is excellent with game meats like venison and smoked duck breast; find the superb '96 if you can. $40-42
Piedmont, Italy
Imported by Commonwealth

Over $40

Giuseppe Mascarello
BAROLO "Monprivato"
Medium- to full-bodied. A profound wine with fabulous perfume and multifaceted character.
Giuseppe Mascarello's son Mauro, the fourth generation at this winery, makes an ultra-traditional Barolo in *botti* (giant old barrels) that penetrates the soul with aromas of truffles, loam soils, dried strawberries, and roses woven into a ripe wine.

Decant and serve with Italian haute cuisine—game birds, crusty veal chops, or braised lamb shanks topped with your favorite mushrooms. The '93 and '97 are in the market, and you'd do well to search them out. $60-70
Piedmont, Italy
Imported by Polaner

Aldo Conterno
BAROLO "Colonello"
Full-bodied. Strong in every aspect, from tannin to alcohol to flavor intensity—the Barolo *ne plus ultra*.
The legendary Aldo Conterno isn't averse to experimentation, but his Barolos remain among the most consistently opulent wines made in Italy. His crown jewel is the Riserva **Granbussia** ($120–700) mostly seen at auctions; but the more approachable Colonnello is the one we know best. Aged three years in oak casks and one in the bottle, it is typically grand: deeply saturated in color, hugely tannic, and

replete with scents of tar, tea rose, leather, and dark chocolate. The '96 was classic and the '97 and '98 were astonishingly rich, but older vintages are more variable. Cellar this and all of Conterno's Barolos patiently and unveil them with game meats or rare roasted lamb. $100-150
Piedmont, Italy
Imported by Vias

Bruno Giacosa
BAROLO "Falletto"
Medium- to full-bodied. Lengthily aged, concentrated, and capped by lasting tannins.
Founded in 1890, Giacosa is on everybody's shortlist of Piedmont's finest and most traditional estates. The "Falletto" is highly scented with baked earth, truffles, and tar (there's even a hint of saltiness in some vintages), and the tannins are unapologetically hard. It needs some time: The '95 and '96 (two great Barolo vintages of the '90s) are still slow to come around. Give it ten years or so in a cool cellar, then decant and serve with thinly sliced rare beef, braciole, and the freshest Parmigiano-Reggiano you can find. $150-200+
Piedmont, Italy
Imported by Winebow/ Leonardo LoCascio

Pinot Noir

*Though notoriously pricey and vintage-sensitive,
Pinot Noir remains the wine most prized by chefs and collectors,
especially in the great growths of Burgundy.*

HEY CALL IT the "heartbreak grape," and for good reason. Pinot Noir is prone to disease and mutation in the vineyard while demanding a lengthy, cool growing season. It's picky about its soils, terribly susceptible to vintage variation and, because of its high acidity, it makes particularly thin, tart wines when poorly handled. Worse, as the wine matures, it's sheer luck whether it turns out magnificent or falls to pieces. As a result, this prima donna is expensive—and if it isn't, it's usually because the wine has been blended with other grapes or chemically altered. Yet the grape still managed to give the world one of its greatest wines: Burgundy.

In the Grand Cru vineyards of Burgundy's Côte d'Or (Golden Slope), a thirty-mile strip of hills south of Dijon, Pinot yields its riches. Its wines turn silken and deep, behaving, in the best examples, like a liquid distillate of the landscape—the reason the large, balloon-like Burgundy wineglass was designed to capture as much of the bouquet as possible. Burgundies from the northern part of the region tend to taste and smell of black fruits, while Southern burgundies and most American Pinots tend toward red ones like strawberry and cranberry. With age, earthy, gamey, and woodsy flavors crop up. Specific flavors and aromas detected by tasters could fill a small book, with truffles, perfume, mushrooms, cedar, cigar, and worn leather often noted.

The coupling of complexity and good acidity makes Pinot Noir one of the most versatile food wines in the world. It spans the divide between vegetables, meat, and fish, encouraging the diner to explore one wine throughout multiple courses of a meal.

Where, beyond Burgundy, is Pinot grown? In Europe, close by in the Loire and in northern Italy, Germany, Austria, and Switzerland. In America, Oregon's Willamette Valley and California's Russian River, Carneros, and Central Coast are the major growing areas, with wines from New York State offering noteworthy variations in style. Some nice Pinots also come from the Southern Hemisphere, though, like elsewhere, getting the best out of the grape is touch and go.

Under $12

Angove's
PINOT NOIR
**Light- to medium-bodied.
All fruit all the time. Simple,
vibrant, and good fun.**
This Aussie wine has a really
interesting aroma of tea
(Red Zinger perhaps?). It's also
unoaked, which seems the right
choice. Nothing serious, this red
still makes a nice foil for Indian or
Southeast Asian curries. $7–9
Australia
Imported by Empson USA

William Cole
PINOT NOIR
**Light-bodied. Bright and simple—
a sipping wine with a juicy edge.**
Sometimes you have to go
below the equator to find tasty,
affordable Pinot Noir. This Chilean
version has a straightforward red
berry character tinged with earth,
plus lovely balance for a meal
centered on veggies or quiche.
$10–12
Casablanca, Chile
Imported by Metropolis

Wyatt
PINOT NOIR
**Light- to medium-bodied.
A wonderful sipping wine with a
gentle, juicy finish.**
This wine is "made to order" for
a New York importer but is
available nationally. Sourced
mainly from the Carneros
appellation, it is not only well
balanced but has delicious cherry
pie flavors and a touch of earth.
It's a choice bargain red for
vegetarian dishes and chicken
dishes alike. $11–13
California

$12 to $20

Carneros Creek
PINOT NOIR
"Fleur de Carneros"
**Light-bodied.
Delicate, yet
very fruity.**

We feel this
inexpensive
bottling from
Carneros Creek
is their best wine—maybe the
reason it sells out every year. The
wine's flavors of tea roses and
strawberries float across the
palate, leaving a sense of
refreshment. A perfect red for
light fish or paella. $12–15
Carneros, California

Blankenhorn
SPÄTBURGUNDER **"Der Kuss"**
**Light- to medium-bodied.
Surprisingly sweet on first taste,
then quickly addictive.**
Fresh and cherry-berryish is this
German Pinot, which has no hard
edges, no oaky distractions, and a
lip-smacking residual sweetness
in deft balance with the whole.
We like it mildly chilled, as a
complement to hot 'n' spicy
dishes, and it's a great summer
sipper as well. $14–16
Baden, Germany
Imported by Wines for Food

Avila
PINOT NOIR
**Medium-bodied. Good, hearty
style with oak in evidence
and plentiful fruit.**
This rich, sappy, earth- and plum-
scented Pinot from warmer climes
has something almost Zinfandel-
like about it. An attractive red for
hearty fare like roast chicken,
charcuterie, and bean dishes.
$14–16
San Luis Obispo, California

Bouchaine
PINOT NOIR
"Buchli Station"
Medium-bodied. Plump, fleshy, soft, and mouthwatering— hard not to like.
Buchli Station made its debut in 2002, apparently as a casual, less-expensive alternative to this winery's premium offerings. It is a lovely red, dripping with cherries and pomegranate. Thanks to its lack of earthiness or heaviness, it's a jubilant match for trendy pan-Asian and

pan-Latino dishes. Its colorful Americana label also makes it a nice Thanksgiving wine. $14–16
Napa

Ramsay
PINOT NOIR
Medium-bodied. Soft and easy to drink, persistent in the finish.
Vintage after vintage, Kent Rasmussen's second label is an elegant, high-quality Pinot. Caramelly oak is balanced nicely with the wine's floral aromas and ripe cherry and cranberry flavors. Delicious with vegetables au gratin, just fruity enough for spicy Chinese and Thai, yummy with fried chicken, and fun to drink in general. $15–17
California

Zenith Vineyards
PINOT NOIR
Light- to medium-bodied. A juicy, jazzy, winningly sweet Pinot.
This delightful sipping wine hails from the north half of New Zealand's South Island. Name your red fruit and it's here. On the culinary front, the terrific acidity that's making your mouth water transforms this Pinot into a

fantastic seafood and vegetable partner. A dish like poached salmon on a bed of braised leeks in cream is the perfect match. Need we say more? Yes: Chill it. $15–17
Marlborough, New Zealand
Imported by Southern Starz

Guy Chaumont
CÔTE CHALONNAISE
Light-bodied. A delicate Pinot that's organically grown and vinted.
Pure, sweet strawberries on the nose and featherweight character will make this appealing to anyone who likes light reds. It chills well and makes a delicate adornment to fish, vegetables, and pasta primavera. $15–17
Burgundy
Imported by Organic Vintages

Warwick Valley Winery
PINOT NOIR
Light-bodied. A dry, graceful, slightly earthy wine for foodies.
Amidst the apple trees and old windmills of upstate New York, the father-son team at Warwick crafts a tasty, pale-hued Pinot whose blanched cherry fruit and fine balance will enhance all kinds of food. Pour it lightly chilled with hors d'oeuvres, pasta with mushrooms, light white meats, fish steaks, rice pilaf, or even sushi. $15–18
Hudson Valley, New York

Henri Bourgeois
SANCERRE ROUGE
"Le Porte de Cailloux"
Light-bodied. A tad deeper than rosé, high in natural acidity, and beautifully delicate.
We call this slender willow of a wine the Gwyneth Paltrow of Pinots. While it's highly vintage-sensitive, like all Sancerre reds, the quality-conscious co-op that makes it does admirably well each year and excels in good vintages like

1997 and 2002. Cranberries and watermelon are the dominant flavors. A fab choice for fish dishes. $15–17
Loire Valley, France
Imported by Monsieur Touton

Willamette Valley Vineyards
PINOT NOIR "Whole Cluster"
Light-bodied. Ebulliently fruity, bordering on sweet.
This distinctive Pinot is fruitier than the norm because its whole berry fermentation method emulates that of Beaujolais winemakers. In some vintages it's like biting down on fresh strawberries. Great for spicy fare, sausages, saucy Caribbean/ Indian/Mexican, or a Cantonese sweet 'n' sour fish. $15–18
Oregon

Ransom
PINOT NOIR
Medium-bodied. Earthy and dry, with honest Pinot character.
Tad Ransom is a one-man show in Willamette, doing great work with both Pinot Noir and Pinot Gris. His red is definitively Oregonian in style, with spice, earth, and leathery scents at the forefront. Fine fruit, too—the woodsy kind. Try this with grilled Copper River salmon or a bowl of polenta with grilled vegetables. $15–18
Oregon

Nicolas Potel
BOURGOGNE "Vielles Vignes"
Light- to medium-bodied.
Fabulously perfumed, silky, and easy to sip.
Famed *négotiant* Nicolas Potel makes great Pommards and Clos Vougeots, but frankly, we're most excited about his least-expensive wine—the basic, everyday Bourgogne. Its gentle cherry- and tobacco-scented palate makes it an amicable pre-dinner sipper,

wonderful with creamy soups and appetizers and with light poultry. $16–18
Burgundy
Imported by F. Wildman

Domaine Sirugue
CÔTE DE NUITS-VILLAGES
"Clos de la Belle Marguerite"
Medium-bodied. Succulent and savory, with bold aromas and a delicately tapering finish.
Redolent of blackberries, woodsmoke, spice, and pepper. Exquisitely juicy, and ready for the table. This is our kind of Pinot! Enjoy with *coq au vin* (its classic partner) or any sort of sauced poultry. It's equally good with white bean dishes. $16–18
Burgundy
Imported by Southern Wine

Piper's Brook
PINOT NOIR "Ninth Island"
Light- to medium-bodied.
A sassy, fun style with cleanly expressed fruit.
Tasmanian Pinot Noir? It turns out that Australia's island state has a cool, hilly, wet climate at its north end, perfect for growing the world's most fickle grape. Piper's Brook is one of the "big three" wineries in what's called Tassie. Enjoy this rosy, berryish, balanced Pinot with all kinds of vegetarian dishes, omelets, and fish. $16–19
Tasmania, Australia
Imported by Lauber

Saint Clair
PINOT NOIR "Doctor's Creek"
Medium-bodied. Fruity, plump and pleasing.
This is a red wine from New Zealand's white wine country, so it's no surprise to find juiciness and the kind of pure, clean fruit that cool-climate winemaking engenders. A touch of oak adds

depth and a sweet vanilla note. Try it with all manner of grilled fare or mild meat dishes like pot roast. $18–20
Marlborough, New Zealand
Imported by Lauber

Au Bon Climat
PINOT NOIR
Medium-bodied. Strongly fruit-driven and mouthwatering.
Jim Clendenen's quirky, forward-thinking winery on California's Central Coast turns out top-notch Chardonnay and Pinot Noir in practically every vintage. Vibrant with cherry and pomegranate fruit and clearly Californian in its "drink-me-now" sensuality, this Pinot is great for the grill. In 2002, the Santa Barbara bottling contained 25% Mondeuse grapes, which added a fantastic brambly fragrance. For those who like a fuller wine, the Santa Maria bottling is usually richer and more chocolatey. $18–20
Santa Barbara, California

Marc Brocot
MARSANNAY "Les Echezeaux"
Light- to medium-bodied.
Ripe, flavorsome Pinot with gentle, pleasing mouthfeel.
This is a bargain Burgundy—lighter in some years, richer in others, but always fragrant and abundantly fruity. At its best, Asian spices, licorice, and hints of real Burgundian *gout de terroir* (taste of the earth) come through. Look for the winsome 2002, a perfect partner for salmon, swordfish, or light poultry. $18–20
Burgundy
Imported by V.O.S.

Didier Fornerol
CÔTE DE NUITS-VILLAGES
Light- to medium-bodied.
Delicate, piquant Pinot with an elegantly balanced finish.
A pleasing café wine with a black fruit theme nicely nuanced by mineral traces, olives, and black pepper. Serve it with smoked cold cuts, cheese toast, or grilled vegetables. $18–22
Burgundy
Imported by Jeroboam

AN AMERICAN IN BEAUNE

Alex Gambal is that rarest of birds: an American making wine in Burgundy. What's more, he's making splendid wines from several top appellations. He moved his family to the Burgundy wine center of Beaune on a whim in 1993, started winemaking in 1996, and came to our attention (and many others') with his superb 1999 vintage. When asked how he got access to Burgundy's hallowed vineyards, Gambal said modestly "I joined the PTA at my kids' school, chatted with the other parents at soccer games, made some winemaker friends…"

Gambal's **Bourgogne Pinot Noir "Cuvée Les Deux Papis"** ($16–19) reveals the most about Gambal's winemaking style: It is strawberryish and friendly, yet aptly expresses the earthy, salty *terroir* of Burgundy. As a complement for food, it's versatile and delicious with stuffed chickens, pastas with sausage, mustardy medallions of pork, or an assortment of soft French cheeses. The estate also makes a fantastic **Chambolle–Musigny** ($40–45), which is satiny, fruity, and serious all at once—a sensuous wine that will benefit from cellaring. Both wines imported by House of Burgundy

Claude Maréchal
BOURGOGNE "Cuvée Gravel"
Medium-bodied. Pure, plush fruit all the way. Fun!
A very pure Pinot for pleasure-seekers—very strawberryish, terrific staying power. Drink it young with vividly flavored fare like pineapple ham, Hunan dishes, and Cajun/Creole. The more structured **"Savigny-Les-Beaune "Vielles Vignes"** ($30+) is also superb, but works better with subtler savory fare like stuffed mushrooms and garlicky hanger steak. $18–22
Burgundy
Imported by Louis/Dressner

$20 to $40

Millbrook
PINOT NOIR
Light- to medium-bodied. A fruit-driven, pleasing Pinot with a juicy finish.
This is probably the best-known Pinot from the East Coast, made under the sure hand of wine-maker John Graziano since 1985. Briefly aged in French oak, it's a tasty mouthful of cherries, cocoa, and strawberries that wants a little food. Try it lightly chilled with grilled or broiled fish steaks. $19–22
Hudson Valley, New York

Calera
PINOT NOIR
Medium-bodied. A drier, earthier style makes for a more "Burgundian" California Pinot.
Winemaker Josh Jensen is considered a benchmark producer of California Pinot. With the exception of his new value-priced **"El Niño"** line ($13–15), we find the wines less about pure fruit than about spice, minerality, and dry earth tones—hardly typical of Pinot grown in California, but very interesting. His exceedingly rare single-vineyard bottlings of **"Mt. Harlan"** ($25–55) receive 30% new oak, while his Central Coast wine sees half that. Cellar the Harlan and drink the regular Pinot with mushroom dishes, pâté, and rich, meat-flecked rice dishes. $20–25
Central Coast, California

François Raquillet
MERCUREY "Vielles Vignes"
Medium-bodied. Great texture, and rich in fruit.
Mercurey lies in the "sweet spot" of the Côte Chalonaise in southern Burgundy, and Raquillet is regularly the top producer there. Exuberant and fruity with cherries and boysenberries, this wine is drinkable right from the get-go. Try it with your holiday turkey or ham, with blackened redfish or other Cajun/Creole specialties, or dine Burgundian style with charcuterie and pungent cheeses. For a few dollars more, single vineyard selections **"Les Chazeaux"** and **"Les Veleys"** ($30–34) are definitely worth seeking out. $24–26
Burgundy
Imported by Bayfield

Gerard Mugneret
BOURGOGNE
Medium-bodied. Shows the great depth and richness of a premier cru (first growth) wine.
Sensational! The fruit in this wine hits you in waves—a sensuous succession of black cherry, currant, and cola flavors. A serious wine for Burgundy lovers that improves with age, it's blessed with a swirling oriental spice bouquet even when young. Mugnerer's **Vosne–Romanée**

($35–50) is fine as well, full of fruit and great with roast pork or Peking duck. $25–30
Burgundy
Imported by Jandell

David Bruce
PINOT NOIR "Vintner's Select"
Medium-bodied. Mouthfilling and saturated in color, with smooth texture but fairly strong alcohol.
Bruce is a forty-year veteran winemaker in Santa Cruz who makes a Pinot striking for its concentrated black fruit, sweet vanilla oak, and integrity of flavor. While he does several bottlings, including two from the Central Coast, we prefer the fruitiness of the Sonoma. A fine match for grilled chops or steaks. $26–28
Sonoma

Adelsheim Vineyard
PINOT NOIR
Light- to medium-bodied. Silky, delicate, easy on the oak, and drinkable now.
As so often happens in wine, this is a case when a winery's most basic bottling is its best. Wine pioneers David and Ginny Adelsheim craft their Oregon Pinot from ten different sites in the Willamette Valley. Its intricately lacy, strawberry-scented character makes it pair beautifully with fish and vegetable dishes. $27–30
Oregon

Lane Tanner
PINOT NOIR "Bien Nacido"
Medium-bodied. Subtle and sophisticated, with a dry palate and lip-smacking acidity.
Ms. Tanner works with small parcels of superb fruit in central California and quietly makes some of America's most renowned Pinots. This carefully crafted example is appealing for its baked cherry/cranberry fruit and the elusive milk chocolate in its finish. It really comes alive with grilled fish steaks, turkey, and roasted root vegetables.
$28–32
Santa Barbara, California

Domaine Chandon de Briailles
PERNAND-VERGELESSES 1er Cru "Ile des Vergelesses"
Light- to medium-bodied. A charming and delicate Burgundy with flavors that linger.
This is the finest wine of its appellation, tended biodynamically on the best plot of ground by a mother and daughter who put passion into their work. The  fruit is almost ethereal on the palate, focusing on blanched cherries, strawberries, minerals, and potpourri. There's hardly a better seafood red in the world.
$30–32
Burgundy
Imported by Jeroboam

Gary Farrell
PINOT NOIR "Russian River"
Light- to medium-bodied. Pale and pretty, very succulent, and a classy style overall.
Gary Farrell, who has one of the most beautiful, most well-run wineries in the Russian River, painstakingly makes a lithe, lissome Pinot with a complex red fruit profile, hints of new French oak, and high-toned herbal flavors like mint and sage. This is a food wine, and a subtle one at that, excelling with grilled and roasted fish, pan-Asian cuisine, and calf's liver, sweetbreads, and other organ meats. $30–33
Russian River, California

Domaine Millot
SAVIGNY-LES-BEAUNE
Medium-bodied. A stylish red Burgundy with robust fruit and terrific mouthfeel.
Jean-Marc Millot is one of the most stubborn traditionalists in all of Burgundy. His wines are organically grown, hand-harvested at very low yields, and see little new oak. We consistently enjoy this lively wine with rich fish steaks of salmon or tuna. $30–35
Burgundy
Imported by Pinnacle

Cold Heaven
PINOT NOIR "Le Bon Climat"
Medium-bodied.
Ripe and voluptuous—
a no-holds-barred style.
Made by Morgan Clendenen (wife of Jim Clendenen from Au Bon Climat), this is back-to-basics winemaking, and to incredible effect. While the focus is on sweetly ripe bing cherry fruit, beguiling whiffs of tea rose and incense, a bit of oak, and a long, lip-smacking finish are also characteristic of this unfiltered, unfined wine. Serve with spicy white-meat dishes, fish, or mild blue cheeses. $31–33
Santa Barbara, California

Capiaux
PINOT NOIR "Widdoes Vineyard"
Medium- to full-bodied. Exotic aromas, very rich mouthfeel, and a deep finish that lasts and lasts.
After winemaking stints in Napa and Sonoma, Sean Capiaux has mastered Pinot Noir in the Russian River valley. The Widdoes Vineyard, of which fewer than five hundred cases are annually produced, is about as close to a great Nuits-St-Georges (Burgundy) as we've tasted in California. Explosively aromatic, earthy, chocolatey, and

long and liqueurlike on the palate, it's great teamed with duck, game birds, or braised short ribs. A little breathing in a decanter is suggested. $32–40
Russian River, California

Coturri
PINOT NOIR "Jewell Vineyard"
Full-bodied. Dazzling fruit and over-the-top ripeness— more like Pinot liqueur.
In this surreal cocktail of perfume, pomegranate, and cherry Kool-Aid, heightened acidity and extravagant alcohol remain tenuously in balance with the wine's sweetness—which makes the dry finish something of a shock. If you're feeling adventurous, explore this organic "über-Pinot" with such sweet-and-sour edibles as Carolina barbecue. It's also good with aged semi-soft cheeses. $35–40
Sonoma

Domaine Philippe Charlopin-Parizot
CHAMBOLLE-MUSIGNY
Medium-bodied. Graceful, lush, and enticing.
Ambitious, skilled, and steadily rising to prominence in Burgundy, Philippe Charlopin-Parizot is known as a vintner to watch. With its concentrated, black curranty fruit, his Chambolle-Musigny feels "slurpy," and the ripe-but-soft tannins allow it to be drunk right away. Serve this amiable Pinot with roasted poultry, slow-cooked meats, and grilled fare of all kinds. Look also for the estate's well-priced, cherryish **Marsannay** ($25), recognizable by its amusingly generic-looking plain brown labels. $35–40
Burgundy
Imported by Fruit of the Vine

ARCHETYPAL MODERN BURGUNDIES

In the village of Santenay, young Vincent Girardin makes fifty thousand cases a year of wines both famous and infamous for their fruit-forward, well-oaked, "international" style. Although traditionalists at heart, we feel there's a well-deserved place at the table for this style, and Girardin does it surpassingly well. He works in an almost organic fashion without fining or filtering, oaks his wines generously but not excessively, and achieves tremendous concentration of fruit, even in difficult vintages. **Domaine Vincent Girardin Santenay 1er Cru "La Maladiere"** ($22–25) is a sappy, leather-scented, red-fruit-driven wine for the table, best served with a simple roast chicken. The **Volnay 1er Cru "Les Champans"** ($40–50) is colored deep magenta and stunningly good, a silky, roasty, liquefied expression of its vineyard—and worthy of a crown rack of pork or veal. Modern or no, Girardin's red Burgundies are wines to be reckoned with, all of them meticulously crafted. *Imported by Vineyard Brands*

Domaine Jean-Luc Joillot
POMMARD "Les Noizons"
Medium-bodied. A wonderfully old-fashioned Burgundy, rustic and hearty as they come.
This Pinot combines the classic funkiness of Pommard with oriental spice reminiscent of jasmine tea. With bottle age, the wine becomes satiny-smooth, floral, spicy, minerally, and very complex. (The 1999, if you can still find it, is fabulous.) Try it with short ribs or pork chops. $35–40
Burgundy
Imported by Bayfield

Domaine Hervé Sigaut
CHAMBOLLE-MUSIGNY 1er Cru "Les Chatelots"
Medium-bodied. A complex Pinot with mild tannin and lots of character.
This enchanter from traditionalist Hervé Sigaut shows pure cherry fruit with peppery notes when it's young, then becomes spicier as it ages. What doesn't change is its clear expression of Burgundian *terroir*, succulent mouthfeel, and gentle, lingering finish. Usually, the wine takes four or five years to reach its peak. Save it, if you can, for small birds, wild mushrooms, or terrines of pork or veal. For a bargain, try the Bourgogne "Les Hattets" ($15–20), the winning kid sister of this wine at half the price. $35–40
Burgundy, France
Imported by Pinnacle

Argyle
PINOT NOIR "Nuthouse"
Medium-bodied. Silky and layered, with flavors that recur persistently in the finish.
Like many of Argyle's Pinots, this wine requires the taster's attention—flavors of strawberry, cranberry, fresh flowers, and earth are there, but they're subtle. They seem to spring to life, however, when this Pinot is paired with salty and savory fare. A fine pick for baked ham with a mustard glaze. $38–40
Willamette Valley, Oregon

$40 to $60

François Buffet
VOLNAY 1er Cru "Les Champans"
Medium-bodied. Sensuous, silken, and tender. The appealing creaminess is typical of Volnay.

Fun to drink when it's young—all sweet red fruit splashing brightly on the palate. That quality recedes as the wine ages into warm Asian spices and a subtler palate overall. This will pair beautifully with any game bird or poultry dish. Also look for the basic **Volnay A. C.** ($25) which, while lighter, is made in the same style. $40–45
Burgundy
Imported by Bayfield

Domaine Henri Gouges
NUITS-ST. GEORGES 1er Cru "Les Chenes Carteaux"
Medium- to full-bodied. The new oak is evident, but so is the dense fruit that absorbs it.
Christian Gouges makes wines that are collectibles for detail-oriented Burgundy lovers. He makes one of the heartier Burgundies we know of, especially in good vintages like '99. Its black fruit is buried under bittersweet chocolate and tar aromas, so this wine needs five or so years in the cellar—and then some charred red meat or game to tame it. $40–50
Burgundy
Imported by Vineyard Brands

Vincent Dancer
POMMARD 1er Cru "Les Pezerolles"
Medium-bodied. Fresh-tasting, lively in the mouth, and enjoyable when young.
This recent import into the U.S. is slick, modern winemaking in the best sense. Dancer crafts a seductive "drink-me-now" Pinot Noir with cranberries, raspberries, and apricots running riot. (A few dollars less and easier to find is **"Les Perrières"** ($40–45), but it's not a premier cru.) Serve with rich fish steaks or dishes flavored with Middle Eastern spices. $50–60
Burgundy
Imported by M. Scott

Domaine Drouhin
PINOT NOIR "Laurene"
Medium-bodied. A rich, sculpted Pinot that often needs cellaring.
Winemaker Veronique Drouhin is the daughter of famed Burgundy *négotiant* Robert Drouhin. (*Négotiants* are buyers of grapes or ready-made wines who then blend, bottle, and sell the wine with their own labels.) Her Laurene bottling—named for her daughter—is her best, consistently offering compact black cherry, blackberry, and oaky chocolate flavors. The wines aren't flashy—just elegant (we liked the gentle '97 vintage). Decant and serve with oily broiled fish like tuna, salmon, mako, and bluefish. $50–60
Oregon

Domaine François Lamarche
VOSNE-ROMANÉE 1er Cru "La Croix Rameau"
Medium-bodied. Surprisingly mellow for cellarable Burgundy.
We called this the "Burgundy of the vintage" in 2001. Lamarche uses 40–60% new oak, filters lightly, and barrel-ages his wines (all from top premier and grand crus in Vosne-Romanée) for about sixteen months. The result is bright, perfumey Pinot with mounds of complex red fruit and florality—the kind of wine that sings with food and drinks well even early in its life. Decant this and enjoy it with Cornish hens or some thick monkfish steaks in a reduction of wine and mushrooms. $60–70
Burgundy
Imported by House of Fine Wines

Over $60

Domaine de la Pousse d'Or
VOLNAY 1er Cru
"Clos des 60 Ouvrées"
Medium- to full-bodied.
Fabulously ripe, sensuous, and
satiny, with a profound finish.
Organically vinted and aged in old
and new oak, this is a glorious
portrait of Great Burgundy. The
fruit is intense, like molten cherries.
Roasted nuts and coffee play
through the finish, and the mineral
complexity amazes. More famed,
but not as hedonistic, is the **Volnay
1er Cru "Clos de la Bousse d'Or"**
($120–160). Both wines are
cellarable for twenty-plus years in
vintages like '96, '99, and '02. Serve
with decadent dishes such as
boeuf bourgignonne. $80–150
Burgundy
Imported by Langdon Shiverick

Domaine Drouhin–Laroze
CLOS DE VOUGEOT Grand Cru
Medium- to full-bodied. Deep in
color, powerful, penetrating,
and in need of cellaring.
Produced by Bernard Drouhin
and his son Philippe from a tiny
parcel of vines, this big, classically
proportioned Burgundy is a
satisfying splurge. Front-loaded
with cherries, berries, cinnamon
spice, and sweet cocoa, it's a
special partner for slow-cooked
beef, duck confit, or grilled organ
meats like sweetbreads. $95–100
Burgundy
Imported by Pinnacle

Domaine René Engel
CLOS DE VOUGEOT Grand Cru
Medium- to full-bodied.
Authoritatively rich and meaty,
with excellent complexity.
Philippe Engel owns, among
several splendid sites, a miniscule
plot of Clos de Vougeot composed mostly of vines planted in
1922. The wine he makes from
there is firm, ruddy, and redolent
of roasted black fruits, soy, and
Asian spice. Cellar it and serve
with stuffed Cornish hens or
peppered filets of beef. $90–115
Burgundy
Imported by House of Burgundy

A SECRET ADDITIVE

Before spilling the beans, let's clear up the confusion over Burgundy and
Bordeaux of times past and the nature of these two wines today. Burgundy
was once the bigger wine, Bordeaux the more delicate (the word *claret* for
Bordeaux referred to its clear, pale color). Today, the opposite is true.

Why the reversal? Because Burgundy used to be regularly adulterated
with wines from other areas to give it color and strength. Much Rhône
Syrah and god–knows–what from Morocco and Algeria were spilled into
Burgundy tanks to beef it up and darken it to the level customers expected.
Today's Burgundy is not only lighter but better regulated and purer than
its antecedents. The worst malfeasance currently occurring is the constant,
little–talked–about addition of beet sugar to many of the wines (even
famous ones)—a practice that boosts alcohol levels and overall weight.

Short of spying on the winemaker, there is no pre–purchase way to
detect a surreptitious dose of beet sugar. The clues come only when 1) you
taste the wine and it seems thin but very high in alcohol or 2) when a
Burgundy that has been cellared doesn't last as long as it should.

Sangiovese

With its myriad subvarieties, the dominant grape in Chianti is also the most widely planted in Italy. The reds it yields are generally high in acid, tannins, and spiciness.

HIANTI—Tuscany's most important winegrowing region—may have put Sangiovese on the map, but this grape grows all over central Italy, appearing on its own or more frequently in blends from Umbria, Emilia–Romagna, Molise, and Abruzzi.

Several other important clones on Sangiovese have made their mark. Prugnolo Gentile, a dark, thick-skinned variation, is the grape of the robust, highly prized, and cellar-worthy Vin Nobile di Montalcino, which some regard as Italy's finest red wine. Wines made from the clone Brunello are traditionally tannic, quite dry, and matured at length in wooden barrels (large and old), while the modern style is more fruit-driven and sweetened and softened by new oak, usually French.

Then there's Chianti, the version of Sangiovese most of us know best. Actually a blend of four grapes (Sangiovese, Canaiolo, Trebbiano, Malvasi), Chianti can be a light, quaffable little cocktail or a rich, oak-aged powerhouse, especially in its most "serious" form: Chianti Classico Riserva. "Super Tuscans" are wines that ignore rules of the Chianti appellation and are made with nontraditional grapes (Merlot, Cabernet), aged in new oak, or both; more than a few are rare and expensive.

Sangioveses are usually red-fruit driven (think cherries, raspberries, and strawberries), though in warmer climes they occasionally taste of blackberry and black cherry (see Morellino di Scansano, page 62). All, however, are fairly high in acidity, savor, and spice, which makes them uniquely appropriate partners for Italian food.

Still, that very acidity makes Sangioveses a great partner for Italian food. Its classic match is steak Fiorentina—a modest cut of beef with olive oil, herbs, and lemon—and it shows a real affinity for roasted birds large and small. Oakier Riserva versions are aged longer than regular Sangioveses and need something heartier, like roast lamb or game.

Until recently, Sangiovese was part of the "Cal-Ital" boom in blends of Sangiovese, Barbera, and Nebbiolo. Though the boom fizzled, a few delicious Sangiovese-based wines resulted and are found in these pages.

Under $12

Farnese
SANGIOVESE DAUNIA
"Farneto Valley"
Light-bodied. Simple, rustic "spaghetti red."
This is a tasty, chillable red with no pretensions but great flavor. Strawberryish, bright, and quaffable, this is pizza/party/picnic wine par excellence. $5–7
Abruzzi, Italy
Imported by Parliament

Villa Diana
SANGIOVESE
Light-bodied. A fun, casual sipping red—nice and juicy.
This wine is probably made by the tankerful, but we can't complain. Bright berries and spice move zestily along your palate, washing down pizza, pasta, and burgers with ease. $5–7
Abruzzi, Italy
Imported by Winebow/ Leonardo LoCascio

Di Majo Norante
SANGIOVESE "San Giorgio"
Light to-medium-bodied. A bright, juicy, very food-friendly style.
From Molise, a little-known Italian province down the Adriatic coast from Abruzzi. Consistent on the palate with soft cherry, strawberry, and fig flavors, this red has a pleasingly tart twist and surprising length. Good with anything light and salty cheese straws, ham, olives, and the like. $6–8
Molise, Italy
Imported by Winebow/ Leonardo LoCascio

Badia a Coltibuono
CHIANTI "Cetamura"
Medium-bodied. Good balance and a sweetish finish make this pleasing to a wide audience.
The wine we now know as Chianti was purportedly invented at the abbey at this estate, and its pricier Chianti Classicos reflect more of that tradition. This little guy, however, is a simple, modern pleasure with meaty red sauces, mac 'n' cheese, and kebabs. $8–10
Tuscany
Imported by Winebow/ Leonardo LoCascio

Renzo Masi
CHIANTI RUFINA
Light- to medium-bodied. Lively and flavorful.
Grapes for this rather berryish style of Chianti come from the highest elevation area in the region. We love it with pizza and spicy chicken wings. The estate's fuller-bodied **"Riserva"** ($12–13) is aged three years in oak and offers amazing value. $8–10
Tuscany
Imported by Lauber

$12 to $20

Baroncini
MORELLINO DI SCANSANO "Le Mandorlae"
Medium-bodied. Dark and musky with deep fruit and a very dry finish.
Morellino is the local name for Sangiovese grown in the village of Scansano in the southeast corner of Tuscany. It's got sappy, blackberry/black cherry fruit—perhaps a little licorice, too—and an honesty we admire. A beautiful wine for roasted hens, and a reasonable lasagna choice as well. $12–14
Tuscany
Imported by Dufour

"MR. TOMATO MAN"

That's what we call **Bernardi Sangiovese di Romagna "Maestro del Pomidoro"** ("Master of the Tomato") from Emilia-Romagna, the Italian wine–growing region north of Tuscany and south of Veneto and Lombardy. A bargain at $7–9, it's Chianti-esque, full of cherries and spice, and just the wine to have when you're dining on—you guessed it—anything with tomato sauce. We like this light- to medium-bodied wine's juicy fruit, its good texture, and touch of  friendly "funk." A mild earthiness also makes it a fitting partner for beans and mushrooms. *Imported by Wines for Food*

Maestro del Pomidoro

La Braccesca
ROSSO DI MONTEPULCIANO "Ceregio"
Medium-bodied.
A savory, hearty wine with traditional Tuscan character.
Here's a big-boned blend of Sangiovese (or rather its Prugnolo Gentile clone) and 20% black-cherryish Canaiolo—like a Chianti but with hair on its chest. Great with a meaty red sauce, steak with Italian seasonings, or Cornish hens stuffed with porcini and sundried tomatoes. $12–14
Tuscany
Imported by J. Given

Terra Nostra
CHIANTI RISERVA
Medium-bodied. Rich with excellent ripeness and surprising complexity at this price.
Made from 90% Sangiovese, 5% Canaiolo, 5% white grapes, and aged one year in barrels, this wine is smooth and seductive in the mouth—some call it sultry. Earth, straw-berry, and violet notes abound. A good-value choice for roasted poultry and veal Parmigiano. $13–15
Tuscany
Imported by Verdoni

TERRA NOSTRA
CHIANTI
RISERVA

Zerbina
SANGIOVESE DI ROMAGNA "Ceregio"
Light to-medium-bodied. A vivacious, fruity style with no oak.
This cherry-berry cocktail red (a 100% Sangiovese aged in stainless steel tanks) can go places that woody Chianti can't—like beside grilled fish and vegetables, mild cheeses, and spicy fare. $14–16
Emilia-Romagna
Imported by M. Skurnik

Ca' del Solo
SANGIOVESE "Il Fiasco"
Medium-bodied.
A fruit bomb—definitely more Californian than Tuscan.
This 100% Sangiovese from Santa Cruz's philosopher–cum–wine guru Randall Grahm is altogether pleasing: the essence of raspberry preserves and just the right balance for copious swigging. It's magnificent with barbecued chicken or stuffed veggies with tomato sauce. $14–16
California

Monti Verdi
CHIANTI CLASSICO
Medium-bodied. Friendly and easy, lush and long.
A year in Slavonian oak and six months in bottle yields a balanced, silky Chianti that's delicious right

out of the gate. Made from 90% Sangiovese and 10% Canaiolo from thirty-year-old vines, it offers a palate of fresh and dried cherries and is tasty on its own or with a platter of focaccia, olives, and salumi (Italian cold cuts). The **Riserva** ($35–40), oak-aged three years, is black, velvety, and a burly red for lamb. $15–17
Tuscany
Imported by Verdoni

Coturri
SANGIOVESE "Weiss Vineyard"
Medium- to full-bodied.
Modest in alcohol and dry, yet still an explosively flavorful red.
California vintner Tony Coturri's usual extremity of style is curbed here to fine effect. His West Coast organic take on Sangiovese is fragrant with sweet berries, leather, and allspice but remains expertly balanced—not to mention versatile at the table. Enjoy with sausage, rotisserie chickens, or braised lamb shanks. A cool Thanksgiving choice, too! $16–18
Napa

Moris Farms
MORELLINO DI SCANSANO
Medium- to full-bodied.
A bold, dark, expansive wine with abundant flavor.
Deepening as it breathes, this luxurious wine lures you in with a host of black cherry and roasted-coffee aromas. Don't fight it. Just enjoy the seduction with a hunk of fresh Parmesan cheese, a pork loin wrapped in pancetta, or roast duck. The estate's **Riserva** ($30–35) is for folks who want all of the above plus lots of oak. $16–18
Tuscany
Imported by Polaner

Fattoria Le Pupille
MORELLINO DI SCANSANO
Medium-bodied.
Rich with fruit and texture.
Le Pupille, made by Elisabetta Geppetti, is perhaps the best-known Morellino, the local variant of Sangiovese from southeast Tuscany. Its complexity and depth, with scents of wild cherry, plum, and leather, plus a palate hinting at black olives and iron, make it a gutsy choice for game meats. $16–18
Tuscany
Imported by Domaine Select

Caparzo
ROSSO DI MONTALCINO
Medium-bodied. Made in the traditional way and boasting plenty of fruit and a suave, elegant feel.
This is a textbook Rosso di Montalcino. Crafted from the young Brunello vines of this famous estate, it's a mouthful of cherry fruit and sandalwood, balanced for early drinking. The '99 was good, and the 2000 was even better. Serve it tonight with hearty lasagnas and manicotti, carpaccio with pepper and olive oil, or an Italian veal dish of your choice. $18–20
Tuscany
Imported by Palace Brands

Concadoro
CHIANTI CLASSICO "Cerasi"
Medium-bodied. With its gorgeous fruit, soft tannins, and lengthy finish, it's virtually the perfect Chianti.
One of our favorites, this organically produced wine (no pesticides, no added sulfites) is bursting with delicious black cherries right up front and fresh, mineral tanginess. The **Riserva**

($24–26) is coffeeish, chocolatey, and weightier, thanks to two years in barrel. Save the Riserva for steaks and drink the regular wine with grilled white meats and pasta Bolognese. Both benefit from breathing time. $18–20
Tuscany
Imported by J. Given

$20 to $40

Corte Pavone
ROSSO DI MONTALCINO
Medium-bodied. As complex and delicious as these wines get.
Call this 100% organic Rosso di Montalcino, made from the young vines of Brunello, a "baby Brunello" if you wish, but it is inarguably serious wine. Toast, leather, and spiced-wood notes surf a rippling wave of red fruit. Classy and ebullient, it deserves a major-league Tuscan feast of balsamic-marinated hens, steak Fiorentina, or rabbit with white beans. $20–22
Tuscany
Imported by Palace Brands

Fanti
ROSSO DI MONTALCINO
Medium- to full-bodied. Especially big and spicy with rich tannins.
This is a traditionalist Rosso built for the long haul, so don't expect

a fun 'n' fruity wine. It's replete with earth, dried red fruits, and the pepper-spice aromatics and tannins that come with two years, aging in new and used oak. It's a great match for slow-braised meats and pungent cheeses. FYI, Fanti's **Brunello** ($60-90) is impressive but often overpriced. $22–25
Tuscany
Imported by Winebow/ Leonardo LoCascio

Valdipiatta
VINO NOBILE DI MONTEPULCIANO
Medium- to full-bodied.
As sexy as Sangiovese gets, with tons of fruit and deep, inky color.
All Vino Nobiles need time, and even this one—made from 80% Prugnolo Gentile (a Sangiovese clone) and 20% Canaiolo and boasting a scrumptious palate of black bramble fruits—wants four or five years to shed its battery of tannins. Serve this big luscious beast with steaks, lamb, or spit-roasted hens. $22–25
Tuscany
Imported by J. Given

CHIANTI CLASSICO

Wines from Chianti Classico, the historical heart of the Chianti growing region, are recognizable by the black rooster that usually appears on the label. They're also said to be a cut above wines from Chianti's subzones. A prototype is the medium–bodied **Rodano Chianti Classico** ($15–17), whose makers don't fool around with new oak or any tricks of the modern wine trade; this is aged in giant, neutral wood casks, picked ripe at low yields, and perfumed with rose, incense, and sour cherries. Firm and juicy, it's great with savory Italian fare like veal or chicken scallopine, eggplant Parmigiano, and spaghetti Bolognese. Rodano's fine, powerful "super–Tuscan" **Monna Claudia** ($35–40) is 50/50 Cabernet and Sangiovese. *Imported by Polaner*

Castello di Bossi
CHIANTI CLASSICO
Medium-bodied. More about spice and earth than fruit— and very dry at the finish.
This is Chianti the old-fashioned way: old-wood flavors, firm mouthfeel, and spicy, delicious figs and dates all the way through. There's also no shortage of tannins, so this wine begs for rich food. Have it with mushroom dishes, sheep's milk cheeses, and hearty stews of beans, pancetta, and Italian herbs. $25–27
Tuscany
Imported by Winebow/ Leonardo LoCascio

Over $40

Pertimali
BRUNELLO DI MONTALCINO
Medium- to full-bodied.
A mouthfilling, multilayered, rounded style.

Livio Sassetti's Brunello shows deeper fruit than most. Aromas of black cherry, leather, and moist earth are underpinned by velvety tannins. Enjoy a bottle with sliced rare duck breast, carpaccio, truffled hens, or a variety of firm, salty cheeses. Your steak wine is Sassetti's **Vigna dei Fili di Seta** ($60+), a blend of Cabernet and Sangiovese—a satiny "super Tuscan" that's judiciously oaked and delivers tremendously concentrated flavor. $45–50
Tuscany
Imported by Vin Divino/Marc de Grazia

Ciacci Piccolomini d'Aragona
BRUNELLO DI MONTALCINO
Medium- to full-bodied.
A lavishly built, hearty wine that needs time.
This superstar traditionalist, a darling of ours since 1993, is revered on both sides of the Atlantic. The smokey, pruney wine is saturated in color and scented heavily with minerals and moist earth. It's also a red meat wine to be sure, for garlicky leg of lamb, standing rib roasts, and so on. The estate's **Rosse di Montalcino "Vinge della Fonte"** ($22–25) is also sensational, and richer than many pricier Brunellos. We'd drink it with a T-Bone any night of the week. Both wines are cellar-worthy. $50–60
Tuscany
Imported by Selected Estates of Europe

Antinori
BRUNELLO DI MONTALCINO "Pian delle Vigne"
Medium- to full-bodied.
Very traditional-tasting, with plush texture and lots of spice.
Aged two to three years in small barrels, this 100% Sangiovese from twenty-year-old vines isn't released until five years after the vintage. The '97 got incredible press, but we like the '98 as well; its warm cherry pie, plum, and cinnamon character is wide open and enticing—unusual for young Brunello. Decant and serve with racks of lamb or beef. $60–75
Tuscany
Imported by Rémy Amerique

Syrah/Shiraz

*In the wine stakes, this grape with two names
truly excels in only three parts of the world—
the Rhône, Australia, and California—
yet it's giving "King Cab" a run for its money.*

*S*YRAH, a sturdy black grape variety, is responsible for some of the world's most "serious" red wines—and some of its most delightfully "unserious" ones as well. In France, the minerally, tannic Syrahs from the northern Rhône Valley taste of pepper, spice, and blackberries and often benefit from cellaring. The lush Australian Shirazes, most for immediate drinking, are thick, fruity, and chocolatey. California, where vintners usually call their wine Syrah, produces rich, ripe wines that fall somewhere in the middle ground.

Regardless of origin, these wines are enjoying a surge in popularity. One reason is their relatively reasonable price, with Rhône Syrahs usually costing much less than their counterparts in Bordeaux and Burgundy, and New World examples priced under $25.

Why the two names? Long ago Syrah was also called Scyras, a name preferred by James Busby, the Scottish viniculturist who took the grape from the Rhône to Australia in 1832. The similarity to "Shiraz," the Persian city, may explain the gradual shift to the latter name. The "Persian connection" also has fed speculation that the grape was brought to France by a Crusader. More likely, it is indigenous to France, where the vines have been grown since the time of the Romans.

Though Syrah is often used in southern France for blending, the northern Rhône is the place for 100% Syrah. The main communes are St. Joseph, where fruity wines are typical; tiny Cornas, home to bold, rustic wines; Côte Rôtie, where powerful, fragrant wines often include Viognier in the blend; the Hermitage, the rock-strewn hillside that makes the world's most renowned Syrah; and Crozes-Hermitage, the vast wine-producing acreage that surrounds it.

Most Aussie Shirazes originate in South Eastern Australia, though some from Western Australia are superb. California Syrah/Shiraz grows statewide, with the central coast producing much of the best.

Outside the "big three" growing areas, Syrah blends are produced throughout southern France, in a few places in Italy, in South Africa (as Shiraz)—and, on these shores, in Washington State.

Under $12

Barefoot Cellars
SYRAH
Medium-bodied. A deep-purple fruit bomb.
Nothing fancy here: just a plump, purple party wine at a great price. It's great with chips, dips, burgers, burritos, cheese, chicken fingers, and other foods of the "fun" sort. $6-8
California

Miranda
SHIRAZ "Firefly"
Medium-bodied. Thick, jammy, and full of sweet oak.
If you have a taste for chocolate syrup, you'll probably go for this wine. Its bargain price makes it possible for you to serve a roomful of guests and still have a bottle or two left over for takeout pizza the next day. $6-8
South Eastern Australia
Imported by Wingara

Alice White
SHIRAZ
Medium- to full-bodied. Great depth and purity of fruit for such an inexpensive red.
This ruby-colored Shiraz has a plum bouquet, lots of flavor, and a clean, fruity finish. A good party wine that's also a great companion to grilled meats (burgers included). $7-9
South Eastern Australia
Imported by Old Bridge Cellars

McGuigan Brothers
SHIRAZ "Black Label"
Medium-bodied. A sweet and juicy chunk of fruit.
Brian McGuigan's unoaked Australian Shiraz is blended with a little Grenache, which makes it one of the jammiest wines around. Try this with favorite casual eats: burgers, pizza, soul food, spicy Tex-Mex, and party snacks. $7-9
South Eastern Australia
Imported by Winebow

Heritage Road
SHIRAZ "Reserve"
Medium-bodied. Plump and soft, with an easy-as-you-go charm.
This flavorsome Hunter Valley Shiraz, with fruit grown in the winery-owned Angle Vine Vineyard, is aged half in French and half in American oak. Satisfying on all counts, with lush red berry fruit all over, it's a great sipping choice and just right for a cookout. $8-10
Hunter Valley, New South Wales
Imported by R. H. Phillips-Hogue

VICTORIAN IN NAME ONLY

If you're looking for an inexpensive Shiraz that consistently offers the sweet, alluring fruit of the variety, you'll find it in **Jindalee Shiraz** ($6-8). In 1997, brothers Vince and David Littore established Jindalee Estate in Geelong, Victoria, using grapes grown in their vineyards in Mildura. In league with most Australian vintners' ultramodern approach to vinification, the Littores' state-of-the-art winery controls its winemaking with an advanced computer system. And the food for this nugget of blackberry goodness? Fried chicken, spicy wings, and Tex-Mex. *Imported by F. Wildman*

Les Hautes Blanches
CROZES HERMITAGE
Light- to medium-bodied. Gentle, savory Syrah in a bistro style.

Looking for a good Crozes that won't break the bank? This one is mild but has true Crozes Hermitage character—smoke, herbs, baked black fruit, and a dry finish. Its excellent balance makes it a hit on its own or with cheese assortments and cold cuts. $9-11
Rhône, France
Imported by Baron François

McManis
SYRAH
Light- to medium-bodied. A soft, easy-drinking Syrah.
Made just south of Lodi, California, by a fourth-generation winemaking family, this wine has a whiff of smoke and spice to keep things interesting. Try it with summertime burgers and franks. $10-12
California

Cartlidge & Browne
SYRAH
Medium-bodied. Sturdy and bold.
This surprisingly Rhône-like Syrah from the West Coast has smoky, lasting black fruit and a shot of espresso in the finish. Pair it with burgers, lean steaks, and roasted poultry. Great value! $10-12
California

Ferngrove
SHIRAZ
Medium-bodied. Plush fruit, modest tannins, and intensity.
From grapes grown in an unusually cool region in Western Australia, this Shiraz has an impressive density of fruit spiced up with herbs, mint, and loads of black pepper. More Rhône-like than classic Aussie, it's elegant with herbed red meats and charcuterie. $10-12
Frankland River, Western Australia
Imported by Bayfield

Guilhem Durand
SYRAH "Vielles Vignes"
Medium- to full-bodied. Thrillingly rich, deeply flavored.

An incredible value, this unfiltered Syrah made from thirty- to fifty-year-old vines is blessed with those great smoky, brambly, leather-scented wafts that you usually get only from the northern Rhône. Serve it with stews and red meats. $10-12
Languedoc, France
Imported by Weygandt/Metzler

Fess Parker
FRONTIER RED
Medium-bodied. Rich, strong, and pleasantly funky.

The nonvintage blend (70% Syrah, 12% Grenache, 6% Mourvèdre, 5% Cinsault, 4% Cab Franc, 3% Counoise) has hints of earth, black pepper, and prune. It pairs handily with burgers, chops, and takeout chicken. $10-12
California

Teal Lake
SHIRAZ
Medium-bodied. A lush, silky-soft, and extremely ripe kosher wine.
You don't drink this kosher wine for its complexity. You drink it because it's basically a caramel-drizzled bowlful of cherries and raspberries that goes down like butter. It's a great foil for sweet

or salty meats like barbecued chicken and glazed ham. $11-13
South Eastern Australia
Imported by Royal Wine

$12 to $20

Chateau Mourgues du Gres
COSTIERES DE NIMES
"Les Galets Rouges"
Medium- to full-bodied. Deep purple, lavish, and mouthfilling.
This knockout Syrah, brimming with black cherries and pepper, is perfect for hearty fare like rotisserie chickens, fried chops, Cuban *ropa vieja,* and anything grilled. The *galets* of the name are round, flat stones prevalent in southern French vineyards, where they do winemakers a favor by absorbing heat by day and then warming the vines by night. $12-14
Rhône, France
Imported by Weygandt/Metzler

Domaine d'Andézon
CÔTES DU RHÔNE
Medium- to full-bodied. An especially saturated, aggressive style.
Black as pitch in the '96 and '99 vintages, this 100% Syrah from sixty- to ninety-year-old vines is worth trying in any year. Laced with dried cherries and licorice, it's great with steaks, Chinese duck, and hard cheeses. We also find it delightful with veal Parmigiano. $12-14
Rhône, France
Imported by European Cellars

Cave de Tain l'Hermitage
CROZES HERMITAGE
"Les Hauts du Fief"
Medium-bodied. Seems restrained at first, but swiftly expands into something rich and savory.

Made by one of the best growers' co-ops in France, this Crozes has a character that's roasty and pepper-scented, with black fruit that grows with airing in the glass. Marvelous for game and French bistro fare—mushroom tarts, pâté, and baked Brie. $12-14
Rhône, France
Imported by Diageo

Mas des Chimeres
COTEAUX DU LANGUEDOC
Medium- to full-bodied.
Wonderful ripeness and balance.
Guilhem Dardé blends 70% Syrah, 20% Grenache, and 10% Cabernet into his wine, which he ages in *barriques* and bottles unfined and unfiltered. (*Barriques* is the Burgundian word for small oak barrels, and an "unfined" wine is one that hasn't undergone the clarification process known as fining.) An array of brown spices and rustic, "peasanty" character make this plump little red very appealing. Drink it with chicken Provençal or pack it in the picnic basket with pâté, olives, and farmhouse cheeses. $13-15
Languedoc, France
Imported by Louis/Dressner

Abbaye de Tholomies
MINERVOIS
Medium- to full-bodied.
Full-flavored and spicy, with a sun-baked feel.
Here's a peppery organic blend (60% Syrah, 30% Grenache, 10% Mourvèdre) that's jammed with fruit and has a lingering baked-berry finish. It is only 12.5% alcohol, which is modest for wines from Coteaux de Languedoc. It goes particularly well with beef stew, roasted vegetables, and Caribbean and other slightly spicy dishes. "The Sanctus" ($13-15) is bigger, and a real teeth-stainer—funny, given

in wood is minimal. The result is a surprisingly fresh, floral bouquet that darkens swiftly into currants on the palate. Red meat and mushroom dishes excel. $45-50
Rhône, France
Imported by Kermit Lynch

Alban Vineyards
SYRAH "Reva"
Full-bodied. Strong and thick, and perhaps America's finest Syrah.
Somehow, John Alban maximizes the luscious fruit typical of California and compounds it with the complexity and earth-driven character of such Rhône Syrahs as Cornas and Côte Rôtie. The high alcohol of Reva is masked by the rolling flavor of cassis and black fig, with results that would impress any lover of red wine. A wine that can be cellared for a decade or more, it's decadent with slow-cooked meats. $50-60
Edna Valley, California

HERMITAGE WINES

The Hermitage appellation, in the northern Rhône just south of Lyon, has produced some of France's greatest wines since the reign of Louis XIV. The Hermitage itself—a rocky, domed hill topped by a humble thirteenth-century chapel—has an intriguing, if hazy, history. Legend has it that Henri-Gaspard de Sterimburg, a knight, returned from the Crusades wounded and in need of seclusion. He retreated to the hilltop, planted vines, and lived as a hermit. Whether he built the chapel is open to question, but man and edifice are of such a piece that the truth is of little import.

Today, father-and-son team Gerard and Jean-Louis Chave craft their **J. L. Chave Hermitage** ($100–200) and other wines much as their family has for over five hundred years. Hand-ploughing the fields using no chemicals and fermenting in open wood vats with native yeasts, they make separate wines from their nine *climats* (vine parcels) on the Hermitage hill and blend them for the final bottling. Given a year to eighteen months in old and new oak for finishing, the resulting elegant, full-bodied wine has fine tannins, perfectly ripened fruit, and a savoriness that showcases its complexity. The classic smoke, blackberry, licorice, leather, flint, and flowers of Syrah are all here, but so are the myriad flavors of the wine's *terroir*. On the culinary side, we'd open a bottle with a simple roast duckling and savor the last of it with a plate of sheep's milk cheese and Roquefort or Danish Blue.
Imported by Kermit Lynch

Another jewel is **Paul Jaboulet Aine Hermitage "La Chapelle"** ($100–200). Muted on the palate when young, it's a very beefy, dry, complex wine built to last. Let it breathe and look for black pepper, wood smoke, green herbs, leather, and above all, the intense minerality of the rocky *terroir*. Cellar and serve with grilled lamb or duck with wild mushrooms.
Imported by F. Wildman

Over $60

Marie–Claude Lafoy et Vincent Gasse
CÔTE RÔTIE "Vielles Vignes"
Medium- to full-bodied. Perfumed and impressive from the first sip.
Vincent Gasse grows vines biodynamically—no pesticides, minimal sulfites, and plantings scheduled to astrological phases and rhythms. Sourced from sixty-plus-year-old vines on the Côte Rôtie ("roasted slope"), this elegant wine releases its violety, country hillside fragrance after extensive breathing. It's a perfect match for roast lamb or osso buco. At least ten years in the cellar will bring out its best. $60-70
Rhône, France
Imported by Weygandt/Metzler

Sean H. Thackrey
ORION
"Rossi Vineyard–Old Vines"
Medium- to full-bodied. Maybe the most cellarable Syrah in California.
Sean Thackrey makes fewer than eight hundred cases of each vintage, eked from century-old Syrah vines. Surprisingly grapey when young, the Orion keeps its fruit as it ages, adding spicy anise, tar, pepper, violet, and complexity with time. Serve with a well-marbled roast encrusted with herbs. Also seek out Thackrey's non-vintage **Pleiades** ($25-30) a blend of Syrah, Grenache, Barbera, and Carignan. It's fantastic with grilled bluefish. $75-100
California

René Rostaing
CÔTE RÔTIE
Medium-bodied. Luscious and very seductive for a Côte Rôtie.
Rostaing is a forward-thinking winemaker who makes very ripe Syrahs with a lot of new oak and clean, deep fruit. (The wines have been so successful they're now hard to come by.) His basic Côte Rôtie offers a lengthy mouthful of black fruit, earth, soy, and pepper. Ideally, drink it two to four years after the vintage, serving it with marbled beef. Collectors prize the fulsome **Côte Blonde** ($100-120) and **La Landonne** ($95-105), both exceedingly rare. $60-80
Rhône, France
Imported by Kermit Lynch

Michel Chapoutier
ERMITAGE "Le Pavillon"
**Medium- to full-bodied.
A biodynamic beauty.**
Michel Chapoutier has been the lead flag-waver of biodynamic viticulture in the Rhône since 1988, taking his cues from the stars. A lovely touch is the planting of rose bushes at the bottom of each vine row (roses, subject to many of the same pests as grapes, act as a bellwether for trouble). He is the largest vineyard owner in the Hermitage (*Ermitage* in French), and his hard-to-find wines from there are his best. All are vibrantly acidic and minerally when young and are focused on elegance and complexity, not power. Le Pavillon may be the most prized, with black depths, powerful tannins, and roasty aromas accented by black pepper. The much less costly "La Sizeranne" ($50-70) is a virtuosic expression of its vineyard but rather dry and stubborn until it's had ten years of cellaring. Both wines are a food lover's fantasy when served with the likes of spit-roasted lamb and olives, sheep's milk cheese, and roasted potatoes. $250-400
Rhône, France
Imported by Jeroboam

Tempranillo

The pride of Spain is the main grape in user-friendly Rioja and aristocratic Ribera del Duero. Reflecting Tempranillo's easy adaptability is its multiplicity of names.

TEMPRANILLO has much in common with its Italian neighbor Sangiovese: a love of warm weather, lively acidity, and the ability to take oak gracefully and yield a range of light to heavy wines. Both also taste of red fruits—Tempranillo of cherry in particular—and go by different names. In Spain, Tempranillo is called, among other things, Ojo de Libre (eye of the hare) in the Penèdes region and Tinto Fino (fine red wine) in Ribera del Duero.

Tempranillo is also known for having a spicy quality, but that may have as much to do with its oak treatment as inherent flavor. The wines of Rioja and Navarra are traditionally aged in American oak, a coarser-grained wood that imparts a malty or chocolatey flavor. In Ribera del Duero, wines are often aged in French oak and tend to be darker, firmer, and more Bordeaux–like in style.

Tempranillo's adaptability extends to blending in a big way. While it is frequently blended with Grenache (known as Garnacha in Spain), the "better" Spanish wines contain more Tempranillo and less (or no) Grenache. By definition, Rioja wines are a blend of up to five grapes: Tempranillo, Grenache, Mazueil (the Spanish name for Carignan), Graciano, and the Spanish white grape known as Viura or Macabeo.

With the exception of Portugal, where the grape is named Tinta Cao, and Argentina, where it's called Tinta Roriz, Tempranillo is rarely grown outside of Spain. Some serious wine lovers wonder why the grape isn't grown more in Australia and California, where all of the conditions are in place to produce some outstanding Tempranillo-based wines. Time will provide an answer.

Under $12

Dominio de Eguren
PROTOCOLO RED
Light- to medium-bodied.
A simple, fresh-tasting
cocktail red.
So many Spanish
bargains, so little
time to enjoy
them! This
cherry-berry
pleasure is a
perfect party and
pizza wine. Serve
it lightly chilled. $5-6
Tierra de Manchuela, Spain
Imported by Tempranillo

Pinord
PENÈDES Clos Torribas
Light- to medium-bodied.
A bright everyday sipper.
Easy-going cherry and strawberry
flavors make this a treat with
Spanish soul food like empanadas,
sliced ham, and plantains. It's a
fine cocktail red, too. Serve
lightly chilled. $7-9
Penèdes, Spain
*Imported by Spain Wine
Collection*

Vicente Gandia
HOYA DE CADENAS Reserva
Light- to medium-bodied.
Smooth as silk and surprisingly
fruity for its age.
Released late (the current
vintage is '97), this inexpensive,
mature Tempranillo, with its
spiced cherry and cocoa finish
is an amazing bargain. It takes
especially well to rice 'n' beans
and party snacks like olives and
mild cheeses. $7-9
Utiel-Requena, Levante, Spain
Imported by Tri-Vin

Viña del Val
RIBERA DEL DUERO
Medium-bodied. Dark and
sturdy, with a plush finish.
In a time when wines from this
region are spiraling up in price,
this Ribera del Duero remains a
fantastic value. Coffeeish and
full of tasty black fruit, it's a
terrific choice for beef and
bean dishes. $8-10
Ribera del Duero, Spain
Imported by Vin Divino

Ramblilla
TEMPRANILLO
Medium-bodied. Bold textured
and bursting with fruit.
The newest appellation in Spain,
Ribera del Jucar (in the north,
near Galicia), has yet to make
the textbooks. This promising
Tempranillo is dark and exciting,
dense with fruit, and accented
with a whiff of oregano;
it's also free of tannins. Great
for drinking with roast pork,
black olives, and Middle Eastern
kebabs and curries. For just a
little more, enjoy Ramblilla's
Crianza ($12-14), which is
oak-aged and spicier.
$8-10
Ribera del Jucar, Spain
Imported by Frontier

Vega Sauco
TORO Crianza
Medium-bodied.
Dark, powerful fruit beefed
up by two to three years
in the barrel.
This balanced, elegant bottling
sourced from seventy-year-old
Tempranillo vines offers up rich
cherry fruit and curlicues of
campfire smoke—a nice match
for burgers and portobello
mushrooms. $9-11
Toro, Spain
Imported by F. Wildman

ALL IN THE FAMILY:
TWO RIOJA GRAN RESERVAS

The 120-year-old bodega of R. Lopez de Heredia Vina Tondonia in Rioja Alta brooks no compromise. The two sisters who run it are steeped in their family tradition, creating singular artisanal wines that fly in the face of the modern "international" style. While they make numerous wines, it is the Gran Reservas for which the bodega is justly famed.

Lopez de Heredia Gran Reserva "Vina Bosconia" spends six years in barrel and six more in bottle before public release. It tends to be the Lopez de Heredias' burliest wine, in contrast to the graceful **Vina Tondonia**, which drinks very much like prized Premier Cru Volnay Burgundy. A rare 1947 Gran Reserva "Vina Tondonia" ($225) sampled from here was saturated purple, completely pure, fresh-tasting, and complex.

All the wines are consistent within the house style, each rather like a perfectly aged little plum cake from a different recipe, variously accented by strawberries, salty minerals, spicy oak, potpourri, and varying degrees of "sherried" character. Many current vintages on the market are twenty years old or more—and at $50 to $250 depending on their age, they are considered bargains. *Imported by Rare Wine*

Bodegas Dehesa Gago
TORO "g"
Medium- to full-bodied.
A big mouthful of dark red wine for not much money.
With an etched white "g," the minimalist bottle design advertises this wine's boldness and modernity. Plenty of new oak and strong, dark, forward fruit fulfills the promise. Fans of "big reds" will love this one, always a willing partner for red meats and mushrooms. $10-12
Ribera del Duero, Spain
Imported by Tempranillo

Palacios Remondo
RIOJA "La Vendimmia"
Medium-bodied. A taste of succulent, vibrant fruit.
Here's an ultramodern Rioja, made partly by whole berry fermentation (which makes the wine fruitier) and then given a quick nap in new French oak. We love it with burgers (beef, lamb, turkey—even buffalo) and Middle Eastern specialties like falafel, kebabs, and merguez sausage. $11-13
Rioja, Spain
Imported by Rare Wine

$12 to $20

Hijos de Antonio Barcelo
RIBERA DEL DUERO Crianza "Vina Mayor"
Medium-bodied. Plump, fruity, and a lot of wine for its price.
From rugged mountain climes, this popular red really satisfies. Nice with pork chops, fried foods, and sandwiches. Also try the non-oaked **Vina Mayor Tinto** ($8-10) for even fruitier sipping. $12-14
Ribera del Duero, Spain
Imported by Tempranillo

Abadia Retuerta
SARDON DEL DUERO "Rivola"
Medium-bodied. A rich, barrel-aged, fragrant blend.
This blend (60% Tempranillo, 40% Cabernet Sauvignon) is warm and smoky. Enjoy it with ketchupy burgers, bistro steaks, and hearty stews of all kinds. $14-16
Castilla y Léon, Spain
Imported by Tempranillo

Gorri Biurko
RIOJA "Los Valles"
Medium-bodied. A modern Rioja with the rich depths of a Reserva, minus the oak.
This 100% organic wine is stuffed with ripe blackberry and black plum fruit, soft tannins, and a load of spicy cocoa flavor. A cool steak wine, extra-cool lamb wine, and an intriguing partner to spicy chicken dishes like the Peruvian *pollo ala brasa*. $14-16
Rioja, Spain
Imported by De Maison

Pagor
TEMPRANILLO
Medium-bodied. Tender, sweetly ripe, ready to drink, and totally delicious.
The grape of Rioja—Spain's noble, historic red—with a California twist. It's alive with aromas of maraschino cherries and pomegranate—a gutsy choice on the part of the winemaker. Enjoy it on its own or with white meats, paella, or fish dishes richly sauced. $16-18
California

Over $20

Pesquera
RIBERA DEL DUERO "Condado de Haza"
Medium- to full-bodied. Seemingly a nod to Bordeaux, but with rich Spanish roastiness.
The Pesquera wines from Alejandro Fernandez remain the touchstones for the appellation. Condado de Haza is his second-label wine, which we prefer because it's less oaked than the main release. Dusty black cherries, cola, and coffee flavors surge through it, especially in older vintages. Serve with garlicky steaks or firm cheeses like cheddar, Leicester, and Jarlsberg. $20-23
Ribera del Duero, Spain
Imported by Classical Wines from Spain

Dominio de Atauta
RIBERA DEL DUERO
Full-bodied. Bordeaux-like in many ways, with good depth and length.
The vineyard where this wine is made escaped Spain's phylloxera louse plague in the 1800s, so the hundred-plus-year-old vines are on original, ungrafted rootstock—each a precious piece of natural history. The wine is dry and full, with bold black raspberry fruit and bittersweet cocoa making a direct hit on the palate. It's also got nice potential for aging. An extraordinary lamb and roast beef partner. $35-40
Ribera del Duero, Spain
Imported by European Cellars

Zinfandel

Zinfandel—also known as "Zin"—is thought of as "America's red wine" because it is grown almost exclusively in California.

THE FORTY-NINERS who flooded California in the Gold Rush of 1849 may have given a push to the wine that today has a huge following. A good percentage of the prospectors took up agriculture, which depended in part on plant material shipped from back East. Among the goodies in the huge shipment of 1852 was Zinfandal [sic], a grape vine that had taken hold in the Northeast after its importation from Europe in 1829. Within a decade, vineyards in both Napa and Sonoma were growing this newcomer. Dozens of those early plantings still thrive and are considered treasures—the reason so many wines on the next three pages are noted as having been made from grapes grown from hundred-year-old (or thereabouts) vines.

Zinfandel is a late-ripener, which makes it sweet yet relatively high in acid. It tends toward high alcohol, the result of high sugar levels at harvest. Zin is also a hard grape to pick: Most bunches have green fruit and red fruit on the same cluster, meaning pickers have to go more than once through the vineyard to harvest enough ripe grapes.

When it comes to aging, American oak is the traditional medium for Zinfandel. The flavor of the finished product is usually described, in order of frequency, as raspberry or blackberry (often paired as "bramble fruits"), black pepper, and spice. For food, Zin is barbecue wine, plain and simple. In fact, there's hardly a better wine-food combo around.

White Zinfandel, the craze that swamped America with sweetish pink wine in the 1980s, grew out of the surplus of Zinfandel California growers found on their hands. In a stroke of marketing genius, Sutter Home turned the surplus to good use, employing the method for making rosé: removing the skin from the grapes just after they are crushed so that just a touch of color remains. (It's the pigment in grape skins that gives red wine its color.) The result was a soft, pink wine sweetened further with a little added sugar. And that's how "blush wine" was born.

Under $12

Moss Bridge
ZINFANDEL
Medium-bodied. In this zesty wine, it's all fruit all the time.
Winemaker Jim Olsen uses no oak in the production of this wine, achieving a pure palate of jammy, raspberry fruit that resembles no other Zins we know. You won't find a better companion for spicy food. $10-12
California

Cartlidge & Browne
ZINFANDEL
Light- to medium-bodied. Easy-drinking Zinfandel for casual sipping.
Seeking bargain Zin with a bright, berryish character for warm-weather sipping? This is it. A spiced bouquet with a hint of anise is the prelude to plummy, brambly flavors. Burgers, kebabs, Tex-Mex, fried chicken, and party snacks find it friendly. $10-12
California

$12 to $20

Benson Ferry
ZINFANDEL
Medium-bodied. Supple, satiny, and gloriously fruity.
Take a sip, and cherries and boysenberries bounce across your palate like ping-pong balls. Surprisingly, the daunting 15% alcohol is overwhelmed by the bright flavors—a miraculous feat of balance. You'll enjoy this wine with foods as dissimilar as Chinese takeout and creamy blue cheeses, but it's also great on its own. $13-15
Lodi, California

Domaine de la Terre Rouge
ZINFANDEL "Easton"
Full-bodied. A fruity, food-friendly Zin with terrific length.
Smartly tended very old vines make an old-fashioned Zinfandel that delivers tasty, sun-roasted blackberry fruit with little tannic distraction.

Drink this with charcoal-grilled fish or chicken, black bean dishes, and stews. $13-16
Amador, California

Blockheadia Winery
ZINFANDEL "Blockheadia Ringnosii"
Medium- to full-bodied. A plump, pleasing Zin with a gentle finish.
The Blockheadia winery is so named because its owners use very specific "blocks" of vineyards to create their blends. The ripeness, richness, and tempting red fruit of their Blockheadia Ringnosii (92% Zinfandel, 8% Carignan), graced with a little black peppercorn, is perfectly balanced for white meats like poultry and pork. Blockheadia's **Napa** Zinfandel ($28-30), with 10% Petite Sirah, is better suited to red meats. $16-18
California

Rancho Zabaco
ZINFANDEL "Dry Creek"
Full-bodied. Grand-scale Zinfandel with intense alcohol and fruit.
A powerful American red wine, this Zin is unfiltered and rapturously deep, with black raspberry and dried fruit flavors. A shot of Petite Sirah adds extra depth and flavor. It's a perfect pairing with grilled rib-eye steak.

CHAPTER TWO

Other Choice Reds

Lacrima di Morro. Abouriou. Malvasia Nera. While you may not be even remotely acquainted with these and other secondary grapes, most are certainly worth getting to know, whether in blends or on their own. In this chapter the wines they yield earn our respect alongside old friends like Barbera, Malbec, and Petite Sirah.

Interestingly, today's obscure also-ran could well become tomorrow's phenomenon. Case in point: Winegrowers never gave much thought to Merlot as anything but a blending grape until the 1980s. So, of the thousands of grape varieties out there, which might be the "next big thing"?

Other Choice Reds

So much red wine, so little time. Surveys show that Americans prefer reds over whites almost three to one—explained, most likely, by the wines' bolder flavors.

ALL IT WHAT YOU WILL—*rouge* (French), *rosso* (Italian), *tinto* (Spanish, Portuguese), or *rot* (German)—red wine is vinted and treasured the world over. Almost anywhere there's a pocket of warmth and arable soil, vines will be planted, grapes will be crushed, vinification will take place, and the bottled product will find its way to a wine store's shelves.

One of the aims of this guide is to introduce you to some choice reds from far and wide, most not as famous as the Cabernets, Pinots, and Merlots (nor in many cases as easy to find). But isn't the discovery of something new one of the most exciting things about wine?

Your search will be abetted by remembering something very basic: Old World wines (i.e., European) tend to be named by their region, while New World wines (those from the Americas and the antipodes) are named by grape. Another word to the wise: Appreciate the beauty of blended wines. Some of the best wines the world has to offer are blends—Bordeaux and Chianti, to name two. Above all, get to know your wines in the company of different foods. That big chewy red that tasted so awful with last night's chicken enchilada may rock your world with tonight's steak Diane. So spread your wings and *explore!*

Still, the territory is sometimes difficult to navigate, especially since wines and their names are anything but cut and dried. Grapevines mutate readily, resulting in numerous subvarieties known as clones. Clonal selection then makes it possible for winegrowers to propagate new strains. Add to this the cloudy history of which grape was imported from where (often centuries and centuries ago), and the branches of the family tree of *Vitis vinifera* and the few other species that provide us with our favorite potable are more than a little tangled.

For example, the Italian grapes Brunello and Prugnolo Gentile fall under the parental umbrella of Sangiovese. Petite Sirah may be either a clone of Syrah or an extinct Rhône variety called Dourif. But in the end, who but a botanist or a wine grower cares? Your focus should be on what you're enjoying at the moment, then expanding your horizons by trying something new, whether a nice sipper or a dinner wine.

Under $10

Casa di Pescatori
SICILIAN RED
Light-bodied. A fun, fruity rosso to drink from carafes.
This bright red is made from Barbera, which juices it up, and Nero d'Avola, which gives it more depth. It's great with lighter Mediterranean foods: pastas, focaccia, olives, cheeses, and *pissaladière,* the pizzalike tart from Nice. An important grape in Sicily, the low-acid Nero d'Avola is often blended with other varieties to right a wine's balance. $5-6
Sicily
Imported by Wm. Grant

Villa Diana
MONTEPULCIANO D'ABRUZZO
Light- to medium-bodied. Perfectly ripe and balanced, and food-versatile.
A steal if there ever was one! This unbelievably underpriced red from the sweet, dark Montepulciano grape goes with any Mediterranean fare you care to throw at it. Ruby red, fragrant, and dry and mellow in taste, it's meant to be enjoyed right away. $5-7
Abruzzi, Italy
Imported by Winebow

Quinta dos Carvalhais
GRAO VASCO
Light- to medium-bodied. A jammy, ripe, cheerfully rustic Portuguese wine.
A tasty blend of Portuguese grapes, this red brings you the pleasure of rich cherry fruit, a shot of café au lait, and the earthiness typical of Portuguese wines. Versatile with food, it's a traditional match for *bacalao,* Portugal's famous dried salt cod. $5-7
Dão, Portugal
Imported by Tri-Vin

Farnese
MONTEPULCIANO D'ABRUZZO "Farneto Valley"
Light- to medium-bodied. An easygoing, fun-to-drink party red.
Here's a fruity *vino di tavola* (Italian table wine) from Montepulciano grapes. Its taste? Berries with a hint of vanilla and smoke. Pure pleasure in a glass at spaghetti dinners and casual get-togethers. $6-8
Abruzzi, Italy
Imported by Parliament

Cataldo
NERO D'AVOLA
Medium-bodied. A whopping mouthful of fruit for its price.
Dark, earth-and-chocolate-scented fruit from the sun-baked hillsides of Sicily is the signature of this red, which has just enough edge to keep it interesting. We bet that if this doesn't put you in the mood for a pizza with the works, nothing will. $6-8
Sicily
Imported by Tri-Vin

Villa Fanelli
PRIMITIVO
Medium-bodied. Delicious fruit at a miraculous price.

Serve this to unsuspecting Italian wine lovers and let them think it's a $20 wine. We love its leathery red fruit and wild, woodsy character with dishes like sausage-and-peppers or polenta with a dollop of red sauce. $6-8
Apulia, Italy
Imported by Verdoni

Domaine de la Chanade
CÔTES DU TARN "Les Rials"
Light-bodied. A delicate wine with a firm touch at the finish.
The grape is Malbec, though the label specifies Braucol—Malbec's name in the local dialect of the

commune of Gaillac in south-western France. This red is floral and wispy, with black fruits so elusive that you'll miss them if you gulp it down. It makes a good conversation-starter at cocktail parties, where the ideal appetizers would include some light pan-Latino bites. $7-9
Southwest France
Imported by Monsieur Touton

Feudo Monaci
SALICE SALENTINO
Medium-bodied. A bargain bottling of southern Italian richness, rusticity, and flair.
This blend (80% Negroamaro, 20% Malvasia Nera) is scented with dried cherries, spices, and sunbaked earth. It is also the wine for sausage-and-peppers. Negroamaro (in Italian, a merging of "black" and "bitter") is traditionally used for blending. Malvasia Nera is the red subvariety of the white grape Malvasia, thought to be native to Turkey and Greece. $7-9
Apulia, Italy
Imported by F. Wildman

L. A. Cetto
PETITE SIRAH
Medium-bodied. Sweetly ripe, with a satiny sheen.
Mexican wine? You've gotta try this. Grown in coastal Baja at high elevation under a hot sun and cool ocean breezes, this is a chocolatey, basso profundo wine for red meats, chipotle chili, and fajitas *al carbon*. The winery's **Cabernet Sauvignon Vino Tinto** ($7–9) is good too, but the Petite Sirah is A+ casual fun. $7-9
Baja, Mexico
Imported by Premier

Château Aiguilloux
CORBIÈRES
Medium-bodied. Full of fruit and complex earthiness and tasting much more expensive than it is.
A blend of mostly Carignan Grenache vinified in the method of Beaujolais, this jumble of cherries, spiced plums, earth, lavender, and leather is a good match for most cheeses, grilled meats, broiled salmon, and bowlfuls of chili or Szechuan noodles. At this price, it's also a great wedding wine. $7-9
Languedoc, France
Imported by Monsieur Touton

Colosi
ROSSO
Medium-bodied. Ruddy, sweet, and remarkably smooth.
This old brand drinks like a concocted brew of raisins, cherry compote, and campfire smoke. It's got that "peasanty" something that makes you want to drink it from tumblers in the Sicilian sunshine. Enjoy it with deep-dish pizza or spaghetti puttanesca, or veer toward Texas and dig into a platter of nachos loaded with cheese. $7-10
Sicily
Imported by Vias

Navarro Correas
MALBEC
Medium-bodied. An attractive luncheon partner with lots of fruit and spice.
This is a great example of the everyday wines from Argentina, made by one of the largest estates there. Enjoy its dusty raspberries and earthy savor with herby bean stews, burgers, and meaty wraps or sandwiches. $7-10
Mendoza, Argentina
Imported by Palm Bay

BARBERA:
PERFETTO CON CIBO!

*I*N CASE your Italian is a little rusty, that means "perfect with food"—
something it pays a wine lover to recognize.

While yet to become one of the world's widely recognized grapes,
Barbera—with its pure cherry bouquet and excellent levels of natural acidity—
may be one of wine's best food partners. It is native to Piedmont, where the locals
drink it young as they wait for their Barolos and Barbarescos to mature. Happily,
that hardly means Barbera's usefulness at the table is limited to Italian cuisine.

Light versions work gracefully with many kinds of seafood and spicy fare,
behaving much as white wines do but with the added dimension of red fruit. They
take a chill nicely, too. Fuller versions, often aged in *barriques* (small, new, French
oak barrels), offer lush ripeness wedded to power and complexity—the holy trin-
ity of great winemaking.

Anyone partial to dishes with fruit or honey and to slow-cooked meats (with
a special kind of sweetness all their own) would do well to complement them with
Barbera. But above all, this wine almost seems created for tomato sauce (lighter
Barberas for light and spicy red sauces, richer ones for meaty red sauces).

For a pure and fruity Barbera to serve with pizza or any other relatively light,
tomatoey fare, try **Gallino Barbera d'Alba** ($13–15, *imported by House of Burgundy/
Lorenzo Scarpone*). For a full-bodied example with ripe tannins and a finish that
stands up to meaty lasagna, duck, or a pork roast, an excellent choice is **Brunco
Giacosa Barbera d'Alba** ($20–25). It's a regal wine, barrel-aged and built to last.
(*Imported by Winebow/Leonardo LoCasio*).

ESTREMADURA FROM PORTUGAL

Estremadura is a *vinho regional,* a Portuguese wine designation similar to that of the French *vin de pays.* But the two examples cited here are no bumpkins. The ripe, medium–bodied **Quinta de Bons–Ventos Estremadura** ($6–7), made from the local grapes Periquita, Camarate, Tinta Miuda, and Touriga Nacional, offers ample black fruit and a bit of sweet cocoa. It's good with any Mexican dish with "mole" in the name, and we've used it as a sangria base with tremendous results. The lighter **Aveleda Estremadura** ($6–8), is made solely from Periquita, Portugal's "parakeet grape." Cherryish and mildly spicy, this nice foil for hard sausages and a bowl of chili is also a good addition to the picnic basket. *Both wines imported by Tri-Vin*

Canaletto
MONTEPULCIANO D'ABRUZZO
Medium-bodied. Gutsy and flavorful. A supermarket red that transcends its peers.
Bargain hunters will think they've struck gold when they taste this little table red from Italy. Dark cherries are the theme, with hints of smoke and leather detected here and there. When it comes to food for this one, it's spaghetti all the way. $7-10
Abruzzi, Italy
Imported by Fine Wines

Feudo Monaci
PRIMITIVO
Medium-bodied.
A smooth red with nice depth and juicy fruit that lasts.
You no longer have to travel to southern Italy to enjoy wines like this. The grape many call Italian Zinfandel is here rendered in a dark, brash style loaded with roasted fruit and black olives. (By the way, Primitivo is almost identical to Zinfandel, as DNA testing proved a decade or so ago.) Serve it with grilled fare, fried pork chops, and southern Italian meats and pastas. $8-10
Apulia, Italy
Imported by F. Wildman

Vinedos Agapito Rico
CARCHELO
Medium-bodied.
A hearty, sun-warmed red.
Southern Spain is hot, both climatically and metaphorically. This little blend of 50% Mourvèdre (or Monastrell as it's known in Spain), 20% Merlot, 10% Tempranillo, 10% Syrah, and 10% Cabernet Sauvignon is one of our favorites from that sunstruck clime. Simultaneously gutsy and grapey, it's a fine choice for fatty meats and all sorts of bean dishes and cheeses. $8-10
Jumilla, Spain
Imported by Lauber

Caves Alianca
ALENTEJO "Alabastro"
Medium-bodied.
Softly rich and warming.
A cherryish Portuguese wine with a sensuous oak-chocolatey finish, this blend of Periquita, Trincadeira, and Cabernet Sauvignon handles the sausages, olives, and rich brown stews of its native cuisine. For something lighter, try the fruity "**Tagra**" ($7-8), a 100% Periquita grown in Terras do Sado. $8-10
Alentejo, Portugal
Imported by Tri-Vin

Coop. Del Masroig
MONTSANT
Negre Jove "Les Sorts"
Light- to medium-bodied. Juicy-fruity and buoyant on the palate.
Spain's answer to Beaujolais, this delightful Spanish blend of Garnacha (Grenache) and Carinena (Carignan) is made in the *negre jove*, or "fresh red" style, with whole berry fermentation and light, cherry and vanilla character. It's very appealing on its own or served with salty or spicy foods. Give it a little chill. $11-13
Montsant, Spain
Imported by Distinct Expressions

Joaquin Rebolledo
MENCÍA "Vina Riva"
Light- to medium-bodied. Mouthwatering with vivacious fruit.
This Spanish wine's faint herbal touch and bright cherry-berry fruit make it a great partner to vegetarian dishes, rich fish, and salty Smithfield ham. $11-13
Valdeorras, Spain
Imported by Signature

Palama
ROSSO DEL SALENTO "Metiusco"
Medium-bodied. Raisiny and enticingly sweet on the palate.
This blend of 50% Negroamaro, 25% Montepulciano, 20% Malvasia Nera, and 5% Primitivo evokes the rugged, sun-roasted hills of Apulia. The wine is rich with ripe black fruit and aromas of dry earth, musk, and cappuccino. Hearty Italian fare is its ideal partner, with an emphasis on mushrooms, olives, sausages, and game meats. Palama's lighter **Salice Salentino** ($8-10) makes a nice sipper. $12-14
Apulia, Italy
Imported by J. Given

Avide
CERASUOLO DI VITTORIA
Medium-bodied.
A seemingly modern style from an ancient place.
A blend of Nero d'Avola and Frappato (a Sicilian blending grape), this wine's chief appeal is its creamy, sensuous smoothness and straightforward cherry aromatics. Ideal for roast pork (especially stuffed and sauced), salty cheeses, or flaky fish fillets grilled with fresh herbs. $12-14
Sicily
Imported by Supreme

Shooting Star
BLUE FRANC
Medium-bodied. A sassy, fruity, palate-awakener.
Made from Lemberger, the grape known as Blaufrankish in Austria. Winemaker Jed Steele, of Kendall-Jackson fame, discovered it growing in Washington's Yakima Valley, anglicized it to Blue Franc, added a touch of oak, and in the process crafted a blueberry-and-plum-scented marvel. Fun with fried foods, pizza, roasted veggies, and picnic fare. $12-14
Washington

Convento di Cappuccini
BARBERA D'ASTI
Medium-bodied. A classic Barbera—savory-sweet and elegantly balanced.
A plump, ripe red with a black cherry theme. Use it to complement dishes with northern Italian sauces like Bolognese and the spicy fra diavola. It also excels with grilled foods and blunts the bitterness of radicchio, the trendy salad leaf. $12-14
Piedmont, Italy
Imported by Supreme

Marietta Cellars
OLD VINE RED
Medium- to full-bodied. Ripe and enticing, with a thick fruit palate.
A non-vintage blend of practically everything but the kitchen sink: Zinfandel, Petite Sirah, Carignan, Gamay, and whatever other grapes the old-timers planted in Sonoma. This delicious mother lode of berries, milk chocolate, and sweet pipe tobacco suggests what Sonoma could do best if vintners would stop yanking out the old vines to plant Merlot. A magnificent soul food choice and a fitting partner for any gutsy, saucy cuisine. $12-14
Sonoma

Domaine Mouréou
MADIRAN
Medium- to full-bodied. A rock-solid, meat-eater's red.
Here's a ripe, rustic blend of Cabernet and Tannat, the indigenous grape of Madiran in southwestern France. The blackest of black fruits (blackberry, black currant) are accompanied by strong tannins—the reason Madiran is best served with something fatty or fleshy, including smoked cheeses and thick, meaty stews.
$12-14
Southwest France
Imported by Wines for Food

Boccadigabbia
ROSSO PICENO
Medium- to full-bodied. A sturdy, modern Adriatic red.
This Montepulciano drinks like good Bordeaux. It's gratifyingly dark, robust, and firm-textured with a smoky element. It's great with a grilled ribeye or firm grana cheeses. $12-14
Marches, Italy
Imported by Marc de Grazia

Cosse Maisonneuve
CAHORS "Les Laquets"
Medium- to full-bodied. Effortlessly combines richness, length of flavor, and enormous power.
This is the legendary "black wine of Cahors," made from Malbec and boasting striking aromas of fresh soil, black pepper, and violets. Not your simple sipper by any means, it begs for fatty fare and smoked sausages and meaty stews. As it matures, its oak becomes more apparent.
$12-14
Southwest France
Imported by European Cellars

Olivares
MONASTRELL "Altos de la Hoya"
Medium- to full-bodied. Full of power and good concentration.
Made from 100% Monastrell (Mourvèdre in France), a red grape capable of yielding big, black-hued wines. This version adds a lovely Spanish earthiness and strong espresso flavors to the finished product. A superb red meat mate at a bargain price!
$12-15
Jumilla, Spain
Imported by Polaner

Château La Caminade
CAHORS "La Commandery"
Medium-bodied. Very dry, savory, and about as elegant as rustic Cahors can get.
La Caminade makes classic Cahors, with its Malbec varietal scents of dried black fruit, lavender, and leather. This example also has great balance, thanks to the beneficial addition of a little Merlot. Excellent with cold cuts, firm cheeses, and duck confit.
$12-15
Southwest France
Imported by Bayfield

Bogle Vineyards
PETITE SIRAH
**Medium- to full-bodied.
Simply put, a big black wine.**
With plenty of fruit and tannins, this is a dense, chocolatey red. What is still California's best deal in Petite Sirah will make you sing hallelujah when you pair it with grilled steaks, burgers, fried pork chops, or pizza with the works. $12-15
California

Hauner
SALINA ROSSO
Medium-bodied. Very earthy and savory, with a finish full of spice.
This super-ripe Sicilian rosso is made from 100% Nerello Moscalese, a grape with a wildly perfumed mix of earth, dried fruit, and the scent that can only be described as cigar box. Try it with ripe cheeses or meaty pot pie. $13-15
Sicily
Imported by Domaine Select

Felline
PRIMITIVO DI MANDURIA
**Medium- to full-bodied.
A big, suavely textured, "modern" Primitivo.**
Creamy black-raspberry fruit and notable oak styling result in a half-Californian, half-Italian variation on traditional Primitivo—irresistible to most folks. Ideal partners are rich, doughy pastas and deep-dish pizza. $13-15
Apulia, Italy
Imported by Domaine Select

Mayol
BONARDA "Vista Flores"
**Medium-bodied.
Fresh and invigorating, with a long, sassy fruit finish.**
An Italian grape now thriving in Argentina, Bonarda has a piquancy that's exceptionally appealing when the grape is properly ripened. Mayol's bright magenta wine offers blackberry and vanilla flavors that seem to glow from somewhere in its depths. Intriguing with Asian dishes, and a regional match with spicy steak chimichurri. $13-15
Mendoza, Argentina
Imported by OmniWines

Battistotti
MARZEMINO
**Light- to medium-bodied.
Fruity, with a pleasing astringency.**
From an Italian appellation far north in the Italian Alps comes this pale, dry Marzemino, which is berryish and flowery up front, then earthier and dry at the finish. It needs food, but what Italian

---

MODERN MALBECS FROM MENDOZA

Malbec is the mainstay grape of Argentine reds, and here are two attractive examples. **Altos Las Hormigas Malbec** ($10–12) is a firm, rich, dry red with an enticing fragrance. Lovers of California wine won't be disappointed by this mouthful of coffee, cocoa, black fruits, and something faintly floral. (Merlot lovers will flip for it!) While steak is its natural partner, it's fruity enough for dishes like fried pork chops with red beans and rice.

    Giaquinta Malbec "Cavas del Valle" ($13–15) is fruitier and more vivacious than many Malbecs, reminiscent of a full-bodied Dolcetto. Though plump and loaded with blackberry fruit, it's what might be called "Malbec Lite." Still, like all Malbecs, it's Grade A steak wine, especially with the garlicky steak chimichurri. *Both wines imported by M. Skurnik*

DOLCETTO: THE "LITTLE SWEET ONE"

While its name translates as "little sweet one," the Dolcetto grape isn't so much sweet as grapey and spicey, making the light wines it yields very easy to drink. The small Piedmont village of Dogliani claims to be the birthplace of the grape, but the wines of Dolcetto d'Alba appellation, home to more high-quality producers, are better known. Still, that doesn't keep Dolcetto di Dogliano from turning out some real winners.

Here are two worth trying. **Francesco Boschis Dolcetto di Dogliani "Pianezzo"** ($13–15) is fragrant, nicely concentrated, and piquant. Its berry aromas and lavender notes make it a good fit for focaccia, pizza, baked chicken, and rich pastas. A bolder Dolcetto from the same vineyard is **Dolcetto di Dogliani "Sori San Martino"** ($15–18), a strong, deep purple, a carnivore's wine that is said to improve with age. *Imported by Marc de Grazia*

---

wine doesn't? Star pairings include sausages, antipasti, roasted red peppers with anchovies, pasta carbonara, and light dishes with herby red sauces. $13-15
Trentino, Italy
Imported by Vias

La Ghersa
MONFERRATO "Piage"
Medium-bodied.
Dark and vigorous, with ample fruit and a meaty finish.
Barbera, Syrah, and Merlot—a weird combination that really works here! While the ripe, juicy, cherry fruitiness of Barbera stands out, the other grapes tone this wine down to something more serious. Good matches at the table include hearty baked pastas and gravied dishes like veal Marsala. $13-15
Piedmont
Imported by Epic Wines

Montes
CABERNET SAUVIGNON/ CARMENÈRE "Apalta Vineyard"
Medium- to full-bodied.
Darker, a tad sweeter, and more exotic than straight Cabernet.
From Montes's "Limited Selection" series, this is a single-vineyard wine made from 70% Cabernet and 30% Carmenère, the grape dubbed Chile's "great red hope." Reminiscent of a roasty, tarry Haut-Médoc from Bordeaux, the blend is a bold companion to garlicky steaks, and lamb. $13-15
Santa Cruz, Chile
Imported by TGIC

Tasca d'Almerita
REGALEALI ROSSO
Medium-bodied. A gentle, juicy, and ultratraditional Sicilian red.
Perhaps the best-known wine of Sicily, this blend of native grapes (90% Nero d'Avola and 10% Perricone) is attractively plump and sings with red cherry and fig notes. Match it with pasta puttanesca and similarly piquant foods. Collectors prize the **"Rosso del Conte"** ($42-45), a reserve bottling of the same blend, enormously rich and matured in new French oak. $14-16
Sicily
Imported by Winebow/ Leonard LoCascio

Vinum Cellars
PETITE SIRAH "Pets"
Full-bodied. Smooth and sun-roasted, with a soft, opulent finish.

for a mushroom risotto or anything baked slowly under layers of cheese. $16-18
Basilicata, Italy
Imported by Opici

Di Meo
IRPINIA AGLIANICO
Medium-bodied.
Fruitier than most Aglianicos and well balanced for food.
This is a soft, voluptuous version of Aglianico—full of those brickish, roasty aromas that characterize the grape but with a surprising amount of cherry fruit at its core. Try it with crusty pork chops, polentas, and pastas with sausage. $16-18
Campania, Italy
Imported by Supreme

Franck Peillot
MONDEUSE
Light- to medium-bodied.
Enticingly perfumed, then pleasantly astringent in the finish.
The grape is Mondeuse, known as Refosco in Italy. Grapey and raspberryish, the wine has a piquancy that makes it a great fish and white meat accompani- ment. Or try it slightly chilled with Thai, Vietnamese, or other Southeast Asian dishes. $16-18
Savoie, France
Imported by Louis/Dressner

Luis Pato
BAGA
Medium-bodied. Nice, rustic, fruity stuff with firm tannins.
Baga is "berry" in Portuguese, so this wine's flavor is self-explanatory. Unfiltered, un-fined, and a little gruff in character, it's just right for fried pork or chicken and hearty

Iberian specialties like paella, *puerco asada* (roasted fresh ham), and the traditional dish of Algarve, Portugal's southernmost region—braised pork with clams. $16-18
Beira, Portugal
Imported by Tri-Vin

Le Terrazze
ROSSO CONERO
Medium-bodied. Fragrant, dry, and elegant—a feasting red.
From Montepulciano grapes grown on the central eastern shore of Italy, this finely balanced wine, briefly aged in large casks, sports smoke-scented red fruit and a juiciness that begs for food. It's a savory companion to chicken or pork dishes and pasta with hearty red sauces. $17-19
Marches, Italy
Imported by M. Skurnik/ Marc de Grazia

Gianni Gagliardo
DOLCETTO D'ALBA
Light- to medium-bodied.
A soft and juicy red with delicious fruit and no hard edges.
This young Italian winemaker crafts a refreshingly unpretentious Dolcetto, fragrant with cherries and mint. It's not only a terrific wine for sipping but also an easygoing companion for pasta and pizza. Chill it first. $17-19
Piedmont, Italy
Imported by Enotec

Coturri
ALBARELLO
Full-bodied. Red-wine density and ripeness, white-wine acidity.
This blend-of-all-blends from Sonoma is 40% Petite Sirah and 40% Zinfandel, with Carignan, Barbera, and Alicante-Bouschet, Early Burgundy, Sauvignon Vert,

105

Sémillon, and Muscat topping it off. A joyful jumble of crushed berries, passion flowers, and marmalade, it excites your palate with intense, juicy character. Drink it lightly chilled with a steaming bowl of gumbo, grilled chicken with roasted red peppers, or a citrusy ceviche. $17-20
Sonoma

Pecchenino
DOLCETTO DI DOGLIANI
"San Luigi"
Medium-bodied.
Purplish, low-acid, fruity—
a mouthfilling pleasure.
Piedmontese locals say that if you analyze a sample of their blood, half of it will turn out to be Dolcetto. They drink this kind of wine young with savory Italian cooking: antipasti, veal and pork dishes, baked pastas, and soft buttered noodles with sage. While Dogliani isn't the preferred zone of production for Dolcetto, this is one wine that far exceeds its appellation. $18-20
Piedmont, Italy
Imported by Vias

Cline Cellars
MOURVÈDRE "Ancient Vines"
Medium- to full-bodied.
Flavorsome and firm,
with rich tannins and
an exotic perfume.
Fred Cline has rescued Mourvèdre from extinction in California with his carefully crafted, savory interpretation. (Mourvèdre produces very dark wines, hefty to the point of carnality.) It's never quite as black as you hope it will be, but it's always a mouthful of tarry, dusty, dried blueberries and currants with a nice touch of cocoa from the oak. Some vintages are more tannic than

others. Cellar it a few years and then unveil it with a five-spice Cantonese roast duck. $18-20
Contra Costa, California

Cusumano
NERO D'AVOLA/SYRAH
"Benuara"
Medium- to full-bodied.
Should satisfy anyone who
loves big Italian reds.
Here's a dark Sicilian blend (70% Nero d'Avola and 30% Syrah) bolstered with new oak. It's intriguing with sweet/savory dishes such as melon with prosciutto or sweet-and-sour pork. It's also a good grilled beef choice. $18-20
Sicily
Imported by Vin Divino

Foradori
TEROLDEGO ROTALIANO
Medium-bodied. Fascinating
rarity with savory character and
excellent concentration.
This is 100% Teroldego—a grape that covers fewer than three hundred acres of soil in the world. Elisabetta Foradori has made it her life's work to turn this forgotten variety into serious wine worthy of cellaring. Low yields and forty-year-old vines lend ample depth and complexity to its herby, red fruit palate. Serve with meaty lasagnas, osso buco, a rich risotto, or steak. $18-20
Trentino, Italy
Imported by Polaner

Domaine de Lagrezette
CAHORS
Medium-bodied. A strapping red
for the cellar.
Scented with black licorice, iron, and dusty black fruits, this blend of 75% Malbec and 25% Merlot is in no sense a cute little sipper. It's a commited carnivore's red,

with tannins that need a few years to mellow. Tackle it at the table with the stuff the locals eat in Cahors: duck confit and cassoulet. $18-21
Southwest France
Imported by M. Scott

Mionetto
RASO SCURO
Medium-bodied. Succulent, balanced, and surprisingly easy to drink for such a complex wine. Inside the flamboyant flask bottle dwells a unique blend of Cabernet Sauvignon and Teroldego, one of the rarest grape varieties in Italy. Raspberries and roasted beef notes appear subtly in the bouquet and seem to expand through the finish. It's an exciting, unusual choice for rich pastas, pepper steak, and northern Italian cheeses like Fontina and Tellegio.
$18-22
Veneto, Italy
Imported by Mionetto

$20 to $30

Renwood
BARBERA
**Medium-bodied.
Ripely sweet and succulent, with abundant fruit.**
Renwood Winery is more famous for its Zinfandels, but we prefer its Barbera, which shows less oak and plenty of cherry, blueberry, and sweet cola flavor. Don't expect anything remotely Italian-tasting. Just pour it with a bacon burger, grilled fare, or spicy Thai or Vietnamese and enjoy the ride.
$20-22
Amador, California

COS
CERASUOLO DI VITTORIA CLASSICO
**Medium-bodied.
Creamy-textured and very plush.**
An important wine made in the Vittoria growing zone at the southeast corner of Sicily. (The "COS" is formed from the initials of the three proprietors' first names.) Cerasuolo is a traditional blend of Nero d'Avola (a thick-skinned black grape) and Frappato, which adds a fruity, peppery note. Serve this mouthfilling mix of roasted cherries and berries with roast pork, salty cheeses, and game birds. $20-22
Sicily
Imported by Domaine Select

Marietta Cellars
PETITE SIRAH
**Very full-bodied.
One of the heartiest, most decadent red wines in California.**
Marietta's old-vine Petite Sirah usually goes into other blends. But when Chris Bilbro bottles it alone, it's an opaque, black elixir that lusciously coats the glass. It's hard to specify fruits here; just imagine a stew of mixed berries reduced to their essence. A magnificent barbecue wine and a perfect duck partner. $20-22
Sonoma

Australian Domaine Wines
PETITE VERDOT
"Coldridge Vineyard"
Medium- to full-bodied. More about fruit and finesse than power.
The fifth grape of Bordeaux in a first-class red wine. Inflected with cocoa and loaded with purple plums and blueberries, this is one of the most interesting and simply delicious wines we've ever

had from Down Under. It's a hit with roast stuffed chicken, meaty Asian dishes, and even sweet winter squashes. Hard to find, but worth the search. $20-22
South Australia
Imported by Grateful Palate

Taurian Vineyards
PETITE SIRAH
"Proprietors Reserve"
Full-bodied. Rustic, juicy, and unpretentious.
Elso Taurian has been growing small amounts of ruddy Petite Sirah for more than thirty years on his two-acre plot of old vines in the Russian River valley. The wine's appealing gaminess and tart black fruit are what you want at a summer cookout starring home-grown vegetables and fresh tomatoes. $20-24
Sonoma

Marziano & Enrico Abbona
DOLCETTO DI DOGLIANI
"Papa Celso"
Full-bodied. An opaque purple super-Dolcetto, with soft tannins and grapey fruit that lasts.
This surprising wine swiftly overtakes your palate and cleverly distracts you with gorgeous aromas of violets and truffles. That's why you'll want to keep it around for your next Piedmontese feast of sheep cheeses and braised lamb or beef. If you can't find the Papa Celso, Abbona's regular **Dolcetto di Dogliani** ($15-17) is an excellent alternative.
$20-25
Piedmont, Italy
Imported by Polaner

Domaine de la Marfée
COTEAUX DE LANGUEDOC
Full-bodied. A super-concentrated, complex wine—as good as Carignan gets.
The deep purple, high-tannin Carignan originated in Spain but is now the most widely grown grape in France. Very limited production and extra bottle age makes this wine—a magnificent old-vines Carignan from a century-old vineyard—an artisanal effort. It is purple bordering on black, intense, rustic, peppery, and wild. This is for people who like an Old World style of wine, the kind not often seen on these shores. At the dinner table, think sirloin, rack of lamb, or smoked sausage. $20-25

Languedoc, France
Imported by European Cellars

Mastroberardino
TAURASI "Radici"
Full-bodied. A bold, firm-textured, old-fashioned red that needs aging.
Mastroberardino is the most renowned interpreter of the Aglianico grape, which accounts for 100% of this wine. With its formidable battery of tannins and pungent palate of scorched earth, dried fruits, and cinnamon, this is not for New World wine fans (though your great-grandfather would probably love it!). It's ideal for traditional southern Italian cuisine, has tremendous cellar potential, and is pricier in older vintages. $20-30
Campania, Italy
Imported by Paterno

Summers
CHARBONO "Villa Andriana"
Full-bodied. Miraculously well-balanced and low-alcohol for such a thick, lush wine.
This red is from Charbono, an obscure Italian grape barely

grown in Italy anymore but lovingly nurtured by a few fanatics in California. Deep, vivid purple, and exploding with blueberry fruit, it's very versatile at the table. Grilled salmon or tuna, bean salads, blue cheeses, barbecue, and spicy fare of all kinds would be delicious with this exotic tipple. $22-24
Napa

Arnaldo-Caprai
MONTEFALCO ROSSO
Full-bodied. A powerful red that in the old days would've been described as "manly."
This heady blend has 70% Sangiovese and 15% Merlot— plus 15% Sagrantino, the most tannic red wine grape in the world. And while that makes for pretty muscular stuff, the wine is also deep, earthy, leathery, and wonderful. A match with a beef tenderloin and earthy ingredients like mushrooms, truffles, and roasted heirloom root vegetables would be fantastic. $22-24
Umbria, Italy
Imported by Lorenzo Scarpone

Zenato
RIPASSA DI VALPOLICELLA
Full-bodied. Thick and velvety, extravagantly ripe, and almost impossible to resist.
In the Ripassa method, fresh Valpolicella wine is pumped over the spent skins of Amarone (basically, raisined grapes), giving it a richer, sweeter, dried fruit character. In both taste and texture this version drinks like chocolate sauce. Yet it reveals an intriguing complexity if you pay attention. Match it with roast beef or venison, a prune-stuffed pork roast, or aged, crumbly blue cheeses. FYI, Zenato's basic **Valpolicella** ($10-12) isn't bad either. $22-25
Veneto, Italy
Imported by Winebow/ Leonardo LoCascio

Girard
PETITE SIRAH
Full-bodied. Jet-black and powerful yet wholly smooth.
Run by various owners since its founding in 1978, Girard is now turning out great powerhouse wines from some of Napa's oldest vineyards. Their Petite Sirah, grown on a rescued plot of hundred-year-old vines,

---

TWO FROM PRIMITIVO DI MANDURIA

Primitivo di Manduria is an Italian DOC in sun-roasted Apulia, and one of its estates—the ultramodern Vinicola Savese—makes some of the best Primitivos around. **Vinicola Savese Primitivo di Manduria "Terrarossa"** ($22-24) is an earthy draught that drinks like a particularly savage red Zinfandel. Notes of dark chocolate, black licorice, raspberry, and damp soil crowd into the glass, jockeying for your attention. Come dinner-time, team this full-bodied red with a no-nonsense red meat extravaganza.

Primitivo (and Zin) lovers should go to extraordinary lengths to locate **Primitivo di Manduria Dolce Naturale** ($30-35), a sweet, late-harvest rarity. Pour it (sparingly, we advise) alongside bittersweet chocolate desserts or a deluxe triple-cream cheese. *Both wines imported by Tricana*

tastes like a bowl of sun-ripened figs with a little Rhônish earth lurking beneath. A great match for barbecue ribs and slow-smoked meats. $22-25
Napa

Cellers Unio
PRIORAT
"Tendral"
Full-bodied. Sun-roasted, luscious, and complex.
This is our favorite release from this quality-driven Spanish co-op. A blend of 60% Carignan and 40% Grenache, it is aged in a combination of used sherry casks and American oak, an interesting recipe for Priorat. The wine is powerful, no question, but its fine balance makes it elegant as well. Let it breathe a bit and pair it with maple-glazed ham, kielbasa, or anything big and gamey. $22-25
Priorat, Spain
Imported by OmniWines

Bodegas Balcona
MONASTRELL
"Partal" 2000
Full-bodied. Very powerful on the palate, sun-ripened but not overripe—in a word, classy.
With its enticing, earthy black currants and the ripe tannic backbone that makes it suitable for long cellaring, this thought-provoking artisanal wine makes one wonder just how high Spain's star will rise in the pecking order of wine nations over the next decade. Try it with chorizo sausage or aromatic Spanish cheeses like Cabrales and Idiazabal. $23-25
Bullas, Spain
Imported by Tempranillo

Domaine du Gros Noré
BANDOL
Full-bodied. A serious, satisfying, flamboyantly rich dinner wine.
That Provençal treat—the Old World big taste of Mourvèdre — is yours when you pour this red. Alain Pascal's version of Bandol is fruitier and smoother than many, with extraordinary elegance. Still, this is no casual sipper. It shows its best side with steaks, duck, and strongly flavored sausages. $24-26
Bandol, France
Imported by Kermit Lynch

San Giuliano
BARBERA D'ALBA
"Fiore di Marcorino"
Full-bodied. Mouthfilling ripe tannins and a huge finish.
Barrel-aged, high-octane, and magnificent! All the slurpy, sexy mouthfeel you could want—a palate of ripe cherries and grenadine with a cool sort of leathery rusticity underneath—makes for great drinking and serious food matching. Explore this Barbera with meat lasagnas, ducks, roast pig, or timbale. $20-25
Piedmont, Italy
Importer by Summa Vitis

Giuseppe Mascarello
BARBERA D'ALBA
"Santo Stefano di Perno"
Medium-bodied. Graceful, yet incredibly full-flavored and fragrant.
Here's an ultratraditional Barbera whose expression of its *terroir* is unparalleled. Aromatic

AMARONE: A LABOR OF LOVE

AMARONE is a *recioto* (reh–CHAW–toh), or dried grape, wine. And like all reciotos, it is a labor of love for the winemaker. In hot, dry years in Italy's Veneto region (maybe three or four in a decade), the three grapes of the Valpolicella blend—Corvina, Molinara, and Rondinella—are left on the vines until they are super-ripe, almost raisined. They're then air-dried

on straw mats to concentrate their flavors. The few drops of juice pressed from them is fermented to dryness, emerging as a robust, high-alcohol red wine for long-term aging.

One of our favorite Amarones doesn't come cheap, but is worth every penny on the right occasion. **Allegrini Amarone della Valpolicella** ($60–65), is a big-hearted wine booming with notes of smoke, prune, dried cherry, leather, and sandalwood. We like it in its first ten years, while some connoisseurs will insist on waiting at least that long. But there's no disputing its magnificence with roast duck and game. It's also an after-dinner luxury with a hunk of Parmigiano-Reggiano.

Less pricey but still superb is **Allegrini's "Palazzo della Torre"** ($20–22), a smooth, full-bodied red made from 70% regular grapes and 30% raisined ones. *Both wines imported by Winebow/Leonardo LoCascio*

clouds of sage, wild mushroom, rich loam, and damp straw float temptingly above a basketful of super-ripe cherries. Vividly fruity when young and earthier and more complex after six to eight years, it's compelling either way. Serve it with lasagna, salty cheeses, and stuffed roasts of pork or veal. $25-30
Piedmont, Italy
Imported by Polaner

Prunotto
BARBERA D'ALBA
"Pian Romualdo"
Medium- to full-bodied. Succulent, deep-fruited, matured in oak, and built to last. Sometimes Barbera is a light little drink. At other times it's rich and kirschlike—red meat required. This one falls into the latter category, so uncork it when carnivorous company comes to dine. $28-30
Piedmont, Italy
Imported by Winebow/ Leonardo LoCascio

Over $30

Château Bouscassé
MADIRAN "Vielles Vignes"
Very full-bodied. Big and meaty, with pure Old World character and ferocious tannins.
Alain Brumont crafts his mightiest Madiran from fifty-year-old vines of Tannat grown near the Pyrenees. (Tannat is among the most tannic of grapes, which may explain its name.) Baked earth, tar, leather, and prunes dominate in this red, with high notes of black tea. It easily lasts (and often needs) fifteen to twenty years in the cellar, and wines from the mid-'90s are quite interesting now; as food wines they make exceptional partners for roast duck. For earlier consumption we recommend the vineyard's slightly more approachable regular **Madiran** ($14–16), blended with Cabernet and Merlot. $30–35
Southwest France
Imported by Signature

Ercole Velenosi
ROSSO PICENO
"Roggio del Filare"
Full-bodied. The ultimate Rosso Piceno and one of the best wines in Italy.
Artisanally crafted from Montepulciano and Sangiovese grown on the Adriatic shore, this wine is redolent of earth, currants, sweet cherries, and roasted coffee, with more flavors surfacing as it breathes. Ripe but not overbearing, big but not muscle-bound, it perfectly balances grace with power. If you can't find it, look for its less expensive sister, **"Il Brecciarolo"** ($13–15), equally compelling at its price. Neither wine garners the attention it deserves because it's hard to compete with the overhyped wines from Tuscany and Piedmont (more's the pity). Enjoy either wine with a steak or your Sunday roast.
$32–35
Marches, Italy
Imported by Domaine Select

Bonny Doon
OLD TELEGRAM
Full-bodied.
Broad, deep, black as pitch.
This red shows the maverick winemaker Randall Grahm at his best. Made from Mataro (a.k.a. Mourvèdre), it is his tip of the hat to Vieux Telegraphe from Châteauneuf-du-Pape—but it trumps that wine with more sweet fruit and texture. It's sourced from old vines and tastes of prunes, smoke, black pepper, and lavender. Be forewarned: Only 1,500 cases are made, and only in good vintages. When it comes to food, it's a rare treat with grilled lamb or game.
$33–35
California

Domaine Tempier
BANDOL "Classique"
Full-bodied. Vibrant, powerful, and seemingly very dry.
A wine in need of time.
Tempier's Bandol, arguably the benchmark for this Provençal appellation, defies both easy drinking and easy description. While its fantastic, aromatic mixture of earth, exotic florals, and stewed plums is tempting, its unrelenting power on the palate suggests that you'll have to be patient and cellar this stern red wine. It's a classic choice for southern French fare like

Provençal *ragout de boeuf* (beef stew) and leg of lamb seasoned with rosemary.
$34-36
Bandol, France
Imported by Kermit Lynch

Di Majo Norante
MONTEPULCIANO
"Don Luigi"
Full-bodied. A flamboyant, barrel-aged, deep-fruited "super-Monte."
The finest wine of its appellation, Don Luigi (80% Montepulciano and 20% Tintilia, another local grape) is a kingly red wine, modern-seeming with its vanillin new oak and languorous black fruit but still expressive of its Italian coastal origins. While it can be cellared, it drinks just fine now with roasted lamb, venison fillets, or a broiled strip steak topped with Gorgonzola.
$35-40
Molise, Italy
Imported by Bacchus

Château Montus
MADIRAN
"Cuvée Prestige"
Very full-bodied. One of the deepest, most intensely saturated red wines in the world.
Alain Brumont's famed Château Montus is constantly compared to the first-growth wines of Bordeaux. Where his Bouscassé wines are all about soil and tradition, Montus is more about pure power. It is matured over two years in new Tronçais oak barrels (Tronçais is a forest in southwestern France), which influences its intense palate of prunes, truffles, and jet-black fruit. No telling how long this wine might evolve in the bottle, but let's just say it may be left to your children to enjoy. The richest duck confits, pâtés de fois gras, and game meats do it justice. Try the less expensive, basic **Madiran** ($23-25) to get the general idea.
$45-55
Southwest France
Imported by Lauber

Paolo Bea
SAGRANTINO DI MONTEFALCO
Secco "Pagliaro"
Full-bodied. Muted by tannin when young, this red becomes hugely flavorful with long cellaring.
Here we have a bottle of India ink spilled from the tough-skinned Sagrantino grape, exclusive to Umbria's vinous hot zone. With a long, exceedingly dry finish of black fruits, tree sap, and tar, this red definitely needs time in the cellar to soften. Once properly matured (at least 5-10 years), it's great with beef and venison. The rare and expensive **Passito** ($250–300) is exceptionally long-lived and a raisiny, liqueur-like partner for a platterful of aged Gorgonzola.
$65-80
Umbria
Imported by Rosenthal

CHOICE ROSÉS

*R*OSÉ is a rosé is a rosé. Or is it?

Modern rosé wines are usually made by one of two methods. The most common involves a shorter maceration period of the skins with the juice after the grapes have been crushed. (It's the skins that give red wines their color—so when they are separated from the juice, the pigment source goes out the window.) Fermentation then proceeds as in the making of white wine. A second technique is to simply blend a small amount of red wine into a white wine—something you can even try at home if you are so inclined. Rosé styles also differ from country to country, as a comparative tasting of those we've chosen to feature here will clearly show.

Rosés come into their own in the warmer months—a nice change of pace from heavier reds and the usual whites. And just because these refreshers are light in color doesn't mean that they lack character. With rosés the secret is in knowing which ones to pick. Once you've stocked up, chill a bottle of this wonderful stuff, loosen up, and enjoy.

Pinord
REYNAL ROSÉ
"Crackling Wine"
Fun, fun, *fun!* "Crackling wine'" is an apt description for this Spanish *frizzante*, lightly fruity rosé. An icy cold refreshment, it's also great for spicy foods, Tex-Mex, and tapas. A good Sangria base, too! $5-6
Imported by Pleasant

Ochoa
GARNACHA ROSADO
Sun-baked cherries, berries, and fresh citrus swirl through this tasty offering from Navarra, Spain—a bold prescription for summer barbecues, ham sandwiches, and chili. $6-8
Imported by Tempranillo

Les Lauzeraies
TAVEL ROSÉ
Tavel, from Provence, is arguably the most famous rosé in the world and also happens to be the traditional choice for serving with bouillabaisse. This version of Tavel is very dry and full-bodied. $9-11
Imported by Monsieur Touton

Senorio de Sarria
NAVARRA ROSADO
"Vinedo No. 5"
From the Navarra region of Spain comes this strawberryish, soft, fresh rosé. It's particularly pleasing with hors d'oeuvres, tomato salads, tapas, and omelets. $9-11
Imported by Spain Wine Collection

Château de la Guimonière
ROSÉ D'ANJOU
Here's a cherry-packed Cabernet Franc rosé from the Loire. With a touch of sweetness and a modest 11% alcohol, it's the best spicy food partner among the rosés recommended here. $9-12
Imported by T. Edwards

Château de Pourcieux
CÔTES DE PROVENCE ROSÉ
This rosé from Provence is juicy and perfectly balanced, with clean, delicate fruit. It's a rosé that behaves like a white, so pair it with fish and crudités. $10-12
Imported by Baron François

Under $12

Carta Vieja
CHARDONNAY
Light-bodied. Balanced, smooth, and far better than the price suggests.
Why this delicious, varietally correct Chardonnay from Chile comes at a bargain-basement price is a continuing mystery—but that's just another reason to snap it up. On the food front, its apple and cream flavors work well with any light fare. It's also ideal for spritzers or sangria. $4-6
Maule, Chile
Imported by F. Wildman

Galluccio/Gristina
CHARDONNAY
"Point House"
Light-bodied. A non-oaked, fresh, easygoing sipper.
Here's a non-vintage pleasure from a small but venerable Long Island winery which is still in transition to its new owners. Think of it as a simple, inviting, apple-scented choice for the cocktail hour. The jury is still out on the winery's more serious selections. $6-8
North Fork of Long Island, New York

Hardy's
CHARDONNAY
Light-bodied. A smooth and pleasant Aussie.
This one's dependable, and good value to boot. A little oak, a little orchard fruit, and a clean, healthy finish make this our favorite of the many inexpensive Chardonnays from Down Under. Try it with fried shrimp, chicken fingers, and other breaded snacks. $6-8
South Australia
Imported by Old Bridge Cellars

Señorio de Sarria
CHARDONNAY
Medium-bodied. Silky, golden in color, and full of fruit.
This wine has a nice balance of acidity and body—what European wine writers refer to as "harmony." Non-oaked (rare in a Spanish wine) and rich with pears and honey, it's a perfect accompaniment for polenta, egg dishes (including Spanish tortillas and Italian frittatas), and other soft foods. $9-11
Navarra, Spain
Imported by Spain Wine Collection

Domaine Jean Touzot
MÂCON VILLAGES
Light-bodied. Lively, refreshing, and elegant.

Here's the ideal light Chardonnay from southern Burgundy: fragrant with flowers, crisp at the finish, and marvelous at brunch with quiches and sandwiches. $9-11
Burgundy
Imported by V. O. S.

Wyatt
CHARDONNAY
Light- to medium-bodied. A juicy, light-textured, extremely food-friendly Chard.
This California wine is sourced mainly from Carneros and fermented in 40% new oak—just enough to soften the edges without rendering the wine, well . . . wooden. At dinner it's a sassy match for salmon and white meat chicken. It's also quite nice on its own. $10-12
California

Blackstone
CHARDONNAY
Medium-bodied. Suavely oaked and easygoing.

This is a classic mid-coast California Chardonnay that's better balanced than most. Smooth and appealing, it boasts a light shot of butterscotch in the finish. Serve it with fish steaks or corn chowder. $10-12
Monterey, California

Novellum
CHARDONNAY
"Reserve Cuvée"
Medium-bodied. A moderately plump, ripe sipper.
Here's a French 100% Chardonnay from the Languedoc appellation St. Chinian. It radiates a floral, bready perfume and is the right stuff for your next shore dinner: grilled fish, kebabs, corn-on-the-cob, potato salad. $10-12
Languedoc, France
Imported by European Cellars

$12 to $20

Rockbare
CHARDONNAY
Medium-bodied. Mouthwatering and brisk, with no oak.
This is really tasty—a cross between a lean, minerally Chablis and a glass of papaya juice. Great with crawfish (better known in Australia as yabbies). Barring that, just scoop some tuna salad into a halved avocado, sprinkle with lemon and thyme, and enjoy it while savoring this vibrant wine. $12-14
McLaren Vale, South Australia
Imported by Mr. Scott

Jean–Paul Brun
BEAUJOLAIS BLANC
"Terres d'Orées"
Light- to medium-bodied. Succulent mouthfeel, no oak.
White Beaujolais? Yes, a kind very rarely seen in the U.S. This 100% Chardonnay, naturally vinified with wild yeasts and minimal sulfur, is clean, juicy, and has a flowery bouquet. A classy bistro-style sipper on its own or with quiches and omelets. $12-14
Beaujolais
Imported by Louis/Dressner

Selaks
CHARDONNAY
Medium-bodied. Smooth, savory, and bright in the finish.
Just lightly oaked and imbued with that green, savory New Zealand character. A lovely food wine, Selak's Chard is a gentle, tasty accompaniment to vegetables (especially au gratin), the Greek spinach-and-feta pie called *spanakopita*, and herbed chicken or pork. $12-14
Marlborough, New Zealand
Imported by American Estates

Ferngrove
CHARDONNAY
Medium-bodied. Exceptional freshness and vibrancy, plush fruit, and great balance.
This Chard comes from an ace producer in the spectacular, unusually cool Frankland region of Western Australia. Fermented in 70% stainless steel and 30% French oak, it boasts a pure tropical fruit palate. A tasty choice for your next grill session. $13-15
Frankland River, Western Australia
Imported by Bayfield

Domaine Maillet
MÂCON VERZÉ
Medium-bodied. Fresh, plump, and incredibly appealing.
With its vibrant combination of green melons, apples, and cream, all held aloft by great acidity, this drinks better than many $50 Chassagnes. Rich enough for roast hens and fish but simply delicious on its own. $13–15
Burgundy
Imported by Bayfield

Toad Hollow
CHARDONNAY
"Francine's Selection"
Medium-bodied. Fruity and fun to drink.

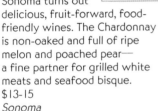

Todd Williams's whimsical, quality-driven winery in Sonoma turns out delicious, fruit-forward, food-friendly wines. The Chardonnay is non-oaked and full of ripe melon and poached pear—a fine partner for grilled white meats and seafood bisque. $13–15
Sonoma

Domaine Billaud–Simon
CHABLIS
Light- to medium-bodied. Very dry, vivacious, and minerally.
At the table this well-priced Chablis performs like a twist of cold, fresh lemon for fish and mixed green salads—not to mention oysters, for which Chablis is the traditional Gallic partner. Fans of richer Chablis should try any of this estate's Premier Cru or Grand Cru selections, all of them superb. $14–16
Burgundy, France
Imported by Langdon-Shiverick

Plunkett
CHARDONNAY
"Blackwood Ridge"
Medium-bodied. Unwooded, crisp, and splendidly balanced.
This oak-free wine is brighter, leaner, and altogether more "Euro" than the oaky Aussie Chards that take their cue from California. We love its fresh, melony style with shellfish of all sorts, vegetarian dishes, and spicy ethnic fare. $14–16
Victoria, Australia
Imported by Verdoni

A HUNTER VALLEY CHARD

The Hunter Valley—a stone's throw from Sydney when you consider the Australian continent's vast scale—has a reputation out of proportion with the amount of wine it produces: less than 3% of the country's total. One reason for the region's cachet is its fabulous, built-for-the-cellar Sémillon, which peaks at ten to twenty years (unusual for white wine). The Hunter is the birthplace of the first Australian Chardonnays, released in 1970.

A Hunter favorite of ours is the medium–bodied **Cockfighter's Ghost Chardonnay** ($18–20). What makes it so? Complex, citrusy yet creamy fruit with just a hint of oak at the finish, plus refreshingly modest alcohol. Pick your mahimahi, swordfish, salmon, or other fish steak and jazz it up with salsas or citrus butters. This producer also has a fruitier second-label Chard called **"Firestick"** ($15–18)—but this one's from way down south, in Adelaide, South Australia. *Imported by Ravensvale*

Colterenzio
CHARDONNAY
"Altkirch"
Light- to medium-bodied.
Delicately perfumed and lively.
This winery has a graceful touch with white wines. The Altkirch is an elegantly made Chardonnay, with subtle apple fruit all over and a nicely mineral etching in the finish. Enjoy it with Italy's lemony pasta, veal, and chicken dishes. $15-17
Alto Adige, Italy
Imported by Domaine Select

Alex Gambal
BOURGOGNE BLANC
Medium-bodied.
A juicy, elegant Chardonnay with a fresh perfume.
Alex Gambal is an American working in Burgundy and making splendid wines from several appellations (see page 54). His white Burgundy is as intricate as lace, a graceful Chardonnay threaded with green apple and citron. It's nice on its own or teamed with a soup, salad, or fresh trout. $17-19
Burgundy
Imported by House of Burgundy

Fitz–Ritter
CHARDONNAY
Spatlese Trocken
"Durkheimer Spielberg"
Medium-bodied. Rich, tangy, bone-dry, and refreshing.
This outstanding Chardonnay is picked very ripe but vinified totally dry. Elegantly balanced with a lovely apricot flavor, citrusy acidity, and a rich vein of minerals, it's delicious with vichyssoise or other creamy soups. It is especially useful for smoked meats or fish. $16-20
Pfalz, Germany
Imported by Chapin Cellars

Roberto Cohen
POUILLY-FUISSÉ
Light- to medium-bodied.
An extremely elegant kosher wine for delicate fare.
The American Roberto Cohen, arguably the best *négotiant* of kosher French wine, selects a very traditional Pouilly-Fuissé from his sources in Maconnais, in southern Burgundy. Minerally, citrusy, scintillating, and devoid of oak, it's ideal for halibut or other firm white fish. $18-20
Burgundy
Imported by R. Cohen

Patricia Green
CHARDONNAY
Medium-bodied. A slender wine that shows how elegant Pacific Northwest Chardonnay can be.
Patty Green and Jim Anderson (formerly of Oregon's Torii Mor Winery) produce small quantities of delicious, refined Chardonnay. With its wisps of fragrance from ocean and orchard, this clean, jazzy wine is for those tired of the oaky butter bombs from California. Try it with a steaming bowl of clam chowder or pan-Asian fish and veggies. $18-20
Oregon

Mount Eden
CHARDONNAY
"MacGregor Vineyard"
Medium- to full-bodied.
Succulent, boldly flavored, and mouthfilling.
This melony, savory Chardonnay hails from the central coast's Edna Valley, an oval-shaped shelf of vines watered each morning by the cool fogs off the Pacific. Smoky oak and sweet herb

---

WINES FROM A *PETIT NÉGOTIANT*

Négotiants are wine merchants who buy grapes, wines, or must (the juice and pulp of crushed grapes that have yet to be fermented), then create wine sold under their own labels. They thrive in Burgundy because so many individual growers produce miniscule quantities from so many different appellations. Numerous *négotiants* now have vineyard holdings of their own. A cadre of smaller winemakers of this sort, colloquially known as *petits négotiants*, aspire to high art in their boutique-style wines. One such wine comes from Jean-Marie Guffens at Domaine Verget.

This busy producer makes dozens of wines, ranging from very expensive Grand Cru Puligny and Chassagnes-Montrachet to bargains from Mâcon, St. Veran, and Pouilly Fuissé. His pure, unalloyed Chardonnays from Chablis, however, show his signature style. The medium-bodied **Verget Chablis "Terroir de Chablis"** ($21–23) is cool and concentrated, with laserlike acidity in most years. An exercise in minimalism, it has clean character, vibrant mouthfeel, enticing leafy aromas, and a rich complement of melony and green appley fruit. Look too for the more opulent **Verget Chablis "Terroir de Fleys"** ($21–23) and any Premier Cru offerings you can find. Pair them with oysters and fine-flaked fish such as sole. They also make complex partners for the cold noodle dishes of Chinese, Thai, and Vietnamese cuisine. *Imported by Winebow*

---

flavors complement chicken and seafood salads. $18-20
Edna Valley, California

Domaine Servin
CHABLIS
"Cuvée Massale"
**Medium- to full-bodied.
Astonishingly ripe and exciting Chablis.**
All of Servin's Chablis are superb, including a very complex and full-bodied **1er Cru "Vaillons"** ($28-32). The hidden jewel, however, is the Massale, an exotic Chardonnay filled with such atypical flavors as pineapple, tangerine, and jasmine. It's also blessed with scintillating acidity and a long finish. Asian or Pacific Rim seafood excels with it.
$19-21
Burgundy
Imported by Weygandt/Metzler

$20 to $35

Au Bon Climat
CHARDONNAY
**Medium-bodied.
Fruit-driven and satisfyingly rich.**
At this idyllic central coast estate, Jim Clendenen crafts a graceful Chardonnay with tropical-tasting fruit, ample oak, and vibrant texture. Match it with glazed fish or pork tenderloin. $20-22
Santa Barbara, California

MacRostie
CHARDONNAY
Medium- to full-bodied. One of the best-balanced Chardonnays in California.

MACROSTIE

CHARDONNAY
CARNEROS

This is one of the few American wineries that achieves perfect synergy between fruit, oak, and acidity on a year-to-year basis. Drunk on its own, it's a rich,

WHITE BURGUNDY

AY "BURGUNDY" to wine drinkers, and ninety-nine out of one hundred will think "red." But the whites of this famous winegrowing region include some of the most important names in winedom. Although they are all made from Chardonnay, they divide basically into two camps: the crisp, austere wines of Chablis, grown in cool, northerly, limestone vineyards, and the opulent, barrel-aged wines of the Côtes de Beaune.

A textbook Chablis vintner is Jean-Marc Brocard. His **Jean-Marc Brocard Chablis Vielles Vignes "Domaine Sainte Claire"** ($20–22) is organically farmed, and, like almost all Chablis, devoid of oak. Stony, lemony, and floral in the nose with a crisp, refreshing finish, it's a classic match with flaky fish and oysters. The Premier Cru **"Fourchaume"** ($26–29) is creamier, richer, and elegant with lobster. Tasters with a scientific bent should also explore Brocard's special bottlings named for geologic eras—**Jurassique** ($18–20), for one. *Imported by Lauber*

In the Côtes de Beaune, opulence is the goal, oak is the rule, and the debate rages between tradition and modernism. Vincent Girardin is the quintessential modernist, making forward wines (wines that taste good young) with lots of new oak and very ripe fruit. His **Vincent Girardin Puligny-Montrachet "Les Enseignères"** ($45–50) is plump and pleasing with zooming aromas of pear, honey, and papaya and an expansive vanilla-oak finish. Other stars in his repertoire are an almost lurid **Meursault 1er Cru "Les Charmes"** ($34–36) and a silky, sensuous **Chassagne-Montrachet "Clos de la Boudriotte"** ($35–40). All are great for grilled seafood or poultry with fruity sauces. *Imported by Vineyard Brands*

Traditionalists prefer the long-heralded wines of Domaine Leflaive, now run as a biodynamic estate by Anne-Claude Leflaive and the formidable winemaking talent Pierre Morey. Whether it's **Domaine Leflaive Puligny-Montrachet** ($70–80) or rarer bottlings of Batard-Montrachet, Chevalier-Montrachet. and Le Montrachet, these are some of the most long-lived, subtly crafted, *terroir*-driven white Burgundies of all. They work best with rich haute cuisine—lots of cream, butter, and white meats on the bone. *Imported by Wilson Daniels*

refreshing glass of Chardonnay. Served with baked ham and buttered noodles, its peach-pineapple fruitiness emerges all the more. At Thanksgiving, this white could elevate your turkey and dressing, cranberry sauce, and candied yams to food-and-wine heaven. $20-23
Carneros, California

François d'Allaines
MONTAGNY
Medium-bodied. Traditional, forceful, earthy, Burgundian style.
François d'Allaines is one of a cadre of Burgundian *petits négotiants* who produce top-quality wines from purchased grapes. We recommend his minerally, exquisitely balanced Montagny—a fabulous complement for chicken, pork, and earthy dishes based on potatoes, mushrooms, or root vegetables. Monsieur d'Allaine's plumper, smokier **Montagny 1er Cru "Les Derrieres Vignes"** ($20-24) and lighter **Rully 1er Cru "La Fosse"** ($24-26), both made from sixty-year-old vines, are also superb. $20-25
Burgundy, France
Imported by Polaner

Clos du Bois
CHARDONNAY Reserve "Calcaire"
Medium- to full-bodied. The opulent, richly oaked Cal style.
The top Chardonnay of the California giant—rich pear fruit, plenty of French oak, buttered toast flavors, and a heady finish. In some vintages it's nicely thick. Among the foods it goes well with are grilled or broiled salmon and double-crème cheeses such as Brie and Petite Gervais. $20-23
Alexander Valley, California

Clos Pegase
CHARDONNAY "Mitsuko's Vineyard"
Medium- to full-bodied. A creamy white wine smartly balanced by acidity.

Better balanced than many of its peers, this Chardonnay is an attractive mouthful (and noseful) of pears, honey, and floral perfume. A third of the production is aged in new French oak before it is blended with the remainder. Serve with richly sauced white meats (it's excellent with pork in an apricot-mustard glaze) and sea bass, red snapper, and other saltwater faves. $22-24
Carneros, California

Foxen
CHARDONNAY
Medium-bodied. A gentle, elegant style with a rich finish.
This is one of the best small-production Chardonnays in California. Cool breezes off the ocean, a late-season harvest, and reasonable use of oak result in a flavorsome wine with a light, buttery quality that goes particularly well with fish steaks and Dungeness crab. $22-24
Santa Maria, California

The Ojai Vineyard
CHARDONNAY "Bien Nacido"
Full-bodied. Abundant fruit and earthiness, plus a juicy finish.
We like winemaker Adam Tolmach's small-production, noninterventionist winemaking philosophy: His Chardonnay comes from vines more than thirty years old and no new oak is used. The toasty aromas, pear fruit, and clayish minerality are just the ticket for herby roast chicken and a buttery sauté of sliced Vidalia onions. $28-30
Santa Barbara, California

Gary Farrell
CHARDONNAY
Medium-bodied.
Firm and opulent, with a
very complex finish.
Gary Farrell's Chardonnays and
Pinots really thrive in the vernal,
misty landscape of Sonoma's
Russian River valley. Honey, peach,
pear, and fresh-sawn wood
permeate his Chardonnay in its
youth, with a little more alcohol
and sweetness evident in the '02
and '03 vintages. For cellaring,
some prefer Farrell's flashier,
oakier effort from the Bien Nacido
Vineyard in Santa Maria: **Bien**
Nacido Chardonnay ($35-38),
which gets nuttier as it ages.
Sautéed skate or monkfish would
be great with either wine. $30-32
California

Over $35

Fernand & Laurent Pillot
CHASSAGNE MONTRACHET
Medium-bodied. Redolent of
the vineyard and terrifically
succulent and vigorous.
This is real Chassagne, with
steely, minerally, complex
aromatics that initiate
conversation at the table.
Serve it now or in the next
two or three years with classic
whitefish dishes—say, broiled
flounder topped with dill butter
or herby mustard. $38-40
Burgundy
Imported by Newcastle

Domaine Vincent Prunier
PULIGNY-MONTRACHET
"Les Garennes"
Medium- to full-bodied.
Fragrant, elegantly balanced,
and minimally oaked.
As revered as they are, wines
of the Puligny-Montrachet
appellation in Burgundy are
either magnificent or terribly
disappointing. So let's opt for
the former for this wine from
an estate worth watching: an
exceptionally ripe Puligny
practically dripping with minerals
and persistent on the palate with
lively apple/pear fruit and lilies.
Any firm-but-flaky fish like cod
will team well with it.
$42-50
Burgundy
Imported by M. Scott

Domaine Maroslavac
PULIGNY-MONTRACHET
"Clos du Vieux Chateau"
Medium-bodied. Excellent
balance, unusually good
acidity, and much minerality.
Masters of restraint, this domaine
makes Chardonnay wines closer
to Chablis in style than to
modern-day Pulignys. The oak is
barely perceptible in this lean,
tightly knit white. The flavor of
crisp green apples lingers nicely.
Enjoy it with crab, squid, mussels,
or any other denizens of the
briny deep.
$46-50
Burgundy
Imported by Lauber

Domaine Lamy–Pillot
CHASSAGNE-MONTRACHET
1er Cru "La Grande Montagne"
Medium-bodied. Excellent
minerality and a dramatic
finish—a reminder of why
Burgundy is so renowned.
René Lamy, originally of Domaine
Lamy and now of Lamy-Pillot,
has been producing Chassagne
since the late 1960s and making
superlative wines since the early
'90s. All of his wines are worth
exploring, but we enjoy the
Chassagnes most for their plump,
honeyed fruit and pronounced
stony character. Serve with rich
seafood on the order of

Coquilles St. Jacques or a sherried crab soufflé.
$55-60
Burgundy
Imported by European Cellars

Domaine Bonneau du Martray
CORTON CHARLEMAGNE
Grand Cru
Medium- to full-bodied. Velvety, and a blue-chip choice for the cellar.
A flagrant display of nuts, cream, toffee, and butterscotch that lasts from the startling initial aroma to the rich, pulsating finish, this white Burgundy is always worth trying, even in poor vintages. You should also know that few whites go better with the creamy, butter-rich dishes of French haute cuisine.
$55-65
Burgundy
Imported by M. Skurnik

Domaine Jean Noel Gagnard
CHASSAGNE-MONTRACHET
1er Cru "Morgeot"
Full-bodied. Lusciousness, succulence, and great staying power.
For some, this top-tier Burgundy producer makes the definitive rendition of Chassagne. There's real harmony and balance here, plus clear expression of the clay and chalk of the Morgeot vineyard. Loaded with pear and complex mineral flavors, the wine drinks beautifully young, but supposedly ages well (we're cellaring the '98). A serious meal match for cod, monkfish, or lobster tails.
$65-75
Burgundy
Imported by Winebow

Domaine Remi Jobard
MEURSAULT 1er Cru "Le Poruzot-Dessus"
Full-bodied. One of the ripest, most honeyed, and opulent French whites we know.
At one of the very best sites in Meursault, the Poruzot vineyard (which some think should have been classed a Grand Cru long ago), young Remi Jobard makes a creamy, superlative white Burgundy. He ages it in 15–25% new oak and gives a good long soak on the lees to add richness and complexity. Unfiltered and unfined, it is redolent of smoke, baked bread, and apple/pear fruit. Cellar for two to five years and serve with salmon, swordfish, or traditional French cuisine, whether "country" or "haute."
$70-80
Burgundy
Imported by Polaner

Talbott Vineyards
CHARDONNAY "Sleepy Hollow"
Full-bodied. Plush and exuberant, flooding the mouth with flavor.

This media darling from the Santa Lucia highlands leads the Chardonnay pack in Monterey, with no serious contenders. Boasting enormous concentration of tropical fruit and pungent butter and oak tones throughout, it's practically more food than wine. Show it off with foods that won't compete: simply prepared poulty, pork roasts, and ham are good choices. Talbott makes many other Chardonnays as well, including the zesty, non-oaked **Kali Hart Vineyard Chardonnay** ($18-20), named for his daughter. $70-80
Monterey, California

Chenin Blanc

Though extensively planted throughout the New World, the grape that gives us Vouvray is a superstar in the Loire Valley of France, its bucolic ancestral home.

MUCH LIKE A TALENTED SINGER, Chenin Blanc has range. *Lots* of range, with its wines running the scale from bone-dry to syrupy sweet (a side of the grape revealed in Dessert Wines, page 210). It is also used in sparkling wines, though very few of them make their way across the Atlantic.

A wine capable of such extremes requires a classification system, and that for Chenin Blanc is much like the one for Champagne: **sec** (dry); **demi-sec** (half dry); and **moelleux** (sweet). The flavors are less variable, with apples, green leaves, and minerals recurring most often in the notes of tasters. Yet the wines are more challenging than they sound: We call Chenin Blanc the most "adult" of white wines because wine drinkers who aren't familiar with it sometimes find it hard to appreciate.

Anyone interested in this grape will do well to learn the characteristics common to its wines' various Loire appellations. Vouvray and Touraine, in the middle Loire, produce wines with aromas of ripe orchard fruits and intense minerality. Neighboring Montlouis-sur-Loire wines are lighter and less important in winedom's scheme of things, though some are absolutely lovely. Saumur offers light, juicy wines, while just a few miles west the tiny Savennières produces some of the driest, most powerful whites in the world. Sweet wines are the forte of Coteaux du Layon, Quarts de Chaume, and Bonnezeaux.

Besides joining Sauvignon Blanc and Riesling as one of the top three most acidic wines (white or red), Chenin is also one of the best whites to cellar. (FYI, the most cellarable Chenins are Vouvray and Savennières, which sometimes need ten years to come around!) Chenin also has a special affinity for seafood—especially crab, shrimp, lobster, and other crustaceans. The sweeter versions of Chenin go best with sweet or spicy cuisine.

Under $12

Caves des Vignerons
SAUMUR BLANC
Light-bodied.
An extremely crisp, vivid Chenin Blanc.
Lemony and somewhat grassy around the edges, this terrific little white adds zest to fried fish, calamari, shrimp cocktail, omelets, and steamed veggies. A steal at this price! $6-8
Loire, France
Imported by House of Fine Wines

Domaine de Vaufuget
VOUVRAY
Light- to medium-bodied.
A simple, soft Chenin with lip-smacking fruit.

Reminiscent of fresh apple cider, this white teams handily with foods that need a little fruit: spicy Southeast Asian dishes, Cajun-seasoned seafood, and Indian or Thai curries. It's also great with autumnal soups made from pumpkin or butternut squash. $6-8
Loire, France
Imported by Monsieur Touton

Baron Herzog
CHENIN BLANC
Light- to medium-bodied.
A fruity and refreshing kosher wine with many uses at the table.
This may be the best value in kosher wine on the market. It's Chenin of the fruity sort—apple-accented and succulent, with a lingering touch of sweetness. Great for spicy foods and gefilte fish. $6-8
California

Domaine Saint Vincent
SAUMUR BLANC
"La Papareille"
Medium-bodied.
Bone-dry, rich, and creamy.
This amazing wine drinks like a Savennières or Vouvray Sec, both of which sell for at least twice the price. Flavors of apples and earth gradually emerge in the glass as the wine is exposed to air. Think of it as a lesson in contemplative enjoyment, then try it with poached salmon or linguini in white clam sauce. $9-11
Loire, France
Imported by Winebow

VIBRANT VOUVRAY

Just east of the French city of Tours, on the northern bank of the Loire, lies the picturesque town of Vouvray, where the local viticulture dates back to the Middle Ages. Until the Vouvray appellation was created in 1936, any wine made in the Touraine region (with monks as the major producers) was called Vouvray. Fortunately, today's narrower definition affords this high-acid wine the individuality it deserves.

A good introduction to its charms is **Chateau de Montfort Vouvray** ($8–10)—medium-bodied, mouthwatering in its acidity, and blessed with a great swell of fruit. Apple and green leaves mingle on the palate, followed by a bit of sweet lemon crème; even better, the creaminess becomes more apparent as you sip. You can serve this wine with most anything, but it seems especially suited to grilled seafood and the spicier cuisines. Value alert: It's also one of the best bargains in this book. *Imported by Diageo*

Vinum Cellars
CHENIN BLANC
"Wilson Vineyards Cuvée CNW (Chard–No–Way)"
Medium-bodied. Plump, creamy, and amiable.

Rich tropical fruit and a pleasing underlying layer of stoniness makes this wine the anti-Chard (note the name). It's appealing with Pacific Rim and Southeast Asian dishes, especially those with sweet ingredients like coconut or sugarcane. It's also a hit with crawdads (crayfish) and spicy steamed crabs. $10-12
Clarksburg, California

$12 to $20

François Pinon
VOUVRAY
Medium-bodied. Fruity, friendly, and gently balanced.

Here's a spring blossom of a wine, made in the *tendre* ("tender") style—that is, halfway between dry and sweet. Aromas and flavors of apples, melons, and lilies combine with creamy texture and gorgeous length of flavor to make this wine perfect for grilled chicken, salmon in a sweet miso glaze, and vegetables of all kinds. $14-16
Loire, France
Imported by Louis/Dressner

Olga Raffault
CHINON BLANC
"Champ-Chenin"
Medium- to full-bodied. A big, dry, earthy white for hard-core Chenin fans.
This austere Chenin, with its firm mouthfeel, is fermented in steel and then aged in barrels. Green leaves and steely notes swirl through the aromas. We think it's a fairly intense lobster wine, but some tasters have found it too dry. Decide for yourself or save it for a seafood risotto.
$14-16
Loire, France
Imported by Louis/Dressner

Domaine Deletang
MONTLOUIS SEC
"Les Batisses"
Medium-bodied. A very dry, richly textured Chenin.
The classic textural descriptor for wines such as this is "waxy," referring to the mouthcoating quality of the beeswax combs one finds in all-natural honey jars. (Taste it and see what we mean.) This estate's Sec, with its bright lemon-zest finish, goes splendidly with crab cakes and firm-fleshed fish like halibut; the sweeter **Demi–Sec** ($18-20) is more appropriate for sweet 'n' sour shrimp, roast pork with apples, or other rich, sweetish foods.
$15-17
Loire, France
Imported by Lauber

Domaine des Aubuisières
VOUVRAY DEMI-SEC
"Les Girardières"
Medium-bodied. Sweet, creamy-smooth, and best drunk young.
In this tasty, easy-to-enjoy Chenin from northern France, caramelized lemon peel, light honey, and custard flavors fill the mouth and last nicely. It's a delicious complement to spicy dishes like blackened red snapper, gumbo, and Maryland crabs with plenty of Old Bay.
$15-17
Loire, France
Imported by Weygandt/Metzler

Paumanok
CHENIN BLANC
Medium-bodied.
Wickedly dry, fresh-flavored, and bracingly acidic.
Here is one New York State producer who understands Long Island's potential to create crisp, food-friendly wines along European lines. Charles Massoud's fiercely juicy Chenin has no oak in sight—just the way we like 'em. Cool and limelike, it's a natural shellfish and ceviche partner. Drink it young. $15-18
North Fork of Long Island, New York

Domaine Bourillon–Dorléans
VOUVRAY SEC Vielles Vignes "La Coulée d'Argent"
Medium-balanced. One of the most pleasingly balanced dry Chenin Blancs available.
Subtly scented with Granny Smith apples and fresh cream. Vouvray Sec is sometimes austere, but this wine is so pleasantly smooth that anyone would enjoy it. It's a triumph with fresh greens and cracked crab. Try the estate's alluring **Demi-Sec** ($16-18) with creamier, sweeter seafood. $17-19
Loire, France
Imported by M. Skurnik

Domaine des Baumard
SAVENNIÈRES "Clos du Papillon"
Medium- to full-bodied.
Firm, very dry, intensely minerally, and long.
Papillon ("butterfly") is the entry-level wine from this estate, but it may be their best food partner. Penetrating on the palate with aromas of green leaves and fresh citrus, it cuts like a knife through oily mackerel and sardines and complements the brininess of oysters. For sheer drama, the **"Trie Spéciale"** ($30-35) is a full-bodied barrage of minerals, baked apple, and ginger, though it needs about five years of bottle aging (and can cellar for twenty or thirty more). Chill slightly, decant, and serve with shrimp or crab risotto, lobster with drawn butter, or roast Christmas goose. $18-20
Loire, France
Imported by Monsieur Touton

François Chidaine
MONTLOUIS "Clos Habert"
Light- to medium-bodied.
Gently sweet, fresh-tasting, and elegant.
Here's a Chenin Blanc in the half-sweet, half-dry *tendre* ("tender") style, with a finishing touch of extra sweetness. Creamy and succulent, with ripe apple/pear fruit and a hint of white honey, it is lighter than a typical Vouvray (its more famous neighbor) and a delicate food partner. Try it with mild squash or pumpkin dishes, stuffed whole fish, or shrimp scampi. $18-20
Loire, France
Imported by Louis/Dressner

$20 to $40

Thierry Puzelat
VOUVRAY "Vin Vrai No. 2"
Medium-bodied. Off-dry and intense, with superlative acidity keeping it fresh.
Organic vinification, tiny production, and manic attention to quality make this a cult favorite. Held back at the winery until it is mature (about four to five years), this complex, briny Chenin is a very personal statement by the winemaker. Serve it with exotica like stuffed zucchini blossoms, roast turkey with oyster dressing, or barbecued oysters. This wine will

probably pitch a sediment, so decanting is suggested. $20-22
Loire, France
Imported by World Wide Wines

Le Clos Baudoin
VOUVRAY "Clos Baudoin"
Medium- to full-bodied.
Richly textured, ripe, and
hefty on the palate.
This historic estate dates from the Napoleonic era, when it was established by the first Prince Poniatowski (1763-1813). The grapes for its Clos Baudoin come from a small plot of old vines located in the Vallée de Nouys, directly above the estate. The wine sees a long, cool fermentation with natural yeasts, leaving it marvelously rich and honeyed. The sheer mass of fruit creates an impression of sweetness, yet this white is essentially dry. While Vouvray can

cellar a long time, many bottles develop a distinct earthiness and faint hints of oxidation—good or bad, depending on your taste. Its best partners? Buttery seafood and very fatty sausages.
   $20-60
Loire, France
Imported by Sussex

Château Soucherie
SAVENNIÈRES
"Clos des Perrières"
Medium- to full-bodied.
Powerful and firm in the mouth,
yet graceful.
You may have to cellar this for a few years before it is ready— but what a wine! A 100% Chenin from vines over thirty years old in a centuries-old walled vineyard, it's leafy green in the nose and redolent of apples, spring flowers, and a twist of lemon peel. Its citric backbone can

---

BIODYNAMIC CHAMPS

Winemaker Nicolas Joly is the preeminent defender of biodynamics, the holistic, decidedly mystical approach to farming created a century ago by Rudolph Steiner—but also the "newest new thing" in winedom. Some think Joly's approach too doctrinaire, but who's to argue when his are some of the most impressive white wines made in the world?

The ultimate Chenin Blanc may be **Nicolas Joly Savennières "Clos de la Coulée de Serrant"** ($70-100, more for older vintages)—a full-bodied, bone-dry, wildly fragrant wine with a deep golden color and a creamy, complex palate. We've also often enjoyed Joly's **Savennières-Roche Aux Moines "Clos de la Bergerie"** ($60-80), a shimmering, minerally, crystal chandelier of a wine and a Dover sole's best friend.

The wine from the historic Coulée de Serrant, a twelfth-century vineyard of chalk and gravel, earns Monsieur Joly most of his admirers. Vintages from the '60s and '70s are gentle and silky now, offering tealike flavors that range from mint to gunpowder to chamomile. "Younger" vintages, such as the '89, are dry as a gin martini yet discreetly honeyed—and about as minerally as Chenin can get. (Drinking anything younger may make you miss the magic of these wines.)

Seafood is the main course of choice, with the focus on oysters, shrimp, and scallops served unadorned or in the most delicate of creamy sauces. Blini with sour cream and Iranian black caviar grow even more tempting when served with these meticulously made wines. *Imported by Paterno*

handle any fish you choose, not to mention wine-challenging foods such as asparagus.
$23-25
Loire, France
Imported by Rosenthal

Foreau
VOUVRAY SEC
Full-bodied. Powerful and expansive in the mouth, with a deep, dry finish.

An exciting, full-throttle Chenin Blanc from a master. Fresh and baked apples dominate an amazingly complex palate that lasts and lasts. On the food front, this is a very "adult" wine for oysters or a whole roasted fish wrapped in fresh herbs. The glossy, deep golden **Demi-Sec** ($24-26), with its glazed-fruit sweetness and deep, earth-and-honey layers, can evolve in the bottle for decades; it's also particularly suited to pâtés, smoked meats, duck confit, and foie gras.
$24-35
Loire, France
Imported by Rosenthal

Foreau
VOUVRAY DEMI-SEC
Full-bodied. Offers a freshness and steely firmness that few sweet whites achieve.

This dramatic Chenin Blanc is replete with sweet apple and grapefruit flavors, plus minerally complexity. Crushed green leaves accent the finish, at least when the wine is young. With age come more baked biscuit-and-honey flavors and a softer, more complete mouthfeel. Sweet and spicy entrées such as whole crab in black bean sauce excel with this Demi-Sec. If you want a full-blown dessert style, choose the

Vouvray Moelleux ($30–35) and enjoy it with fruit crêpes or your favorite cheeses.
$27–30
Loire, France
Imported by Rosenthal

Domaine de la Sansonnière
ANJOU "La Lune"
Full-bodied. Richly layered, with penetrating ripeness and great length of flavor.

To call vintner Mark Angéli quality-driven and meticulous is an understatement. His methods are biodynamic, a mode of organic winemaking based on the holistic theories of Rudolph Steiner. Angéli's production is miniscule, his vine plantings incredibly dense so that the vines will compete to survive, and his late-harvest wines (like this one) are picked *one grape at a time!* It isn't sweetness in La Lune that makes an impression but rather depth, both of *terroir* and structure. Dried apricots, vanilla, and a bready aroma lurk intriguingly in the finish. Among the foods that do the wine justice are broiled lobster and salty blue cheeses.
$35-40
Loire, France
Imported by Louis/Dressner

Gewürztraminer

Most think it German, and indeed it once was. But most modern "Gewürz" comes from France's Alsace region, where it makes profound, perfumed dry whites.

LSACE'S VERSIONS of the exotically scented wine Gewürztraminer are huge in every respect—taste, alcohol, perfume. And with the exception of the late-harvest versions, most are very dry. German Gewürzes, on the other hand, are lighter, juicier, more minerally, and not so wildly fragrant.

Does that make one superior to the other? Well, as with any wine, it all depends on what you like. What we *can* say is that as food wines, the German Gewürztraminers win hands down.

That needn't be seen as heresy in a day when Alsace is ground zero for great Gewürz. On its own, the Alsatian version is a big-boned, flamboyant beauty whose alluring flavors, finesse, and complexity are rarely matched. Yet it is simply indisputable that the wines that best complement food are those which approach it gently. That largely has to with what they are not: too heavy, too alcoholic, too sweet, too acidic. The bolder the wine, the more likely it is to hang around on the palate and overpower, rather than enhance, the taste of food.

Gewürztraminer (geh-VURTZ-truh-mee-nuhr) is a particular clone of Traminer, a lighter-skinned grape named for Tramin, a town in the Alto Adige—the DOC zone that covers the northern portions of Italy's Trentino and is home to a German-speaking majority. The word *gewürz*, German for "spicy," was added to the name, though in this case "spicy" refers to the multiplicity of flavors packed into the grape—among them lychee, gingerbread, and roses.

Gewürztraminer can challenge wine lovers, most of whom seem to either love it or hate it. Not surprisingly, our picks on the next few pages are based on which currently sold versions go best with food, though several are also great sippers on their own. The ideal dinner (or lunch), pairings are the Germanic classics, including leek and onion tart, ham and German sausages (wursts), potatoes and other root vegetables, and rich fish dishes such as whitefish with apples and onions.

Under $12

Alexander Valley Winery
GEWÜRZTRAMINER
"New Gewürz"
Light-to medium-bodied.
At a modest 12% alcohol,
a fruity, easy-going sipper.
It's easy to like this clean,
balanced glass of sunny fruits
and perfume——the opposite
of the "more-is-better" style.
It's also terrific for curries
and pad Thai. $9-11
North Coast, California

Hugelheim
GEWÜRZTRAMINER
Spätlese Dry
"Hugelheimer Hollberg"
Medium-bodied. Surprisingly
dry and subtle for Gewürz
and more elegant than many.
This wine is an exercise in
minerality. While its bouquet
is blessed with a kitchen rack
full of spice, it is not a spicy
food wine. Try it instead with
firm-fleshed fish like skate and
halibut, creamed potatoes
with parsley, or lemony veal
or chicken cutlets. $11-13
Baden, Germany
Imported by Wines for Food

Martin Zahn
GEWÜRZTRAMINER
Medium-bodied. Soft, smooth,
and prettily perfumed.
As Gewürz goes, this is styled
fairly modestly——yet it's still a
gorgeous-smelling drink with
peppery, floral, honeyed qualities
to spare. The traditional partner
for Alsatian leek-and-onion tart,
it also works wonderfully with
pâté, fried potatoes, and fish
steaks. $13-15
Alsace, France
Imported by Weygandt/Metzler

Von Franckenstein
GEWÜRZTRAMINER Kabinett
Medium-bodied. Delicately sweet,
exotic, and scintillating.
Don't let the name scare you:
The only thing
brought to life
in this German
winery is great
Gewürz. This
one's particularly
delicious, teeming

with tropical fruits dusted
with jasmine and rose petals. Its
exotic palate and low-to-modest
alcohol make it a willing partner
for cuisines that span the globe,
from India to West Africa to the
Caribbean. $14-16
Baden, Germany
Imported by Wines for Food

Domaine Trimbach
GEWÜRZTRAMINER
Medium-bodied. Firm, fleshy,
and dry at the finish.
This giant of Alsace makes a
full range of high-quality white
wines. Their surprisingly dry
Gewürz is perfumed with flowers
and talcum and shows just a
touch of fruit—a fine wine for
baked ham and potato salad.
Collectors prize the sweet
Gewürztraminer Vendanges
Tardives ("late harvest", priced
at $60-80); we've enjoyed
deliriously rich, still-fresh-tasting
examples that date back to the
1950s. $14-16
Alsace, France
Imported by Diageo

Fitz-Ritter
GEWÜRZTRAMINER Spätlese
"Durkheimer Nonnengarten"
Medium-bodied. Pleasing and
plump, with good ripeness.
Here's a great introduction to
Gewürz from the large, historic
estate of Konrad Fitz and his
American wife, Alice. An amiable

jumble of apple/pear fruits, flowers, and minerals, it's wonderfully refreshing with hot 'n' spicy Hunan pork, garlicky sausages, and chicken satay. $17-19
Pfalz, Germany
Imported by Chapin Cellars

Willm
GEWÜRZTRAMINER Reserve
"Cuvée Emile Willm"
Medium-bodied. Fragrant, deeply flavorful, and lasting.
What an aroma! Roses and more roses, with a little lychee, honeydew, and gardenia floating around. Also, the wine's acids and alcohol are in good balance—rare to find in a Gewürz. It's an exotic (yea, erotic?) wine for savory tarts and authentically pungent Alsatian Münster cheese. $18-20
Alsace, France
Imported by Monsieur Touton

Lucien Albrecht
GEWÜRZTRAMINER
Medium-bodied. Weighty style with earthy complexity in a wine to cellar.
Jean Albrecht, representing the nineteeth generation at this estate, works in a grand, traditional style. His Gewürz is enormously concentrated and dry, more akin to Grand Cru Burgundy than anything recognizably Germanic. Cream, dried apricots, and mineral pulse powerfully through the finish. Serve this one with the traditional sausages, tarts, and creamy dishes of Alsace. Albrecht's sweeter *vendange tardive* Gewürzes are expensive but sensational. $18-20
Alsace, France
Imported by R. Kacher

$20 to $30

Jean-Baptiste Adam
GEWÜRZTRAMINER
"Kaefferkopf-Cuvée Jean-Baptiste"
Medium-bodied. A sleeper in most years, this graceful, dry wine is nicely lifted by acidity.
Though he works from a Grand Cru site, Monsieur Adam pursues a subtle, mineral-driven style that seems under-appreciated by the wine press. That's a pity, since the wines perform heroically at the table. Relish this flinty, floral Gewürz with rich fish dishes, white meats, and vegetables in fragrant sauces. $20-22
Alsace, France
Imported by Chapin Cellars

GRAPEFRUIT AND ROSES
Young Bernard Schoffit, a pioneer at Domaine Schoffit in Alsace, is making his mark in the world of wine. The Rieslings, Tokays, and Gewürztraminers from the domaine's Harth vineyard are late-ripened and possessed of incredible density, opulence, and an appealing natural sweetness. **Domaine Schoffit Gewürztraminer "Harth"** ($20–25) is dizzyingly aromatic and rich—all grapefruit and roses on a steely spine of minerals. At the table, it's best paired with sturdy foods like *choucroute garni* (Alsatian sausages and sauerkraut) and roasts of veal or pork. *Imported by Weygandt/Metzler*

RIPE, FLAMBOYANT, THICK!

Maurice and Jacky Barthelme, who succeeded Albert Mann (Maurice's father-in-law) in the 1980s, have catapulted their predecessor's estate onto every top ten list in Alsace. Their **Domaine Albert Mann Gewürztraminer Grand Cru "Furstentum"** ($33-36), grown organically and late-harvested from old vines, smells like some improbable distillate of liquid wildflowers. In the mouth, its concentration of flamboyantly ripe peach, papaya, and passion fruit lends an impression of sweetness but stops short of becoming a dessert wine (a formula that's just right for foie gras). You'll also find this Gewürz so full-bodied that it practically coats the wineglass. *Imported by Weygandt/Metzler*

Pierre Frick
GEWÜRZTRAMINER
Medium-bodied. Fantastically flavorful and succulent, with a bright finish.
Biodynamically farmed, this superb, small-production Gewürz bursts forth with floral aromas mixed with red berries and lychee. Thanks to its unusually fine acids, it's balanced beautifully for seafood. Try it with a baked bluefish wrapped in pancetta. $20-22
Alsace, France
Imported by M. Scott

Over $30

Domaine Weinbach
GEWÜRZTRAMINER
"Clos des Capucins–Cuvée Theo"
Medium- to full-bodied. Some of the classiest, driest, most elegant wine in Alsace.
Colette Faller and her two daughters, Laurence and Catherine, produce great whites that eschew the heaviness and perfumy excess of some of their Alsatian peers. This Gewürz, often needing four to five years to blossom, is prettily scented with lychee and pear and shows a bit of tannin in the tail. Decant

to breathe and then serve with veal, chicken, or duck dishes.
$35-40
Alsace, France
Imported by M. Skurnik

Domaine Zind Humbrecht
GEWÜRZTRAMINER
"Herrenweg de Turckheim"
Full-bodied. Densely concentrated and glycerous in texture, with a whopping finish.
The king of Alsace wine, Olivier Humbrecht is a perfectionist, obsessed with eliciting the essence of each vineyard in which his wines are grown. Even the Herrenweg, his basic Gewürz, is a powerhouse—heady and thick-textured with caramelized-tasting fruit and a bouquet straight from the rose garden. It's an excellent choice for lobster, braised pork loin, or your favorite smelly cheeses. Olivier's multiple single-vineyard selections from **Hengst, Heimbourg,** and **Clos Windsbuhl** ($50-150) are all extremely rich and generally have over 15% alcohol. Such wines don't need food; they *are* food.
$35-45
Alsace, France
Imported by Kermit Lynch

Pinot Grigio/ Pinot Gris

On the white wine stage the spotlight has been turning to the light, fresh wines of this European grape, and the reviews of its performance are mixed.

MASTER OF DISGUISE, the grape most folks know as Pinot Grigio has at least four different identities. It is Pinot Grigio in northern Italy, Tokay Pinot Gris in Alsace, Grauburgunder in Germany, and Pinot Gris in Oregon (and most other places). Not surprisingly, the wines from each region are distinctly different, mainly because of the vast differences in *terroir*.

The Tokay Pinot Gris of Alsace is the most flamboyant. Very rich, very floral, high in alcohol, and often vinified in a sweet, perfumy style, it demands the attention of the taster from first sip to last. The Alsatians themselves use it only for very rich fare, or, in sweeter versions, for pastries and cheeses. (Mysteriously, although the grape is known as Tokay, it has no relation to the Hungarian wine Tokaji, pronounced the same but spelled differently.) Oregon Pinot Gris seems to take its inspiration from Alsace, but offers less in the way of honeyed richness and more in the way of fresh fruit—mostly stone fruits like peach and apricot. The German version, alias Grauburgunder, is mostly of local interest to the Germans, the best examples emanating from Baden. Grauburgunder is invariably bone-dry, and often rather earthy and austere on the palate.

By far the most popular is Italian Pinot Grigio, grown abundantly in the northern provinces of Alto Adige, Friuli, and the Veneto. Some versions (including several noted here) offer interesting character and pair well with fish, pastas, and any dishes that take a light, dry white. But as a rule, Pinot Grigio is a cocktail wine, inexpensive and conveniently made for chilling and swigging. Just like vodka, it offers itself as a neutral, inoffensive beverage you can pitch a couple of ice cubes into without a hassle. It is no surprise that it is catching up to Chardonnay as the bar pour of choice, both in America and internationally.

Riesling

Learning to love wine made from this German grape requires a little work—but only in finding the style that best suits your taste. That done, prepare to fall in love.

HERE'S A REASON for our unbounded enthusiasm for Riesling, and we're more than happy to share it: It's simply the best food partner in the world.

There are several reasons why. First, there is no wine grape translated with such variety. Riesling can be rich or light; simple or profound; intensely dry or voluptuously sweet. You can match it to every course of a meal, appetizer through dessert. Its aromatic range is, for all intents and purposes, infinite. That means it is as complex as any wine you care to mention. Technically speaking, it has better acidity than any other wine grape, which makes it mouthwatering, which in turn makes it an aid to digestion and palate sensitivity. High acidity also means Riesling cellars better than any white wine on earth—and many reds. It is usually lighter than other wines, thus serving as a graceful partner for food rather than an adversary. Its lower alcohol, averaging 7% to 11%, makes it a balm for the spicy dishes that few other wines can handle.

Above all, Riesling is a completely transparent vehicle for its *terroir*. Granted, it is picky, and won't thrive everywhere. But on its home turf, in the vineyards of Middle Europe, it triumphs. In Alsace it makes rich, sensuous wines with a certain "Frenchness" about them, exotic yet still earthbound, sunny wines from sunny climes. In Austria, the wines reflect the austere, rocky slopes of the Danube—dry, zestful Rieslings with restrained character and significant alcoholic strength. Then there's Germany, where inarguably the finest wines are made. In brown bottles from the Rhine come the historic, firm, nervy wines of the Rheingau; the friendlier, sometimes berryish offerings of the Rheinhessen; and the fat, slurpy fruit bombs of the Pfalz, where the slopes are gentler and the weather warmer. To the west flows the River Nahe, home of graceful, citrusy wines that never shout but whisper persuasively. Finally comes the wild squiggle of the Mosel, where sunlight is scarce and the pebble-strewn vineyards slope down at seemingly impossible angles to the river below. Wonderfully delicate wines flow in green–glass bottles here, balletic balancing acts of fruit and slate. The Saar and the Ruwer, the Mosel's tributaries, are sources of the most ethereal wines of all.

Under $12

Willm
RIESLING
Light- to medium-bodied.
Hints of fruit and mineral,
and a dry, zippy finish.
This is easily the best deal in
Alsace Riesling. Lively, fresh
tasting, and light-handed in style,
it pairs well with any food that
likes a dry white with a bit of
fruit to it, from chips 'n' dips,
shrimp cocktail, and pâtés to
entrée salads and poultry. $9-11
Alsace, France
Imported by Monsieur Touton

Max Ferdinand Richter
RIESLING
"Estate"
Light-bodied.
Pure, fresh,
and delicate,
with a faint hint
of sweetness.
Made in an old-fashioned style at
a three-hundred-year-old estate
on the River Mosel, this ethereally
delicate wine is kissed with
green apples and honeysuckle. It
sips easily with seafood salads,
boiled shrimp with remoulade
sauce, and cold cuts. The

aromatic **Kabinett "Wehlener
Sonnenuhr"** ($8-10) is a
textbook rendition at a great
price—and fantastic with rare
tuna. **Spätlese "Brauneberger
Juffer-Sonnenuhr"** ($10-12) is
earthier and more honeylike—an
unlikely but perfect companion
to southern soul food. $10-12
Mosel, Germany
Imported by Langdon-Shiverick

Eugen Wehrheim
**RIESLING SPÄTLESE
"Niersteiner Orbel"**
**Medium-bodied. Fun,
frolicsome, loaded with fruit.**
Ribbons of ripe peach and
apricot swirl through the core of
this bargain Spätlese, giving it an
almost sherbety character. It's
balm for spicy ethnic dishes and
highly seasoned sausages—
German currywurst and Spanish
chorizo, for two. $10-12
Rheinhessen, Germany
Imported by Winebow

Johannes Ohlig
RIESLING TROCKEN "Nikki"
**Light- to medium-bodied.
Zing! A bone-dry, generously
fragrant pleasure.**
This excellent, affordable
Rheingau Riesling comes from a

TRANSLATING A GERMAN WINE LABEL

When buying a German wine, the most important thing to understand is
the difference between ripeness (the amount of sugar at harvest) and sweetness (the amount of sugar in the finished wine). German wine labels tell you
both! The first level of ripeness is **Qualitatswein** or "quality wine," light
and fruity. **Kabinett** is riper at harvest than Qualitatswein, usually off–dry
and light to medium–bodied. **Spätlese** (literally "late picked") is riper, richer, and usually sweeter. **Auslese** is hand–picked when very ripe, definitely
sweet, and may have botrytis (noble rot). Here's the catch: Any of the above
may be fermented to total dryness (labeled **Trocken**), or near total dryness
(**Halbtrocken**). In practice, a Kabinett Halbtrocken tastes about as "sweet"
as Brut Champagne. See Dessert Wines (pages 210–21) for **Beerenauslese**
(B.A.), **Trockenbeerenauslese** (T.B.A.) and **Eiswein** (ice wine).

four-hundred-year-old family estate. It's a bright little wine—pear-scented and a great match with sushi. The **Spätlese Halbtrocken "Johannisberger Erntebringer"** ($14-16) is a riper, fuller-bodied jumble of oranges, minerals, and cloves. Good partners for this one are paella, shrimp gumbo, and pork-and-veggie stir fries. $10-12
Rheingau, Germany
Imported by Wines for Food

Joachim Flick
RIESLING
Medium-bodied. Fruity, firm, and lasting.

JOACHIM FLICK
RIESLING RHEINGAU

The Flick wines owe their filigreed character to a rare vein of pure limestone found in their corner of the Rheingau. The Riesling is graceful, plump with apricot/peach notes, and balanced on a dime. Bottled in liters, it's an astonishing value and seems almost made to order for Chinese food. $10-12
Rheingau, Germany
Imported by Wines for Food

Dr. Loosen
RIESLING "Dr. L"
Light- to medium-bodied. Sleek, balanced, and easy to like.
Because of its consistent quality and availability, this wine has been many wine lovers' introduction to fine German Riesling. Ernie Loosen's entry-level version offers a glimpse of his craftsmanlike style. Its precise flavors, juicy acids, and off-dry fruity character are just what the doctor ordered for pâtés, fried fish, and summer seafood. $10-13
Mosel, Germany
Imported by Valckenberg

Stephan Reuter
RIESLING Dry
"Krettnacher Altenberg"
Light- to medium-bodied. Very dry, with razorlike acidity.
Here's a wine that hits you with an icy laser beam of apple-pear fruit and citrus—a waker-upper, for sure. It is also one of the juiciest, driest, most penetrating Rieslings around. Use it as a racy match for oysters, salads, and salmon roe. $11-13
Saar, Germany
Imported by Wines for Food

$12 to $20

Dr. M. Prüm
RIESLING "Estate"
Light- to medium-bodied. A friendly, fresh, vigorous white for all occasions.
What vintner Manfred Prüm calls his "casual wine" is still better than half the traditional Kabinetts in Germany. With its bold aroma, it's an elegant glass on its own or a knockout Asian food partner. Some bottles may need breathing time. $12-14
Mosel, Germany
Imported by Vin Divino

Dr. F. Weins–Prüm
RIESLING Halbtrocken
Medium-bodied. Dry, stony, refreshing, and firm.
Crafted by Bert Selbach at his tiny, ten-acre Mittelmosel estate, this Mosel Riesling is dry as you please, with suggestions of mineral water and citron. It's a zestful apéritif or a cool mate to crab or shrimp salads and smoked trout. Also try his delightfully refined **Kabinett** ($20+) or the sherbety **Spätlese "Wehlener Sonnenuhr"** ($25+). $12-14
Mosel, Germany
Imported by Cellars International

Gysler
RIESLING KABINETT
"Weinheimer Holle"
Medium-bodied. A blast of fruit that awakens the palate.

Never have we tasted a Kabinett Riesling with such high sugar and acidity levels: It may remind you of the most intense, delicious lemonade you've ever had. Food isn't needed—just chill and enjoy. $12-14
Rheinhessen, Germany
Imported by M. Skurnik

Joh. Haart
RIESLING KABINETT
"Piesporter Goldtropfchen"
Light- to medium-bodied. Enticingly fresh, pale, and lovely.
This gossamer wisp of a wine comes from a legendary Mosel vineyard. Crystalline flavors of flowers and green apples abound, supported by a touch of enticing sweetness. Hard not to like! Drink it for refreshment or serve with light fish, vegetables, and main-course salads. $13-15
Mosel, Germany
Imported by Winebow

Dr. Konstantin Frank
JOHANNISBERG RIESLING Dry
Light- to medium-bodied. Fresh and zesty.
You wouldn't guess it from the German-sounding name, but this is a delicious American Riesling from a New York wine pioneer. Green apple and melon fruit tickle your taste buds all the more as you savor pâtés or smoked fish. Fans of sweeter whites could try the **Riesling Semi-Dry** ($12-14), perhaps with a New York State blue cheese. $13-15
Finger Lakes, New York

Josef Leitz
RIESLING
"Rudesheimer Drachenstein"
Medium-bodied. Sexy and luscious.
If fresh ripe pears were picked and reduced to their purest essence, you'd come close to the jolting flavor of this wine. Few wines are this complex while staying so downright *fun*. Any spicy food will excel. Those curious about Leitz's "serious" side can search out the liqueurlike **Spätlese Rudesheimer Berg Schlossberg** ($32-40), a sweet wine for the cellar. $13-15
Rheingau, Germany
Imported by M. Skurnik

Schloss Gobelsburg
RIESLING
Medium-bodied. A firm, fleshy white with a dry finish.
This affordable Austrian Riesling is very Burgundian—that is, graced with good, earthy minerality and a rich finish. The difference comes with the lemony burst of acidity at mid-palate. It would soar with a crab casserole. Still more

Nonnenberg, which adds citrusy brightness. Dry and strong, it's a serious partner for richly sauced ocean fish or scallops. $22-24
Rheingau, Germany
Imported by Classical Wines

Willi Haag
RIESLING SPÄTLESE
"Brauneberger Juffer–Sonnenuhr"
Medium-bodied.
Creamy, plump, and mellow.
Young Markus Haag makes soft-spoken wines from the steep, slaty Juffer ("old crone") vineyard in Brauneberg.
At its best, his Spätlese is pleasingly sweet with apples, honeysuckle, and that extra-ordinary slate spine. Enjoy it chilled with a whole poached fish on a bed of greens. $22-25

Mosel, Germany
Imported by M. Skurnik

Franz Prager
RIESLING FEDERSPIEL
"Weissenkirchner Steinriegl"
Medium- to full-bodied.
Concentrated, bone-dry, and cellar-worthy.
About as traditional as Austrian Riesling gets, the Riesling from the Steinriegl vineyard seems cool, almost minty in character, with deep mineral layers. Its acidity is so finely integrated into the wine that you don't detect it right away. Superb with lemony fish, breaded veal cutlets, and rich crab or lobster dishes. $23-25
Wachau, Austria
Imported by Vin Divino

Freiherr von Schleinitz
RIESLING SPÄTLESE
"Koberner Weisenberg"
Medium-bodied. Generous in flavor and extremely ripe.

This estate at the far north end of the Mosel crafts a piquant Spätlese, weighty on the palate and rife with gorgeous green apple, mint, and lemonade scents. Decanting may be necessary to avoid the (harmless) tartrate crystals that often form in the bottle. Serve with spicy fare, shrimp scampi, or Greek seafood with plenty of lemon. $23-25
Mosel, Germany
Imported by M. Skurnik

Egon Müller
RIESLING KABINETT
"Scharzhofberger"
Medium-bodied. Firm, subtle Riesling in need of cellaring.
This legendary winery (est. 1797) owns seven hectares of the Scharzhofberg, one of Germany's top vineyards. The wines need years in the cellar but reveal a crisp, citron-and-stone palate and supreme class. Best served with simply prepared trout, sole, or cod. $24-30
Mosel, Germany
Imported by Cellars International

H. Donnhoff
RIESLING Kabinett
"Norheimer Dellchen"
Light- to medium-bodied.
Some of the most graceful Rieslings in Germany.
Helmut Donnhoff, the undisputed king of the Nahe, has a motto: "Das ganze Ding muss klingen!" ("The whole thing must harmonize"). This particular wine has been taut and firm in some years, delicate in others, yet it always sustains that precious harmony of acidity, sweetness, and mineral backbone. Perfumed with tangerines and potpourri, it goes well with light food—even the raw kind (ceviche, sushi, sashimi). The collector's wine from the estate is the **Spätlese**

"Niederhauser Hermannshohle"
($55-65), so cellarable it might
outlive you. $25-35
Nahe, Germany
Imported by M. Skurnik

Schafer–Frohlich
RIESLING SPÄTLESE
"Bockenauer Felseneck"
Medium-bodied.
A Spät to
reckon with.
This startlingly
ripe peach-and-
tangerine bomb
comes from Tim Frohlich, a 30-
year-old wunderkind. Those
who prefer their wines less sweet
can try his perfectly balanced
Schafer–Frohlich "Estate"
Halbroken ($16-18). There's
no shortage of acidity here, so
serve both with intense-tasting
food—say, sauerbraten.
$28-32
Nahe, Germany
Imported by Cellars International

Brundlmayer
RIESLING
"Zobinger Heiligenstein"
Medium- to full-bodied.
Powerful, with perfectly
integrated acidity.
Willi Brundlmayer, considered
the best winemaker in Austria by
many wine writers, makes
Rieslings that have a tendency to

age well for many years. This one
is dense with earth and apples,
but hints of tropical fruits
emerge in warm vintages like '99
and '02. It's great with mustardy
swordfish or salmon. Also look
for the cellarable, extravagant
"Alte Reben" ($50-65), made
from old vines, or **Langenloiser**
Steinmassel ($25-30), a
friendlier, fruitier cuvée with
just 12% alcohol and an incredibly
pure streak of pear in the finish.
$29-34
Kamptal, Austria
Imported by M. Skurnik

Domaine Zind–Humbrecht
RIESLING
"Herrenweg de Turckheim"
Full-bodied. Dry and headily
perfumed, with more soil on
display than fruitiness.
Olivier Humbrecht is the king
of Alsace wines, thanks to his
obsession for detail and quality.
His Riesling is redolent of stones
and fresh earth, underwritten
by ripe citrus and fruits and
surprisingly high alcohol. Save
this for richly sauced fish, white
meats, or bratwurst. His **Riesling**
"Rangen de Thann" ($28-30),
from old vines in volcanic soils,
is the one to cellar.
$36-40
Alsace, France
Imported by Kermit Lynch

THE ULTIMATE MODERN RIESLING

Robert Weil is on everyone's short list of the best winemakers in the
Rheingau (or possibly all of Germany), and his **Robert Weil Riesling**
Spätlese "Kiedricher Grafenberg" ($50-60) is the top of his line as far as
dinner wines are concerned. With sheer power wedded to flamboyant fruit,
this full-bodied Spät is endlessly long on flavor—the *ne plus ultra* of modern
Riesling. Sweet pears and white peaches, clover honey, ginger, and passion
flower are the start of its aromatics, and you're sure to detect others. But it's
that great minerality that's the big reward. Ham, game birds, and whole fish
are good food mates. Incidentally, Weil's simply labeled but powerfully built
"Estate" Trocken ($20+) is one of the best dry wines in Germany.

Château de la Presle
TOURAINE Blanc
Medium-bodied. Fiercely aromatic, boldly flavored, and zingy.
Now this is the kind of Sauvignon we like: *sauvage* (wild), as the French say, totally dry, and loaded with minerals, acidity, grassiness, and a little grapefruit. It's an exciting wine for greens, grains, pesto, tomatoes, goat cheeses, and *pizza bianco* (cheese, but no tomato sauce)—and a hit with oily fish like mackerel or sardines. $9-11
Loire, France
Imported by Bayfield

$10 to $20

Château Lamothe de Haux
BORDEAUX Blanc
Light- to medium-bodied. Crisp and elegant.
A citron-scented Sauvignon/ Sémillon blend with a fresh finish. It's a marvelous dry white with first courses, vegetable dishes, or a creamy pasta tossed with smoked salmon. $10-12
Bordeaux
Imported by Bayfield

Henri Bourgeois
SAUVIGNON BLANC
"Petit Bourgeois"
Medium-bodied.
Crisp and revivifying.
A "baby Sancerre" from Chavignol, a village in France's Sancerre district. Racy, citrusy, and tinged with an herbal note, this one will please even your pickiest wine-loving guests when it's served alongside flaky fish, vegetables, hors d'oeuvres, or chèvre. $10-12
Loire, France
Imported by Monsieur Touton

Sacchetto
SAUVIGNON BLANC
Light-bodied. Ethereally delicate—a Mediterranean take on Sauvignon.
This gentle dry white entices you with an elusive floral-herbal theme and fresh flavors throughout. Serve with sautéed greens, gnocchi with pesto, or flaky fish with a splash of lemon. $10-12

Veneto, Italy
Imported by J. Given

Blanco Nieva
SAUVIGNON BLANC
Medium-bodied.
Penetrating on the palate.
This Spanish SB is bold, grapefruity, and unbelievably aromatic, with rapierlike acidity. It's a great solution for such "problem" wine foods as asparagus, artichokes, or sardines and other oily fish. $10-12
Rueda, Spain
Imported by Frontier

François Cazin
CHEVERNY
"Le Petit Chambord"
Light- to medium-bodied. Crisp, plump, and piquant.
Here's a unique blend of 90% Sauvignon Blanc and 10% Chardonnay. Very dry and kissed with herbs and earth, it often shows a light nuttiness in the finish. Try it with endive spears stuffed with goat cheese. $10-12
Loire, France
Imported by Louis/Dressner

ZEST FROM MARLBOROUGH

It wasn't until the 1980s that Marlborough, the winegrowing region on the northern tip of New Zealand's South Island, came to the wine world's attention—and then because of one grape: Sauvignon Blanc, which thrives on the area's combination of warm days, cool nights, light rainfall, and lots of sunshine. A wine that lives up to the region's growing reputation is **Vavasour Sauvignon Blanc "Dashwood"** ($12–14), an addictive combo of freshness, grace, and lively fruit. Zesty and fragrant, it offers grass and minerals in the nose and threads of grapefruit and kiwi on the palate.

Practically the paradigm of a great food wine, it goes with everything: fish, fowl, vegetables, and even red meat dishes—particularly roast leg of lamb with garlic and rosemary. *Imported by Lauber*

Shenandoah
SAUVIGNON BLANC
Light- to medium-bodied.
Seductively fragrant and smooth.
What really makes this fun is a shot of 20% Viognier in the blend, which adds richness and a sexy pear perfume. It's an exotic American white wine with great potential for crab dishes and spicy seafood. $10-12
California

Domaine du Tariquet
SAUVIGNON BLANC
Medium-bodied.
Bright, juicy, and flavorsome.
This bone-dry Sauvignon, from Cognac country in southern France, is an electric jolt to the senses. A winning apéritif at a great price, it's also a hit at the table with foods as varied as shrimp Creole, stuffed grape leaves, and pasta with pesto. $10-12
Côtes de Gascogne, France
Imported by Baron François

Red Hill
SAUVIGNON BLANC
Medium-bodied. Enticingly fragrant and versatile.
The moment you open the bottle, this Sauvignon fills the room with its melon and fresh citrus perfume. A vibrant and succulent wine, it exhibits a balance and integrity of flavor that benefits light food of any kind, from herbal cheeses to bitter greens to pesto to fish and shellfish. $10-12
Marlborough, New Zealand
Imported by Bayfield

Stoneleigh
SAUVIGNON BLANC
Medium-bodied. Tingly and refreshing, with lots of flavor.
A widely available old favorite. This wine remains as tasty and grassy as it should be, with that grapefruity Sauvignon character coming through in spades on the finish. A super white for vegetable lasagna, Greek salad, or *moules meunière* (mussels cooked with lemon, herbs, and white wine). $10-12
Marlborough, New Zealand
Imported by Commonwealth

Marc Brocard
SAUVIGNON BLANC
DE ST. BRIS
Light- to medium-bodied.
Savory and crisp.
A bit of a rare bird, this Sauvignon is sourced near Chablis, which is usually Chardonnay's turf. The producer does with Sauvignon what he perfects in Chablis, making a crisp, slightly earthy, and very interesting wine with no

oak and plenty of pleasure to give. A great choice for an omelet or Cobb salad. $11-13
Burgundy
Imported by Lauber

Château La Blancherie
GRAVES Blanc
Light- to medium-bodied. Juicy, dry, and elegant.
This blend of Sauvignon Blanc and Sémillon is made in a crisp, non-oaked style, with a dash more complexity than Bordeaux Blanc. It is versatile for foods that like a rich, dry white— among them, white meat chicken, pierogi, seafood terrines, and pâté. $12-14
Bordeaux
Imported by
Cellars International

Babich
SAUVIGNON BLANC
Medium-bodied. Fresh and juicy mean "no worries, mate."
This kinder, gentler New Zealand Sauvignon is very melony in flavor and quite refreshing overall. It's a natural with vegetables, chowders, and seafood salads. $12-14
Marlborough, New Zealand
Imported by Select Brokers

Selaks
SAUVIGNON BLANC
Medium-bodied. Pungent, richly textured, and mouthwatering.
One of the pioneers of New Zealand Sauvignon, the Selaks winery (est. 1934), consistently crafts assertive, take-no-prisoners wines. If you love "dirty martinis" (with olive brine), you'll love this white. It's unique and delicious with fish steaks, tarragon chicken, or any herby, savory fare. $13-15
Marlborough, New Zealand
Imported by American Estates

Saint Clair
SAUVIGNON BLANC
Medium- to full-bodied. A big, ripe Sauvignon that makes red wine loyalists convert to white.
Stunning richness coupled with vibrant acids makes this one of the most dramatic food wines imaginable. It explodes with the classic herbaceous, olivelike tones of New Zealand Sauvignon and is a marvelous choice for grilled fare, creamy risottos, or lobster in its every form. $13-15
Marlborough, New Zealand
Imported by Lauber

Goisot
SAUVIGNON DE ST. BRIS
Light- to medium-bodied. A bright, rich rarity that excels at the table.
Here's an anomalous Sauvignon Blanc from Burgundy, the ancestral home of Chardonnay. The end product? A Chablis-like minerality tacked onto SB's minty, grapefruity varietal character. The wine is not only organic but extremely well made. Try it with lemon sole or a leek-and-goat-cheese tart. $14-16
Burgundy
Imported by Polaner

Villa Maria
SAUVIGNON BLANC
Medium-bodied. Vibrant and savory, with a lip-smacking finish.
This is penetrating stuff, bursting with grapefruit, juniper, and gooseberry. It's particularly good with "green" foods like veggies and pesto and mesclun. And, like many noteworthy New Zealand wines, it's a screw-cap! $14-16
Marlborough, New Zealand
Imported by M. Skurnik

Domaine de Chatenoy
MENETOU-SALON
Medium-bodied. Sometimes drier, sometimes fruitier, but always vivacious.
This intriguing Sauvignon hails from centuries-old vineyards abutting Sancerre. More pungent than typical Loire Sauvignon, it is almost aggressively herbal. Pair it with fresh vegetables, stuffed peppers, smoked salmon, and tomato dishes. $14-16
Loire, France
Imported by VOS

Henry Pellé
MENETOU-SALON
"Morogues"
Medium-bodied.
Full-flavored and savory, with palpable fruit in the finish.
A vivid Sauvignon Blanc awash with lime, crushed mint, and mineral notes. While certainly dry, it is fruitier than Sancerre or Pouilly-Fumé. Mediterranean and Middle Eastern foods are among its best partners. $14-16
Loire, France
Imported by Chapin Cellars

Thelema
SAUVIGNON BLANC
Medium-bodied.
Silkiness balanced with some earthy complexity.
From one of the highest and probably coolest vineyards in the Stellenbosch area of South Africa comes an SB with no oak but plenty of grapefruit, citrus zest, and steely 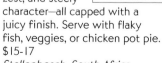 character—all capped with a juicy finish. Serve with flaky fish, veggies, or chicken pot pie. $15-17
Stellenbosch, South Africa
Imported by Cape Classics

Nautilus
SAUVIGNON BLANC
Medium- to full-bodied.
Ripe and rather intense.
Nautilus works in a rich style, crafting wines for the table. Their SB boggles the palate with waves of lime, kiwi, green olive, and cut grass. (Sip it as an apéritif only if you're in the mood for something really gutsy.) Exciting with lobster, monkfish, or grilled seafood sausages. $15-17
Marlborough, New Zealand
Imported by Négociants USA

Domaine Mardon
QUINCY
Medium-bodied.
Elegant and lingering.
Quincy, situated on the River Cher in the southern part of the Loire Valley, is the savvy wine lover's alternative to Sancerre and Pouilly-Fumé. Mardon's version is a steely, flinty delight. The perfect goat cheese partner, it also complements steamed mussels, freshwater fish, herby omelets, and the classic quiche Lorraine. $15-17
Loire, France
Imported by Jeroboam

Framingham
SAUVIGNON BLANC
Medium-bodied.
Boisterously ripe, fruity, and well-rounded at the finish.
Sourced from the Wairau Valley in New Zealand's Marlborough region, Framingham SB is more plump and fruit-driven than its peers, with limeade and melon aromas aplenty. A superb salmon partner (especially for gamier wild salmon), it also pairs well with garlicky foods. $15-18
Marlborough, New Zealand
Imported by Bayfield

Brancott Vineyards
SAUVIGNON BLANC
"Reserve"
Medium- to full-bodied. Rather hearty for white wine.
This frequently intense dry white is packed with herb, olive, grapefruit, and fresh cut grass flavors. It's heart-racing with salmon or spinach pie. When your guests *only* drink white wine but you're serving red meat, this white is up to the job. $15-18
Marlborough, New Zealand
Imported by Bayfield

Allan Scott
SAUVIGNON BLANC
Medium- to full-bodied. An electrifying, wildly fragrant Sauvignon.
The intensity of the 1997 vintage of this wine was almost unimaginable—daunting, to say the least. The '03 was a little more civilized, with its succulent acidity, martini olive aromas, and salty minerality. It's the answer for foods that need aggressive wine pairings: smoked or oily fish, spicy ceviche, and entrée salads full of greens and zesty dressings. As of '03, the bottles are screw-capped.
 $15-17
Marlborough, New Zealand
Imported by Uniqco

Domaine Sautereau
SANCERRE
Medium-bodied. Utterly elegant and well made, yet barely known in the United States.
This wine always evolves the same way. Its first few weeks on the U.S. market see it through a lemony, "jumpy" phase; the edge then relaxes and it becomes one of the great Sancerres. Its bracing mineral bouquet is like a blast of fresh air. Crisp, racy, and dry, it's a fish wine par excellence. $15–17
Loire, France
Imported by Grand Cru

Girard
SAUVIGNON BLANC
Medium-bodied. Very finely balanced and succulent.
A clean, bright, minimalist white, in high contrast to the oaky style popular in Napa, this SB is built more like a Loire wine but shows the melon, orange, and saturated fruit quality of its warmer origins. Serve with tuna steaks, baked Brie, or cracked crab. $16-18
Napa, California

Frank at Jean–François Bailly
SANCERRE
"Cuvée Chavignol"
Medium-bodied.
As elegant and impressive a Sancerre as any we've tasted.
In this artful Sancerre, fabulous aromatics of herbs and flowers are accompanied by gorgeous, mouthwatering texture and a long, full finish. A classic fish wine, it's also able to handle asparagus. $16-19
Loire, France
Imported by Lauber

Dalton
SAUVIGNON BLANC
Medium-bodied.
Fruity and seductively aromatic, it's dry—but just barely.
This is our favorite kosher wine for food: marvelously juicy, with exquisite green melon and lime flavors, an aroma that billows out of the glass, and a crisp, lip-smacking finish. Drink it with anything from the sea or the vegetable garden. $17-20
Galilee, Israel
Imported by Abarbanel

Koura Bay
SAUVIGNON BLANC "Whalesback"
Full-bodied. An impressively bold, perfumy wine that commands attention.

This outlandishly ripe, succulent wine has a huge bouquet of the "greenness" (grass, green peppers, etc.) that makes New

Zealand wines such wonderful partners for vegetables and herbed fish and fowl. The '01 and '02 vintages, both with thick finishes, were amazing. The '03 was lighter but no less distinctive. $18-20
Marlborough, New Zealand
Imported by Weygandt/Metzler

Philippe Raimbault
SANCERRE "Apud Sariacum"
Medium- to full-bodied. Dense, vigorous, full-flavored.

Here's Sauvignon at its purest, made complex by the gravelly, chalky soils of the Loire Valley. The nautilus shell on the label suggests what to serve: anything fresh and briny from the sea. It's also splendid with poultry—say, chicken breasts in a tarragon cream sauce. $18-20
Loire, France
Imported by T. Edward

Domaine Girard
SANCERRE "La Garenne"
Medium- to full-bodied. Rich, round, and highly elegant.

A "complete" wine from start to finish, this SB is for people who appreciate balance and evidence of *terroir* in their wines. Mineral layers and deep, creamy fruit invite thoughtful sipping. A grown-up choice for crab cakes, halibut and other firm fish, or Montrachet and other creamy goat cheeses. $18-20
Loire
Imported by M. Skurnik

Domaine Hervé Seguin
POUILLY-FUMÉ
Medium-bodied. A Pouilly notable for its delicacy and underlying strength.

Hand-harvested from vines over thirty years old, then minimally handled, this wine is delightfully crisp and lemony, with a distinct vein of minerality. Think seafood salads (especially spooned into avocado halves) and fillets of sole or other flaky fish. $18-20
Loire, France
Imported by R. Kacher

$20 to $40

Domaine Cailbourdin
POUILLY-FUMÉ "Les Cris"
Medium- to full-bodied. Astonishingly fragrant and rife with refreshing acidity.

This drinks like a dry gin and tonic—easy on the lime. Wonderfully refreshing and true to its *terroir*, it's an aristocratic choice for lobster or soft cheeses. $20-22
Loire, France
Imported by Lauber

Pascal a Nicolas Reverdy
SANCERRE "Les Coutes"
Medium- to full-bodied. That elusive creature: a Sancerre with assertive Sauvignon Blanc character.

Exquisitely balanced, rich, and pulsing with fruit and minerality, this is truly a white wine for grown-ups. It is hand-harvested from fifty-year-old vines, and bottled without filtration. The finish is tremendously long. Enjoy with rich seafood (lobster!) or aged goat cheeses. $20-22
Loire, France
Imported by Weygandt/Metzler

Under $10

Sogrape
Gazela VINHO VERDE
Light-bodied. Ultra-crisp, ultra-light, and absolutely refreshing.
This is a sit-by-the-pool or picnic-in-the-park wine. Especially refreshing on a hot day, it treats you to floating clouds of lemon and apricot. A touch of carbonation makes it a particularly nice foil for spicy foods. $4-6
Vinho Verde, Portugal
Imported by Evaton

Domaine de Cassagnoles
CÔTES DE GASCOGNE
Light-bodied. A touch of fruit and a bright, vigorous finish.
This wine hits the palate running with juicy, jumpy, pearlike fruit. It's refreshing both on its own and with Greek *mezedes* (assorted appetizers), picnic sandwiches, and chips 'n' dips. The grapes? Ugni Blanc (an alternate name for the Italian Trebbiano) and Colombard, its constant companion in this part of France. $5-7
Gascony, France
Imported by Weygandt/Metzler

Caves Aliança
VINHO VERDE
Light-bodied. Mild, creamy texture and a bit of sparkle.
This simple white, best drunk within a year after release, is faintly scented with apples and wafts into your mouth while sending your soul to the beach. In fact, pack a few in your seashore basket: It's only 9% alcohol, so you and your beach-going buddies may want to take more than one bottle. $5-7
Vinho Verde, Portugal
Imported by Tri-Vin

Domaine de la Chanade
LOIN DE L'OEIL
"Les Rials"
Light-bodied.
Brisk and full of character.
This venerable wine is made from Loin de l'Oeil (Len de l'El in the old spelling), a grape found near Gaillac in south-central France. Popular in the sixteenth century but little known in the twenty-first, it's a drink worth rejuvenating. Try this graceful, dry bistro sipper (vaguely reminiscent of Sauvignon Blanc) with omelets, quiches, and *frites*. $6-8
Southwest France
Imported by Monsieur Touton

Caves Plaimont
CÔTES DE GASCOGNE
Light-bodied. Lively, modest in alcohol, and very refreshing.
This fruity little number from a Gascony growers' cooperative is made from the local white varieties Colombard and Ugni Blanc—the grapes that give us Cognac. Sip it in warm weather with a salad of tomatoes and mozzarella. (For a peek at the lavender screw cap, see page 188.) $6-8
Gascony, France
Imported by VOS

Quinta da Romeira
BUCELAS
Light-bodied.
Iridescent with acidity.
This eye-watering, lemony, lively specialty of the Bucelas region, near Lisbon, is made from Arinto, a high-acid local grape. If Portugal's Vinho Verde is too wimpy for you, wrap your lips around this and enjoy the ride. Oysters, anyone? $7-9
Bucelas, Portugal
Imported by Polaner

Domaine Duffour
VIN DE PAYS DES CÔTES DE GASCOGNE
Light- to medium-bodied. A ripe, juicy white with a mineral finish.

This typical regional blend of Colombard and Ugni Blanc (Trebbiano) benefits from the touch of richness imparted by a dose of Gros Manseng. Pears and earth stay the course on the palate. Perfect for mushrooms, hearty salads, and picnic fare. $7-9
Gascony, France
Imported by M. Skurnik

Vegadeo
VERDEJO
Light-bodied. Nice acidity and easy, quaffable character.

Verdejo is the aromatic, high-acid grape of Spain, Portugal, and Madeira. There's something appealingly floral in this wine, and a fresh, clean fragrance reminiscent of evergreen. It teams well with seafood, stuffed grape leaves, sardines—any light Mediterranean fare. $7-9
Rueda, Spain
Imported by Distinct Expressions

Blankenhorn
GUTEDEL Trocken "Gertie and Max"
Light-bodied. A crisp, delicate apèritif.

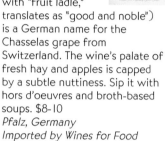

Gutedel (rhymes with "fruit ladle," translates as "good and noble") is a German name for the Chasselas grape from Switzerland. The wine's palate of fresh hay and apples is capped by a subtle nuttiness. Sip it with hors d'oeuvres and broth-based soups. $8-10
Pfalz, Germany
Imported by Wines for Food

Colonnara
VERDICCHIO DEI CASTELLI DI JESI "Lyricus"
Light- to medium-bodied. A bright sipper with a pleasing twist.

The Verdicchio grape has been grown in the Marches region of Italy since the fourteenth century. This Verdicchio, from vineyards near the coast, is as precise and full of character as Italian white wine gets. Its palate? Lemon streaked with licorice. Try this one alongside greens, fresh fennel, or linguine

---

ALLURING ALBARIÑO

The noble grape of northeastern Spain's Galicia region, a land of rocky seacoasts and wet valleys, yields wines that are peachily aromatic, high in acidity, and, unlike most Spanish whites, untouched by oak. They can also be on the expensive side. A bargain labeling from Spanish vintner Martin Codax is from the Salnes Valley, a subzone of the DO (appellation) that made Albariño famous: Rias Baixas. **Vilariño–Cambados Albariño "Burgans"** ($11-13) is brisk, juicy, and perfumed with peach, orange, and wildflowers. People often do a happy double take when they try this for the first time—especially considering the price! It's a traditional paella partner.

The Rias Baixas—grown **Martin Codax Albariño** ($15-17) is a renowned interpretation of the grape. With its floral bouquet, exquisite balance, and lingering finish of apple–pear fruit, it's a glorious lobster wine and a pleasing companion to seafood salads. *Both wines imported by Tempranillo*

with shellfish and parsley. $8-10
Marches, Italy
Imported by Winebow/
Leonardo LoCascio

Cuevas de Castilla
RUEDA "Con Class"
Light- to medium-bodied.
Piquant and refreshing.
Exotically scented with bay leaf
and apples, this is a sublime thirst-
quencher in the hot summer
months. Pair it with the zesty
seafood of the Mediterranean.
$8-10
Rueda, Spain
Imported by D. Polaner

Moncaro
ESINO BIANCO "Terrazzo"
Light- to medium-bodied.
Lively, boldly scented, and dry.
Here's a briny little white from
the Verdicchio
grape, with its
inescapable
licorice and
lemon drop
character. Drink it in carafes by
the seashore, with mussels,
or with cioppino, the Italian fish
stew adopted by Californians.
$8-10
Marches, Italy
Imported by Matt Brothers

Château de Chesnaie
MUSCADET
Sèvre et Maine sur Lie
Light-bodied. Snappy, feather-
light, and vividly refreshing.
The original oyster wine, Muscadet
has a citrusy, talclike freshness
that makes it a fine predinner
drink. At the table it's a bracing
counterpoint for salads and one
of the very best wines to serve
with mussels, clams, and oysters.
Must be drunk fresh!
$8-10
Loire, France
Imported by Monsieur Touton

Domaine du Tariquet
CÔTES DE GASCOGNES
"Cuvée Tardive"
Light- to medium-bodied.
Delicately sweet and succulent.
Made from the Basque grape Gros
Manseng, this "late-picked cuvée"
from an erstwhile Armagnac
maker in southern France is a
honeyish, flowery, mouth-
watering white. Vinified off-dry,
it's a gentle accompaniment to
assorted pâtés and fruits. $8-10
Gascony, France
Imported by Baron François

Hatzimichalis
HATZIMICHALIS WHITE
Light-bodied. Crisp and
cleansing on the palate,
with faint minerality.
Here you have America's most
popular imported Greek wine.
Pleasantly lemony and good in
every vintage, it's a nice surprise
for many wine lovers, especially
when served with a platterful
of *mezedes* (assorted Greek
appetizers)—stuffed grape
leaves, sardines, green olives,
and taramasalata. $9-11
Greece
Imported by Athenée

Casale Marchese
FRASCATI Superiore
Medium-bodied.
Rich for Frascati—almost fat in
the mouth, with staying power.
Tropical, flashy, and evocative of
fresh fruit and almonds, Frascati
could be called the official white
wine of Rome, even though it
originated in the nearby
eponymous town. If you can't
enjoy a tumblerful while
munching on crunchy calamari in
a sunny Roman piazza, a few sips
just might transport you there.
$9-11
Lazio, Italy
Imported by Bayfield

Koster–Wolf
MÜLLER-THURGAU
Halbtrocken
Light- to medium-bodied.
Soothes and refreshes.
It's hard to imagine anyone not liking this wine made from the Müller-Thurgau grape from Germany. It's dry and palate-pleasing from start to end, with just a hint of white peach and a lovely, balanced finish.
An unbeatable sipper, it's also nice with tartly flavored dishes of any sort. $9-11
Rheinhessen, Germany
Imported by Chapin Cellars

Blanco Nieva
RUEDA
Light-bodied. Zesty, faintly candied, and almost sparkly.
Vintners in Rueda, on Spain's Duero River, have been uprooting cheaper grapevines and planting the Verdejo grape to make fresh, juicy, exotically perfumed white wines. You might sense a little watermelon-flavored candy in the aromas of this example—a scrumptious addition to a beach party or cookout. $9-11
Rueda, Spain
Imported by Frontier

Château de la Carizière
MUSCADET Sèvre et Maine sur Lie "Sirènes"
Light-bodied. One of the lightest, driest wines in France.
This may be the quintessential seafood white, complete with a salt air tang derived from the proximity of the Muscadet vineyards to the North Atlantic. It's inexpensive, and it's organic— all the more reason to feel satisfied as you swig it down with a dozen oysters. $9-11
Loire, France
Imported by Wines for Food

Sharpe Hill Vineyard
BALLET OF ANGELS
Medium-bodied. An off-dry white with perfumed character.
A Connecticut wine? You betcha! Apart from the trippy label, this

---

VERDICCHIO: THE TART ITALIAN

The eastern Italian region of Marches (Marche in Italian) is home ground for Verdicchio, the ancient yellow–green grape produced in two DOCs, or appellations. Near the Adriatic Sea and the region's only city of size, Ancona, lies Verdicchio dei Castelli di Jesi, whose lemony wines became famous for their green, urn–shaped, two–handled bottles. A good introduction to its wines is also the best bargain Verdicchio on the market: **Marchetti Verdicchio dei Castelli di Jesi** ($7–9). Rather light, zingy, and mouthwatering, it has the typical lemon-zest character that cuts easily through the oily fish dishes of coastal Italy, while its licoricey, herby element makes it a hit with pesto. *Imported by Monsieur Touton*

The Verdicchio di Matelica DOC, farther inland at a higher altitude, produces fuller-bodied wines that are also supremely rich and capable of aging. A prime example is **Bisci Verdicchio Matelica** ($13–15), a wine of crystal clarity, length, and underlying strength. It boasts the telltale Verdicchio "snap" in the finish and a strong anise aroma. It's a great partner for sardines with raisins and pine nuts or pasta with broccoli rabe and sausage. The massive single-vineyard **Bisci Vigneto Fogliano** ($18–29) is for wine lovers seeking powerhouse whites. *Imported by M. Skurnik*

soft, fruity blend of Chardonnay, Muscadet, and Vignoles has a strangely enticing quality, which probably explains

why it is one of the few New England wines to become popular. We like its refreshing style with spicy foods. $9-11
Connecticut

Argiolas
VERMENTINO DI SARDEGNA "Costemolinas"
Light-bodied. A popular Sardinian specialty, highly crisp and savory.
Vermentino is an aromatic white grape grown in Sardinia, Corsica, and Liguria in Italy, and the Languedoc-Roussillon region of France (where it is called Rolle). Something herbal and snappy lurks within this white, which is great with pesto and a fitting partner for grilled veggies and light seafood. $9-11
Sardinia
Imported by Winebow/ Leonardo LoCascio

$10 to $15

Red Newt Cellars
RED NEWT WHITE
Light- to medium-bodied. Bright, fun white with a touch of sweetness and modest alcohol.
The grapes responsible for this white are East Coast American hybrids, Vidal Blanc and Cayuga, so we're way out in left field with this one. But you've got to love its wildly fruity nature. The kind of wine to stay up late with, it's also a refreshing foil for grilled fish and Indian curries. $10-12
Finger Lakes, New York

Rocca di Fabbri
GRECHETTO
Light- to medium-bodied. Gentle, juicy, and faintly floral.
Made from the age-old grape of the same name, Grechetto is less famous than Orvieto (Umbria's other white specialty) but noticeably more aromatic. Its softness and honeysuckle nose make it a pleasure with a light, garlicky clam sauce. $10-12
Umbria, Italy
Imported by Vias

Michael Frohlich
MÜLLER-THURGAU "Belle Amie"
Light- to medium-bodied. Succulent, clean as a whistle, and totally refreshing.
Müller-Thurgau, the humble workhorse grape of Germany, occasionally gets respectful treatment. This serious version is on the dry side, with an herby, grapefruit palate vaguely reminiscent of Sauvignon Blanc. It comes in a Bocksbeutel, the traditional vessel of the Franken region but whose flagon shape many Americans associate with Mateus. It's a quirky, delicious choice for parties and a good picnic partner. $10-12
Franken, Germany
Imported by Wines for Food

Domaine de Cassagnoles
CÔTES DE GASCOGNE "Cuvée Gros Manseng"
Medium-bodied. Tangy-rich and mildly sweet.
Côtes de Gascogne wines excel when slightly sweet. This example, made from the Basque grape Gros Manseng, delivers a jet stream of apples, honey, and minerals from the first pour.

Drink it well chilled with sesame noodles, spicy snacks, or a platterful of figs, dates, and almonds. $10-12
Gascony, France
Imported by Weygandt/Metzler

Sartarelli
VERDICCHIO DEI CASTELLI DI JESI
Medium-bodied. Firm in texture, with a pleasingly astringent finish.
Verdicchio is paired traditionally with the fresh seafood of the Adriatic, but with its intense anise aroma and fierce mouthwatering acidity, we happily drink good versions like this one with such hard-to-match vegetables as fennel, broccoli rabe, and radicchio. $10-12
Marches, Italy
Imported by Vias

Domaine de Mauvan
CÔTES DE PROVENCE
Light- to medium-bodied. Softly textured and fragrant, with a delicate finish.
This white is made from Marsanne and Roussanne, grapes redolent of the lavender- and rosemary-flecked hills of Provence. Just lovely all around, it can be sipped on its own or paired with creamy dishes, savory tarts, or poultry roasted with herbs.
$10-12
Provence, France
Imported by Bayfield

Geografico
VERNACCIA DI SAN GIMIGNANO
Light-bodied. Refreshing with a light, bitter snap in the tail.
This wine was a favorite of Michelangelo, who wrote in 1643 how it "kisses, licks, bites, tickles, and stings." (Presumably, he'd had a few glasses.)

This large producer makes a wine in a simple, brisk style. Faintly nutty, it's an evening quaffer with pasta *aglio e olio* (garlic & oil), fresh vegetables, or linguini with clams. $10-12
Tuscany
Imported by Matt Brothers

Scarbolo
TOCAI FRIULANO
Medium-bodied. Savory, earthy, and long on flavor.
Some call Scarbolo the definitive Tocai, pointing to its characteristic lime-and-apple flavor and telltale nuttiness. We call it good, savory stuff for pasta primavera, antipasti, and stuffed fish. $10-12
Friuli, Italy
Imported by Domaine Select

Ca' del Solo
BIG HOUSE WHITE
Light- to medium-bodied. A juicy blend of aromatic grapes.
Maverick California vintner Randall Grahm blends Riesling, Muscat, Malvasia Bianca, and red Grenache (hence the faint blush) in this intensely fragrant, pretty wine. It's a surefire hit with spicy Indian dishes and picnic fare.
$10-12
California

Botromagno
GRAVINA
Light- to medium-bodied. Amazing floral, with a touch of sweetness.
This is a capricious blend of 60% Greco (dry, floral, juicy) and 40% Malvasia Bianca (powerfully aromatic, fruity, and rich). You do the math. Gravina is also one of the only white wines from southern Italy that doesn't weigh your tongue down. As such, it's the perfect refreshment with

spicy seafood, Cajun specialties, and very garlicky fare. $10-12
Apulia, Italy
Imported by Winebow/
Leonardo LoCascio

Bayer
WEISSBURGUNDER
Medium-bodied. Icy-crisp, fragrant, and firm.
This Pinot Blanc from the Neusiedlersee, a vast inland sea in Austria, is a little nutty, a little lemony, and a lot of fun. The opera singer on the label may seem stern and serious, yet the wine within is anything but. This brisk refresher is especially good with such healthful vegetarian fare as brown rice, tempeh, hummus, and falafel. $10-12
Burgenland, Austria
Imported by Wines for Food

Pierre Boniface
VIN DE SAVOIE "Apremont"
Light- to medium-bodied.
A very dry white with an almost sparkling personality.
Made practically on the Franco-Swiss border from the indigenous grape Jacquere, this white tastes like Champagne without the bubbles. Great with light fish, clams and other mollusks, and greens. Try the richer, more mouthfilling **Roussette** ($14-16) with fondue. $10-12
Savoie, France
Imported by House of Burgundy

Aragosta
VERMENTINO DI ALGHERO
Light-bodied. Pale in color but vigorous and piquant in the mouth.
The rather clinical diagram of a langoustine on the label of this white suggests serving it with seafood, and we concur. But the piney, savory character shines through even more when the wine is drunk with any dish that includes pesto. $10-12
Sardinia
Imported by J. Given

Franzen
ELBLING DRY
Light-bodied. Crystal-clear, bone-dry, and brisk.
Elbling is a German specialty that thrives in ancient soils composed of fossilized seashells.  With its delicate, neutral palate and zesty finish, it's a good choice for serving with sushi and shellfish. $10-12
Mosel, Germany
Imported by Wines for Food

Domaine Le Mas de Collines
CÔTES DU RHÔNE BLANC
Medium-bodied. Rich, buttery, and balanced, with suave mouthfeel.
Here's a 100% Roussanne, the perfumed, richly textured white grape of the Rhône. Great price, great balance, and no detectable oak make it an interesting alternative to Chardonnay (it shares many of that grape's nutty, buttery aromas). The best food matches? Soups, creamy dishes, and poultry. $10-12
Rhône, France
Imported by Bayfield

P. A. Ohler'sches
SCHEUREBE Kabinett "Munsterer Dautenpflanzer"
Light- to medium-bodied.
The lighter side of "Scheu," fruity, simple and appealing.
Funky and *good*, if you like a Scheurebe that has a very strong pink grapefruit flavor with some Sauvignon Blancesque greenness

and savor thrown in. Whatever you call it, down it with something spicy or sweet—well-sauced barbecue, Tex-Mex, Hunan or Szechuan. $10-12
Rheinhessen, Germany
Imported by M. Skurnik/
Terry Theise

Domaine de la Pepière
MUSCADET
Sèvre et Maine sur Lie.
Light-bodied. Perhaps the most complex and scintillating Muscadet of all.
Old vines and intense expression of its chalky *terroir* make Marc Ollivier's Muscadet taste like a $30 Savennières. An oyster and shellfish wine of the first order, it's also tasty with a leafy salad, a variety of sushis, ceviches, and crudités or a plateful of fresh mozzarella and tomatoes. The exceedingly rare **Clos des Briords** ($12-14), which can evolve for a decade or more, virtually *breathes* minerality. Pair it with oysters or tuna tartare. $10-12
Loire, France
Imported by Louis/Dressner

Di Lenardo
TOCAI FRIULANO
"Vigne San Martin"
Light- to medium-bodied.
Intriguingly fruity, crisp, and dry.
This isn't your typical wine made from Tocai—the grape that's way too rich and earthy for some tastes. Crafted for easy drinking and versatile food matching, this one's a hit on its own or with pasta, fish, and summer vegetables. $10-12
Friuli, Italy
Imported by Lauber

Liegenfeld
OTTONELLA
Medium-bodied. Ripe, and extravagant in its fruit.
Roughly two-thirds Muscat Ottonel (a cross between an obscure strain of Muscat and Chasselas) and one-third Müller-Thurgau, this wildly aromatic and delicious jumble of peaches, mandarin oranges, and Chinese five-spice is the ultimate answer to curries and all things Asian. It's also a cool choice for no-holds-barred classics like Chicken with Forty Cloves of Garlic. $10-12
Burgenland, Austria
Imported by Wines for Food

Alois Lageder
PINOT BIANCO
Medium-bodied. Glides over the palate smoothly, then lingers.
Like a glass of little green apples and lemon flowers, this non-oaked wine's scintillating balance and fleshy texture make it a hit with seared scallops, sole Véronique, and other rich, fragrant seafood dishes. The winery's **Hablerhof** ($18+), a powerful wine from a shelf of vines perched at 1,500 feet, improves with brief cellaring and excels with poultry and pork. Pinot Bianco is Italian for Pinot Blanc, a Burgundian mutation of the Pinot Gris grape. $10-12
Alto Adige, Italy
Imported by Dalla Terra

Sommer
GRÜNER VELTLINER
Kabinett Dry
Light- to medium-bodied.
Crisp and savory,
with surprising length.
This scintillating, herb-kissed Veltliner is refreshingly citrusy.

Even better, it's casual enough to start with tuna salad sandwiches at lunch and serious enough to finish with roast chicken and greens at dinner. $10-12
Burgenland, Austria
Imported by Wines for Food

Martine's
VIOGNIER
Full-bodied. A California Viognier of impressive richness and aroma.
The Viognier grape yields legendary wines in the northern Rhône, and this California version has all the pedigreed aromas of ripe pears and gardenias, but without oak. Its relatively high alcohol and sheer concentration of fruit leave an impression of sweetness, so plan your meal accordingly—rich dishes of fish, chicken, or pork with aromatic herbs. $10-15
California

Domaine Peyrilhe
PICPOUL DE PINET
Light- to medium-bodied. Zippy and fresh.
Picpoul (in its original French form, *piquepoul*, or "lip-stinger") is an ancient grape from Languedoc. But don't be put off. The wine from this estate is just marvelously refreshing, jumping with flavors of fresh grapes and lemon crème. And take note: It may be the world's best white for chicken salad. $11-13
Languedoc
Imported by Grand Vintage

Villa Girardi
LUGANA
Medium-bodied. Lush, sensuous, and pure.
The Trebbiano clone they grow in Lugana seems to be jet-propelled with flavor and richness. Here notes of stone fruits and mineral recur through a long, smooth finish. It's perfect for pasta in a cream sauce and the richer seafood dishes. $11-13
Veneto, Italy
Imported by Verdoni

Aveleda
VINHO VERDE "Alvarinho"
Light-bodied. Crisp with the scents of the garden.
Here's the perfect summer wine. Alvarinho is the Portuguese name for the Spanish Albariño grape, a floral, mouthwatering, Iberian specialty. Enjoy this delicate and gorgeous white with seafood paella, cold crab, or raw shellfish. $11-13
Vinho Verde, Portugal
Imported by Tri-Vin

Stefano Massone
GAVI "Masera"
Medium-bodied. Light in alcohol and dryly refreshing at the finish.
Acidic in a pleasant citrusy way and clean as a whistle, this traditional shellfish wine is equally attractive with fried food, flaky fish, pasta primavera, and feta or goat cheese. $11-13
Piemonte, Italy
Imported by M. Skurnik

Marotti Campi
VERDICCHIO DEI CASTELLI DI JESI "Luzano"
Medium- to full-bodied. Dry, tangy, and forceful with food.
Citrons, bitter herbs, celery, anisette, stones, sea-brine . . . Is this a wine profile or a Wiccan's grocery list? This singularly intense white wine zooms over the palate, refreshing as it goes, and elevates the taste of vegetables like broccoli rabe, fennel, cabbages, chard, and cilantro. $11-13
Marches, Italy
Imported by Lorenzo Scarpone

Sella & Mosca
VERMENTINO DI SARDEGNA "La Cala"
Light-bodied. A vibrant, simple white with a savory finish.
This limey and juicy white, made from the aromatic Vermentino grape grown in Sardinia, is becoming a staple on Italian restaurants' wine lists. That's hardly surprising, since it works well as both an apéritif and spirited food partner. Serve it with lemony fish, calamari, or pasta with tomatoes and herbs. $11-13
Sardinia
Imported by Palm Bay

Zenato
LUGANA "San Benedetto"
Medium-bodied. Characterful dry white with a satiny finish.
Zenato is our favorite producer of Lugana, the formidable white wine made on the south shore of Lake Garda in northern Italy. Rich as any Chardonnay, crisp as a Gavi, and delicately fragrant as Pinot Blanc, it's marvelously multifaceted. Serve it as a complement to crab, chicken, or soft cheeses. $11-13
Veneto, Italy
Imported by Winebow/ Leonardo LoCascio

Sessa
LACRYMA CHRISTI BIANCO DEL VESUVIO
Medium-bodied. Dry, lightly acidic, and minerally.
The words *lacryma Christi* in this ancient white wine's name mean "tears of Christ." Made from Coda di Volpe and Verdeca, local varieties of grapes grown in the volcanic Neapolitan soils of Mount Vesuvius, it's a minerally, mildly earthy choice for ocean fish (preferably from the Amalfi coast!) or a cheese-laden *pizza bianco*. $11-13
Campania, Italy
Imported by Verdoni

Gysler
SCHEUREBE
Halbtrocken "Weinheimer Hölle"

Medium-bodied. Dry and zesty, brightly aromatic, and just a little fruity.
Very, very cool. There's something leafy here, and some pink grapefruit, too. Even better, this Scheurebe has terrific balance for food matching. Enjoy it with your next entrée salad (seafood, Niçoise, Cobb), sausages 'n' sauerkraut, or anything fried and salty. The liter bottle is a bargain. $12-14
Rheinhessen, Germany
Imported by M. Skurnik/Terry Theise

A GEWÜRZLIKE GREEK

The ancient Greek grape Moscholfilero is grown on the high plateau of Mantinia in the Peloponnese and is used to make a perfumy white wine with the aromatics and acidity of a Gewürztraminer. Conditions on the plateau are so cool that the grape harvest is sometimes delayed until late October.

The peachy, plump-cheeked, cherubic personality of **Domaine Tselepos Moscholfilero "Mantinia"** ($13–15) makes us smile. Crisp, pleasingly scented, and easy to enjoy, it's great with grilled fish (especially in a salt crust) or any kind of jazzy Greco/Turkish fare—falafel, hummus, tabbouleh, *spanakopita*.
Imported by Wines We Are

Prà
SOAVE Classico Superiore
Medium-bodied. Gently
refreshing with a *frizzante*, or
faintly sparkling, mouthfeel.
The ancient recipe for
refreshment from the Veneto—
crisp, clean, apple-scented Soave.
Packed with plenty of Trebbiano,
this white is best served icy cold
with a plate of *frito misto* or
calamari—or all by itself. Soaves
from the Classico Superiore zone
must be aged eight months
before release. $12-14
Veneto, Italy
Imported by Vinafera

Kurt Darting
MUSKATELLER Kabinett
"Durkheimer Steinberg"
Medium-bodied. Forceful in
perfume and flavor, slightly oily,
and brilliant with the right food.
Darting is a master magician of
strange grapes. His Muskateller
(Muscat) seems to start out
sweet, offering honey, apricot,
figs, and flowers in delirious
excess—yet it finishes relatively
dry. What a curry wine! It may
also be the long-awaited answer
to such starchy, hard-to-match
Eastern European dishes as
potato latkes, stuffed cabbage,
and *kasha varnishkes* (buckwheat
with noodles and egg). $12-14
Pfalz, Germany
Imported by M. Skurnik/
Terry Theise

Jacky Renard
ALIGOTÉ
Light-bodied. About as light and
dry as white wine gets.
The "other white grape of
Burgundy," Aligoté is grown in the
north of the region in cool climes
and chalky soils. It is lighter, more
minerally, and more acidic than
Chardonnay, all of which makes
it a perfect oyster white and

apéritif. It is also the traditional
base wine for a Kir cocktail.
$12-14
Burgundy
Imported by Bayfield

Tamellini
SOAVE Superiore
Light- to medium-bodied.
A gentle, creamy white.
The Tamellini brothers produce
some of the best Soave around.
Elegant and breezily scented with
lemon blossoms and blanched
almonds, it's a natural with
gnocchi, versatile with mild
cheeses, and perfect for oven-
baked cauliflower Parmigiana.
$12-14
Veneto, Italy
Imported by Vin Divino

Fritz Salomon
GRÜNER VELTLINER
"Hochterrassen"
Medium-bodied. A dry,
savory food wine.
In the world of trend-watchers,
just holding a glass of this wine
makes you seem chic. Think
Sauvignon Blanc with a little hint
of white pepper, and you've
basically got it down. Citrusy,
a little grassy, and incredibly
refreshing, it's the choice for
salads, sushi, and mixed greens.
$12-14
Kremstal, Austria
Imported by M. Skurnik/Terry Theise

Cavalchina
BIANCO DI CUSTOZA
Light-bodied. A cheerful white
with refreshing character.
A Trebbiano-based blend of
varieties from the shore of Lake
Garda, this white is similar to Soave
(the popular café drink of northern
Italy), but grapier and more floral.
It's perfect for antipasti. $12-14
Veneto, Italy
Imported by Vin Divino

Ca' del Solo
MALVASIA BIANCO
Light- to medium-bodied.
Smells like a dessert wine but
winds up dry and elegant.
With Madeleine on the label and
succulent, floral-scented joy in the
bottle, how can you resist this
white? Pair it with fried fish and
crab or Asian dishes seasoned with
coriander or lemon grass. $12-14
Monterey, California

Terre de Trinci
GRECHETTO
Medium-bodied. Richly textured,
dry, and peculiarly aromatic.
The distinctive "varnish-scented"
character of this ancient white
is wonderfully idiosyncratic but
seems to make sense paired with
the area's local strong cheeses
and fish dishes. Try it with pasta
tossed with breadcrumbs, pizza
with anchovies, and foods that
call for plenty of grated Parmesan.
$12-14
Umbria, Italy
Imported by Artisan

Gysler
SILVANER Halbtrocken
"Weinheimer Hölle"
Medium-bodied.
Vivid acidity and great,
high-toned refreshment.
Rheinhessen winemaker Alex
Gysler's Silvaner zigzags across
your palate like a pinball. Racy and
grapefruity, it's a wonderful meal
starter and a vegetarian's friend.
The liter bottle is a bargain. $12-14
Rheinhessen, Germany
Imported by M. Skurnik/
Terry Theise Selections

Giovanni Struzziero
GRECO DI TUFO "Villagiulia"
Medium- to full-bodied. A big
wine with an earthy personality.
The grape Greco Bianco, vinified
in Campania since the age of the

Caesars, is named
for the Greeks who
brought it there.
Smoky and rich, this
Struzziero rendition
is classic. Pair it with soft, earthy,
or oily foods like polenta, fatty
fish, and crumbly cheeses. $13-15
Campania, Italy
Imported by Opici

Ch. W. Bernhard
SCHEUREBE Kabinett
"Hackenheimer Kirchberg"
Medium-bodied. Ripe, highly
aromatic, and mouthfilling.
Hartmut Bernhard specializes in
soft yet fruit-saturated whites
with gorgeous flavors. Scheurebe,
the genetic cross of Riesling and
Silvaner grapes, is clearly the
thing he does best. The satiny
mouthfeel, unique muskiness, and
intriguing flavors of mint and red
berry are emphasized by a little
sweetness, as they are here. Serve
the Kabinett with sausages or a
beet and goat cheese salad. Use
the fabulously ripe, honeyed
Spätlese ($15-17) for meats
in a cherry glaze or Kung Pao
chicken. $13-15
Rheinhessen, Germany
Imported by M. Skurnik/Terry
Theise

Capay Valley
VIOGNIER
Medium- to full-bodied. Golden-
hued, rich, sleek, and flavorful.
The winery's name is pronounced
CAY-pay, and its wine is intense.
Redolent of pears in syrup,
slightly nutty, oaty, and
languorous on the palate, it calls
for some serious food. Think
dishes like roast pork or chicken,
salmon stuffed with breadcrumbs
and toasted sesame seeds, and
turkey cutlets slathered with
mustard. $13-15
Capay, California

SOAVE CLASSICO

Spreading out from the Veneto town of Soave is the vast DOC, or appellation, of the same name. What puts it on winedom's map? The production
of Italy's most popular dry white wines, most of which come from
cooperatives—winemakers who pool their production and marketing costs.
This helps explain why Soaves are usually of middling quality.

The dominant grape in Soave is the indigenous Garganega, blended
with varying amounts of Pinot Bianco, Chardonnay, and Trebbiano. As a
rule, your best bet is to choose a Soave Classico, made in the
original (and smaller) Soave zone. Classico wines are drier,
more complex, and richer than the often bland, run-of-the-
mill issue. One of the best is **Gini Soave Classico** ($14-16),
a medium-bodied, golden-hued, heady elixir simmering
with the flavors and aromas of poached pears and nuts.
What to serve with it? Creamy pastas and fin fish sautéed in
butter are a good start. *Imported by M. Skurnik*

Ca dei Frati
LUGANA "I Frati"
**Medium- to full-bodied. A rich wine
with soft, luxurious mouthfeel.**
The Trebbiano clone planted in
Lugana is special—indeed, local
growers are trying to legislate the
renaming of the subvariety to
Lugana to establish its identity.
This version is a prime example of
a good Lugana—richly perfumed,
pearlike, gently earthy, and very
ripe. It's lovely with creamy
gnocchi and pastas. $13-15
Veneto, Italy
Imported by Bayfield

Colle dei Bardellini
PIGATO
**Light- to medium-bodied.
A perfumed, soft, distinctive
white with modest alcohol.**
A rarity, the Pigato grape is grown
in the rocky coastal vineyards just
southwest of Genoa. It's a little
steely in the nose but surprisingly
gentle and subtle in the mouth.
If you want to be regionally
authentic, enjoy it with fresh
ocean fish and dabs of creamy
pesto. $14-16
Liguria, Italy
Imported by Vias

Fausto Gemme
GAVI DI GAVI "La Merlina"
**Light- to medium-bodied.
A crisp, slender sipper from
the Cortese grape.**
This has all the minerally tones
and citrusy freshness you want
for salads, pasta primavera, or light
appetizers. It's also a mouthwatering
apéritif. The grape responsible,
Cortese, has been grown in the
southeastern Piedmont for almost
three hundred years. $14-16
Piedmont, Italy
Imported by Artisan

Paul Vendran
VIOGNIER
"La Ferme Saint Pierre"
**Full-bodied. A velvety
white nectar for hedonists.**
Here's Viognier with plenty of
alcohol, thick texture, and a
bouquet of fresh pears drizzled
with caramel—a mixture of sweet
and fresh aromas that excites deep-
down senses. Serve with triple-
crème cheeses, broiled lobster,
or roasted chicken or pork with
something fruity, like applesauce.
$14-16
Rhône, France
Imported by T. Edward

Sergio Mottura
ORVIETO Secco
Medium-bodied. At once rich, bright, and admirably pure.

At this winery in Umbria, three local grapes—Procanico (believed to be a superior subvariety of Trebbiano), Verdello, and Grechetto—are grown free of chemical additives or fertilizers and then harvested by hand. Though rich, this dry (secco) wine from the Orvieto DOC shows exceptional clarity and brightness, making it a real refresher with sole amandine or a plate of garlicky spaghetti. The sweet **Amabile** ($14-16) version is appropriate for fresh fruit and honeyed desserts like baklava. $14-16
Umbria, Italy
Imported by Domaine Select

Didier Fornerol
ALIGOTÉ
Medium-bodied. Splendidly silken and rich, with vivid acidity in the finish.
Fornerol makes a fetish of delicacy in his Burgundies, yet his Aligoté is lifted by a brilliant lemony freshness. It's "just a dry white wine" in the same sense that Gershwin was "just a piano player." Pair it with oysters simmered in cream, a salad of fresh tomatoes, or crisply fried fish with a squirt of lemon. $14-16
Burgundy
Imported by Jeroboam

$15 to $30

Brüder Dr. Becker
SCHEUREBE Spätlese "Dienheimer Tafelstein"
Medium-bodied. Ripe, honeyed, and pungently aromatic.
The grape Scheurebe, a genetic crossing of Riesling and Silvaner, holds romance and mystery for many German wine fans. And why not? Ripe to a point of oiliness, with additional dimensions of smoke and surprisingly *red* berry fruit, the wines are downright weird. Dr. Becker's version is organic, shamelessly red-fruity, and terrific for ham, glazed meats, squash dishes, pulled-pork barbecue, and even duck. Fascinating! $15-17
Rheinhessen, Germany
Imported by Metropolis

Poggio Pollino
ALBANA DI ROMAGNA "Monte di Cambro"
Medium-bodied. Fragrant, strong, dry white with a firm finish.
This is a serious rendition of the wines of Albana di Romagna, the first white-wine-growing area to be granted a DOCG—*Denominazione di Origine Controllata e Garantita*, the premium category in Italy's appellation system. Fairly neutral in flavor but equipped with lively acidity and a waxy, balanced mouthfeel, it's a particularly good choice for serving with sardines, mackerel, and other oily and salty fish dishes. $15-18
Emilia-Romagna, Italy
Imported by OmniWines

Broglia
GAVI DI GAVI "La Meirana"
Medium-bodied. An especially pungent Gavi with concentrated fruit and smooth character.
Light, dry whites made from the Cortese grape are the specialty of Gavi di Gavi, a small town in the Piedmont. In this one, a combo of minerals, beeswax, and lemon zest hits the bull's-eye. And what a fabulous food wine! We've found it wonderfully refreshing with edibles as varied as calamari, risotto, mushroom pizza, and artichoke with oil and lemon. $16-18
Piedmont, Italy
Imported by Vias

Txomin Etxariz
TXAKOLINA DE GETARIA
Light-bodied. Fabulously refreshing, with a bright sparkle.
Txakolina ("chock-oh-LEE-nah") is the name of this wine's home turf in the Basque country.
The grapes are equally obscure: Hondarribi Zuri (85%)  and Hondarribi Beltza (15%)—but that just makes us love this exotic tipple even more. Incredibly crisp, lemon-scented, and a little spritzy, it's the world's most exciting oyster partner. It's also quite good with shrimp, clams, mussels, and salads. $16-18
Getaria, Spain
Imported by Tempranillo

Marco Felluga
TOCAI FRIULANO
Medium-bodied. Lively, assertive, and lasting on the palate.
Here's a classically made Tocai, with distinctive earthiness, a citrusy middle, and almonds in the finish. It's a natural match for the region's signature antipasto— thinly sliced prosciutto with fresh melon. $16-18
Friuli, Italy
Imported by Dalla Terra

La Zerba
GAVI "Terrarossa"
Medium-bodied.
Ripe-fruited and vigorous.
A late-ripened version of the classic Piedmontese white. Strong aromas of minerals, lemon verbena, and a basketful of white peaches jump out at you. It's a dramatic white for spicy, garlicky seafood and veal piccata. $16-18
Piedmont, Italy
Imported by Paramount

As Laxas
ALBARIÑO
Light- to medium-bodied.
Lots of fruit and tangy acidity.
With its signature fragrance of peaches and wildflowers joined with fresh acidity, modest alcohol, and light texture, this happy-go-lucky wine is equally companionable with sushi, a fish on the grill, or a plateful of linguini with red or white clam sauce. $16-18
Rias Baixas, Spain
Imported by Frontier

Di Meo
GRECO DI TUFO
Medium-bodied. Weighty and firm, it's balanced for the table.
The winemakers at the little Di Meo winery in Italy suit our philosophy, making wines from indigenous grape varieties that emphasize grace, balance, and versatility in food pairing. Their Greco is gently floral, expressive of its volcanic soils, and a tasty accompaniment to the local

GRÜNER–VELTLINER: THE CHIC AUSTRIAN

On the wine/food front, the grape-of-the-moment harks back to the days of the Austro–Hungarian Empire, with the Emperor Franz Joseph and his courtiers no doubt enjoying its wines in the opulent salons of Vienna. Modern Austria's premier grape, Grüner Veltliner is also cultivated in Hungary, The Czech Republic and Slovakia, and Slovenia.

Despite the grandeur inferred from its imperial provenance, Grüner can be refreshingly light and simple—a crisp, slightly spicy white that joins Pinot Grigio and California Chardonnay as the ideal nonthreatening cocktail white and a good match for salads and other light fare. But wines made from this amazingly versatile grape can also be the spiciest and most monumental of dry whites.

To start light, try **Lorimer Grüner Veltliner "Lois"** ($10–12), from the Austrian wine town of Langenlois in the Kamptal winegrowing area. With its aroma of white pepper and flavors of lemon–lime zest and minerals, it's a fresh and zippy match for omelets, crêpes, and green veggies. *Imported by Vin Divino*

You could then go to the other extreme with the monumental (and much pricier) **Brundlmayer Grüner Veltliner "Ried Lamm"** ($45–50). The Lamm vineyard is at the bottom of a large hill called the Heiligenstein (also in Kamptal), and the wines from this site are exceedingly ripe. In vintages with high acidity you've got it all: great tingly mouthfeel wedded to rich pear and apple fruit, "woodsy" aromatics, and high alcohol. Either enjoy it now as a formidable fish and lobster partner or cellar it for drinking years hence. *Imported by M. Skurnik/Terry Theise*

cuisine of ocean fish, earthy pastas, and potatoes. $16-20
Campania, Italy
Imported by Supreme

Nigl
GRÜNER VELTLINER "Gartling"
Medium- to full bodied. Rich, dry, and shimmeringly acidic.
In this white, herb, white pepper, and citrus notes are chiseled into the palate like stone carvings. Though Martin Nigl's entry-level wine, it's still more profound than half the Veltliners out there. For a mind-blowing experience, try his **Senftenberger Piri** ($18-20)— in practically every vintage

there's a mélange of forest aromas and multitiered complexity. Crab, lobster, or oily fish like bluefish or tuna, and a mixed grill of vegetables with high-quality olive oil are excellent partners at the table. $17-19
Kremstal, Austria
Imported by M. Skurnik/Terry Theise

Remondo Palacios
RIOJA "Placet"
Medium-bodied. Fantastically balanced, aromatic, and supple.
Instead of the oaked, oxidized, heavy, dry wine typical of whites from Rioja, this is devoid of oak,

utterly graceful, and clean on the palate. Bewitching aromas of flowers, pears, and fresh hay leave a refreshing finish. Serve it with delicate fish or fowl, crab cakes, or mild cheeses. $18-20

Rioja, Spain
Imported by Rare Wine

François Cazin
COUR-CHEVERNY
"Cuvée Renaissance"
Medium-bodied. Honeyed, musky, and lightly sweet.

As delicious as it is obscure. Made from Romarantin, a grape that grows essentially in Cheverny and nowhere else, this white has succulent apple fruit, clear

minerality, pleasant sweetness, and a luxurious finish. Foie gras works beautifully with it, as do blue-veined and triple-crème cheeses. $16-18

Loire, France
Imported by Louis/Dressner

Kurt Darting
SCHEUREBE Spätlese
"Durkheimer Spielberg"
Medium-bodied. A love-it-or-hate-it wine, with considerable sweetness and oily mouthfeel.

Very apple-cidery, very honeyed, and very seductive, this Scheurebe is outrageously ripe because of its late harvesting. The right food makes the difference, and your glassful will balance with fruit-sauced fatty meats (duck, sausage, and so forth). It will also quell the heat of spicy Szechuan or Indian dishes and temper the sweetness of mango or tamarind

chutney. Food or no food, this Scheurebe tastes rapturously delicious. An adventure! $18-20

Pfalz, Germany
Imported by M. Skurnik/ Terry Theise

A. & P. de Villaine
BOUZERON DE ALIGOTÊ
Medium- to full-bodied. Prodigious complexity and depth from a grape not known for it.

Aligotê, the "other white grape" of Burgundy, typically makes light apéritif wines. They're traditionally used for the Kir cocktail—but in this case, that would be a waste. This oak-aged, opulent giant is better matched with baked oysters, coquilles St. Jacques, or poached poultry. $18-20

Burgundy, France
Imported by Kermit Lynch

Fefinanes
ALBARIÑO
Light- to medium-bodied. Juicy, slender, and refreshing.

Grown in the remote coastal vineyards of Rias Baixas in Galicia, on Spain's north shore, this is an appealing glassful of orchard fruits and flowers. It's particularly handy as a crisp foil for assertively flavored shrimp scampi or tempura. $18-20

Rias Baixas, Spain
Imported by Artisan

Cornarea
ARNEIS
Medium- to full-bodied. Concentrated and creamy.

A wondrous dry white made in the Piedmont from Arneis, a local grape that almost disappeared in the 1970s but was revived when it found a solid base of devoted fans. In this extravagant rendition, peaches, pears, and licorice wash over the palate in waves. Explore its charms with a seafood risotto

VIOGNIERS THAT SING

Californian Morgan Clendenen, wife of Jim Clendenen of the popular Au Bon Climat winery in Santa Barbara, strikes out in her own direction at her biodynamic Viognier vineyard, Le Bon Climat. Her full-bodied, mineral-drenched **Cold Heaven Viognier "Le Bon Climat"** ($30–35) is balanced to a tee–no mean feat with this variety. She avoids new oak and achieves a great balance of acidity in a peary, flowery wine that sings standing alone or with rich fish and lobster.

Her most intriguing project is an international Viognier blend whose name means "two Cs": **Viognier Deux C** ($60–70), with half the wine coming from the Sanford & Benedict Vineyard in the Santa Rita Hills and the other half from Condrieu Rhône vintner Yves Cuilleron. It's a whoppingly rich, extraordinarily complex achievement that grows and evolves in the glass over several hours. At the dinner table it deserves deluxe cuisine on the order of salmon or pike in truffled cream.

or rich marinated steaks of tuna, swordfish, or shark. $18-20
Piedmont, Italy
Imported by Vias

Mauro Sebaste
ARNEIS
Medium-bodied. Zesty, with good acidity and clean, modern character.
Sebaste's interpretation of what is now the most widely grown white grape in the Piedmont is pleasingly subtle and scented with the variety's typical green apples and anise. At the table, natural partners for this appealing wine are fennel bulb, flaky fish, and savory antipasti. $19-21
Piedmont, Italy
Imported by Opici

Terradora
FIANO DI AVELLINO
"Terre di Dora"
Medium- to full-bodied. Firm and dry, with mild viscosity at the finish.
Perhaps it's the faint honeyed quality of the local Fiano grape that earned it the moniker "the vine beloved by bees." Like many southern Italian whites, this wine from the Fiano di Avellino DOC is

also meaty and earthy. A strong foil for oily sardines, mackerel, and bluefish, it also goes well with Taleggio cheese. $19-21
Campania, Italy
Imported by Vias

Franck Peillot
ROUSSETTE DE BUGEY
"Altesse"
Medium- to full-bodied. Suave and mouthcoating, with a dry finish.
Made near France's Swiss border, this is 100% Roussette, an indigenous white grape more often used for sparkling wines. It's honey and pears all the way in this example, and a match with pork chops with applesauce would be perfect. It's also an intriguing partner for double- and triple-crème cheeses. $20-22
Savoie, France
Imported by Louis/Dressner

Lusco do Mino
ALBARIÑO "Lusco"
Medium-bodied. Classy rendition, with lavish aromas and harmonious balance.
Awash in apricot and lemon sorbet scents, this works effortlessly with all kinds of fresh

seafood and any preparations of lobster and crab. It's also a clever choice for fusion and Pan-Asian cuisine, which often needs a fragrant white. $20-22
Rias Baixas, Spain
Imported by Tempranillo

Lucien Albrect
PINOT AUXERROIS "Cuvée"
Medium-bodied. A dry wine with a surprisingly sweet impression on the palate.
An opulent, honey-textured rarity from thirty- to thirty-five-year-old vines. Amply ripe and well crafted, it smells enticingly of fresh hay, clover honey, and fresh bread baking. Have it with a simple cow's milk cheese or a bowl of creamy corn chowder and biscuits. $20-22
Piedmont, Italy
Imported by R. Kacher

Domaine Schoffit
CHASSELAS "Vielles Vignes"
Medium- to full-bodied. Aromatically fascinating and graceful on the palate.
The most esoteric wine from this master vintner—and one of his most enjoyable. While Chasselas (a.k.a. Gutedel in Germany), is mainly used as a blending grape in Alsace, Schoffit took the time and trouble to nurture a parcel of old vines and crafted a fantastic wine. Alluringly scented with pears and roses, it's great with French bistro fare of any kind: pâté, savory tarts, charcuterie, soft cheeses. It also elevates a brook trout to a princely feast. $20-24
Alsace, France
Imported by Weygandt/Metzler

Adegas das Eiras
ALBARIÑO "Terras Gauda"
Medium-bodied. An especially rich Albariño.
Clearly, this producer is trying to make a more structured, serious wine from Albariño. He succeeds. Firmly textured, redolent of peaches and apricots, and rather minerally, it reminds us of a Halbtrocken Riesling from Germany's Rheingau. A splendid salmon steak white. $20-25
Rias Baixas, Spain
Imported by AV Imports

Schloss Gobelsburg
GRÜNER VELTLINER "Steinsetz"
Medium-bodied. Firm, dry, filigreed white from gravelly soils.
Veltliner is Austria's premier grape. Gobelsburg's is racy at first sip, then fleshes out in the mouth with gorgeous fruit and woodsy, herbal flavors. This is a serious dinner wine, deserving of the likes of mushroom-smothered pork tenderloin or roasted whole fish. Muskier, fuller, and more in need of cellaring is Gobelsburg's **Grüner Veltliner "Renner"** ($30-32), a superb choice for roast veal. $21-23
Langenlois, Austria
Imported by M. Skurnik/Terry Theise

Ch. W. Bernhard
AUXERROIS Spätlese Halbtrocken "Frei–Laubersheimer Fels"
Medium-bodied. Dry, aromatic, and vibrant.
The Auxerrois grape, closely akin to Pinot Blanc, is a German and Alsatian specialty. Rendered here in a dry white of startling intensity, it combines complex floral, apple, and citrus notes with a savoriness that works well with richly sauced veal or vegetable dishes. $23-25
Rheinhessen, Germany
Imported by M. Skurnik/Terry Theise

Villa Russiz Superiore
TOCAI FRIULANO
**Full-bodied. Outsized white
wine, powerfully built and
completely dry.**
There's almost something carnal
about a good Tocai, and this is a
formidable example. The nuts,
the flowers, the tingling acidity
are all there, but it's that deep-
down earthiness that makes this
wine so fascinating—especially
with a plate of mushrooms, salt
cod, garlicky pastas, cured meats,
or pungent cheeses.
$23-25
Friuli, Italy
Imported by Dalla Terra

Château Rahoul
GRAVES
**Medium- to full-bodied.
Sparingly oaked, elegant,
and perfectly smooth.**
This distinctive wine is crafted
from 100% Sémillon. Melon melds
with green herbs, Granny Smith
apples, and minerals. A classy dry
white for tuna steaks, grilled
vegetables, or delicate white
meats (rabbit included).
$24-26
Bordeaux
Imported by Wine Symphony

Manincor
MOSCATO Giallo
"Enzenberg"
**Medium-bodied.
Very dry, temptingly fragrant,
and one of a kind.**
Here's an Italian Moscato with
a Germanic sensibility. Sternly
dry yet perfumed with orange
oil, florals, and minerals, it
makes most Muscats taste like
.ne grape juice off a super-
ma ket shelf. Save its savoriness
for delicate seafood dishes
flavored with capers, saffron, or
cumin. $24-26
Alto Adige, Italy

Imported by M. Skurnik

Clelia Romano
FIANO DI AVELLINO
"Colli di Lapio"
**Medium-bodied. A firm, dense
white with subtle layers.**
A little nutty, a little honeyed,
very dry, and *not* a quaffing
wine, Fiano is a food-lover's
choice for dishes with strong,
salty flavors (think anchovies
or Parmigiano-Reggiano).
$25-28
Campania, Italy
Imported by M. Skurnik

Domaine Georges Vernay
VIN DE PAYS DES COLLINES
RHODANNIENNES
**Full-bodied. A flamboyant
white with vivid perfume and
gorgeous balance.**
Christine Vernay—daughter of
Georges Vernay, famous for his
Viogniers from the tiny Rhône
appellation of Condrieu—now
makes a wine from vineyards
nearby. A lively tumult of
apricots, honeysuckle, and
fresh minerality, it is lighter
than Condrieu Viognier with
no chemical treatments or new
oak styling marring its purity.
(The *vin de pays* in the name
indicates a "country wine,"
the third tier in the French
appellation system.) Either a
firm fish braised in wine or
roast turkey with oyster
stuffing would be a great
match come dinnertime.
$28-30
Rhône, France
Imported by Bayfield

Under $35

Charles de Cazanove
CHAMPAGNE Brut Azur
Medium- to full-bodied.
Opulently rich and lengthy.
Crafted at a tiny, two-hundred-year-old family-run estate in the north of the Champagne district, this *très élégant* Champagne deserves to be better known. Its finish is toasty, almost malty in flavor, and very dry. A stylish partner for soups, poached salmon, and most any dish with a rich cream sauce. $28-30
Épernay, France
Imported by Grand Cru

Pol Roger
CHAMPAGNE Brut
Medium-bodied. Known for its
elegance and utter reliability.
Winston Churchill was so taken with this Champagne that he had it made specially for him in pint-size single servings. The blend (roughly half Chardonnay, half Pinot Noir) is vinted in a crisp, balanced style. With its aromas of fresh-baked brioche and a bevy of orchard fruits, it's an excellent choice for cream-laden shellfish dishes. The estate's **Brut "Reserve" Vintage 1996** ($60-70) is a bold, toasty knockout, as are earlier vintages such as '93, '90, and '88 (all of which should be drunk now, not stored). The **Brut Rosé Vintage 1995** ($60-70) is one of the very best. $30-35
Épernay, France
Imported by F. Wildman

Laurent-Perrier
CHAMPAGNE Brut
Light- to medium-bodied.
Ethereally fine, dry, and delicate.
This lacily intricate Champagne is so lightly floral and pale that its high proportion of Pinot Noir comes as a surprise. What's more, the winery is huge yet manages to craft artisanal-tasting Champagnes. The extraordinary **"Cuvée Ultra-Brut"** ($45-50) is bigger-boned and bracingly dry with no *dosage*, making it super for caviar. The **Grand Siecle "La Cuvée"** ($85-110), rich and cellar-worthy, is the *tête de cuvée* (top bottling) Champagne from this house. $32-36
Champagne
Imported by Winebow

A SECRET SPILLED

The best-kept secret in Champagne? The wines of Paul Goerg, the name for a remarkable co-op in Vertus that sells much of its juice for use by the *grand marques*, including the too-chic-for-words Roederer Cristal. The wines they bottle under their own name are some of the best values in the region.

Made from 60% Chardonnay and 40% Pinot Noir, the fresh, crisp **Paul Goerg Champagne Brut "Tradition" 1er Cru** ($25-28) is subtly elegant, with almond and bread notes in the finish. Try it with crumbly, salty cheeses. The **Brut Blanc de Blancs** ($25-28) is like liquid marzipan—dry, yet somehow confectionery. This one's a natural with Camembert.

The **Brut Rosé** ($30-35) is all strawberries and fresh flowers, bringing a splash of color to exotic hors d'oeuvres or *moules marinière*. Finally, the vibrant, toasty **Brut Vintage 1996** ($30-35) is a tremendous bargain—bright on the palate, very minerally, and almost Riesling-like. It sings even more sweetly with chanterelle mushrooms sautéed in butter. *All wines imported by M. Rinaldi*

TINY BUT USEFUL INITIALS

Anyone who wants to ferret out the best Champagnes on the market (and that in no way means the most expensive) will do well to check the abbreviations attached to the license number at the bottom of the label.

Most labels show **NM**—for a *négotiant-manipulant* (dealer–producer) who may own vineyards but usually buys most of the grapes. This is the designation you'll find on the Champagnes of all of the mass market houses, meaning that N. M. Champagnes vary the most in quality.

Small–production, handcrafted Champagnes are designated **RM** (*récoltant-manipulant*, or grower–producer). It's these initials that should grab your attention, since so–called "grower" Champagnes are always interesting and frequently superb.

MA (for *marque d'acheteur*, or buyer's brand) indicates a brand owned by a third party, such as a restaurant or hotel that orders a private label. These are the cheapest Champagnes, with no guarantee of good quality.

The other two designations are **RC** (*récoltant-coopérateur*), growers who make and sell Champagnes with the help of cooperatives, and **CM** (*coopérative-manipulant*) with some 11,000 growers pooling their resources and marketing approximately 150 of their own brands.

E. Barnaut
CHAMPAGNE BLANC DE NOIRS
Extra Brut Grand Cru Medium- to full- bodied. Deep, bold, and fragrant.
This top-quality RM, or "grower," Champagne is made from Pinot Noir. Extremely rich and fine, with a citrusy flair and no *dosage*, it finishes with almost austere dryness. We find it brilliant with all kinds of seafood, from fried oysters to ceviche. The house's magenta-colored **Brut Rosé Grand Cru** ($33-36) is a bubbling swirl of ripe, tangy berries. $33-36
Bouzy, France
Imported by SDG

Over $35

Guy Larmandier
CHAMPAGNE CÔTES DES BLANCS 1er Cru à Vertus
Medium-bodied. Austerely dry at first, but quickly expands to exquisite richness.
This is a gorgeous, limited production "grower" Champagne from one of our very favorite houses. Wickedly dry and profoundly minerally, it's capped by a delicate essence of fresh pears in the finish. Flawless! Relish it with icy oysters or spoonfuls of sevruga caviar on blini. The powerful **Blanc de Blancs Brut Grand Cru** ($45-50) is a richer, fuller wine with cellaring potential. $35-38
Cramant, France
Imported by Rosenthal

Pierre Gimonnet et Fils
CHAMPAGNE BLANC DE BLANCS
Brut 1er Cru Medium-bodied. Bone-dry and soul-satisfying.
A 100% Chardonnay from a single grower-producer using forty- to eighty-year-old vines in three exciting *terroirs*, this shows wine lovers just how good Champagne can get. The *dosage* is very low, allowing the flavors to come across as clear, practically

crystalline. Citrusy and densely layered with minerals, it's the ideal accompaniment to caviar. $35-40
Cuis/Cramant/Chouilly, France
Imported by M. Skurnik/
Terry Theise

Bollinger
CHAMPAGNE Brut
"Special Cuvée"
Full-bodied. The deepest, richest, toastiest of all nonvintage Champagnes.
James Bond drinks it in the movies, and half the British Parliament probably sips it every New Year's Eve. What are you waiting for? Malty, biscuity, Pinot Noir-driven, and stunning, this Champagne would team beautifully at the table with creamy soups and lobster. (And then there are those Champagne flutes to clink in a sudsy, candlelit bathtub. . . .) Some devotees opt for the **Brut "Grande Annee"**

Vintage ($100-120), a benchmark bubbly regardless of year. $45-50
Ay, France
Imported by Dreyfus Ashby

Bruno Paillard
CHAMPAGNE Brut
"Chardonnay Reserve Privée"
Medium-bodied. Silken and substantial on the palate, with a long, clean finish.
The bottle looks old-fashioned, but Bruno Paillard, founded in 1981, is the youngest estate in Champagne. This special cuvée is 100% Chardonnay, rendered in a *pétillant* (frothy) style with significantly less sparkle than traditional Champagne. Buttery, faintly earthy, savory, and smooth, it's particularly alluring with food. Salmon in pastry and triple-cream cheeses are attractive partners. $48-52
Reims, France
Imported by D. Polaner

Domaine Pierre Moncuit
CHAMPAGNE BLANC DE BLANCS Brut Grand Cru
Full-bodied. Toasty and wonderfully long yet with palate-lifting freshness.
A foodie's Champagne if there ever was one, this 100% Chardonnay is a "grower" wine from a renowned site. Its rich, mouthwatering character and notes of dried hay, caramel, malt, and minerals make it thrilling with roasted game hens and cold smoked meats. Some tasters prefer it with further bottle age— but who could wait? $48-52
Le Mesnil sur Oger, France
Imported by SDG

Gatinois
CHAMPAGNE Brut Grand Cru "Tradition"
Medium- to full-bodied. Deeply aromatic, satiny in texture, and gorgeous.
This superb grower sells half his production to Bollinger for their top cuvées and privately bottles the remainder. Largely Pinot Noir, the wine is a pale straw color— but if you close your eyes, you might think you're smelling red Burgundy. Enjoy this superb dinner companion with roast chicken, salmon, or thinly sliced cold beef.
$38-40
Ay, France
Imported by D. Polaner

René Geoffroy
CHAMPAGNE Brut 1er Cru
Medium-bodied. An extremely creamy Champagne, fresh and alluring.
Jean-Baptiste Geoffroy, a master of detail, winds up making a lovable cream puff of a Champagne that's so much fun you might miss just how intricate and complex it is. Appley, yeasty, and *terroir*-driven, it makes a fine foil for creamy soups and sauces. Geoffroy's **Brut Rosé** ($45-50), made by the *saignée* ("bled") method typically used for rosés, is a vivid, excellent wine. $40-45
Cumiéres, France
Imported by M. Skurnik/Terry Theise

Egly-Ouriet
CHAMPAGNE Brut "Tradition— Non Filtré" Grand Cru
Medium-bodied. Made from Pinot Noir in a lush, mouthfilling style.
Die-hard bubbly fans buy this out fast—the reason it's hard to obtain. Few sparkling wines are as sensuous or primordially satisfying than this Champagne, with its expansive mouthful of vanilla-scented pastry, red fruits, and fresh yet woodsy elements. Enjoy it at brunch with an omelet or cold cuts or at supper with hearty mushroom soup and a baguette. $45-55
Ambonnay, France
Imported by North Berkeley

Other Bubblies

*Before briefly explaining how sparkling wines
are made, let's take a deep breath
and sort out the various kinds.*

*S*PARKLERS given the most pressure during winemaking, like Champagne, are classified as fully sparkling, as opposed to semi-sparkling. They are categorized as *spumante* in Italy and *mousseaux* in France ("foaming" or "frothy" in both languages, or "sparkling" when applied to wine). Moderately sparkling *crémant* ("creaming") wines are made with just over half the pressure given Champagne. Then come the lightly effervescent, or semi-sparkling, wines described as *pétillant* in France, *frizzante* in Italy, *spritzig* in Germany, and "crackling" in America. Wines with even less sparkle are called *perlant* in France and *perlwein* in Germany, denoting their pearl-like bubbles.

More technical but easier to keep straight are the two main methods for making sparkling wine. The first is the traditional method, more elegantly called *la méthode champenoise*. After blending and fermentation, the wine is immediately bottled with a starter of yeast and sugar—the *tirage*. A second fermentation then takes place in the bottle, resulting in additional alcohol and the carbon dioxide that gives sparkling wine its effervescence. The new sediment is removed, a dash of sugar called the *dosage* is added to adjust the Champagne's sweetness or dryness, and it is then resealed with a cork and wire cage to protect it from exploding when it is shipped to market.

The other most commonly used bubble-making method, developed just after the turn of the twentieth century by Eugène Charmat in Bordeaux, is much quicker and less expensive. Alternately called the Charmat or bulk process, it uses large tanks to retain the pressure created by carbon dioxide during fermentation. It isn't as suitable for wines that benefit from aging, and sparkling wines made by this method often lose their bubbles quickly once poured.

One thing to keep in mind: Some sparkling wines do outshine Champagne in their versatility with food. The richness and full sparkle of Champagne limit its ability to complement many things on which you dine or nibble, whereas the gentler textures and varying flavors of other bubblies offer endless variations at the table.

Under $15

Jean-Paul Trocadero
BLANC DE BLANCS Brut
Light-bodied. Crisp, vivacious, and utterly refreshing.
This French sparkler is made from Ugni Blanc (Trebbiano), Chenin Blanc, Macabeo (a Middle Eastern grape that spread to France by way of Spain), and a splash of Chardonnay. The Trocadero estate somehow manages to keep the quality of the Blanc de Blancs high while producing huge quantities. This version is a citrusy, bubbling pleasure for mimosas or predinner cocktails. $6-8
Savoie, France
Imported by Lauber

François Montand
BLANC DE BLANCS Brut
Light- to medium-bodied. Dry, but with discernible fruit.
Chardonnay and Ugni Blanc grapes make this very appealing sparkling wine, which is sourced from vineyards across the French countryside. To our minds, it's a terrific Champagne alternative. Try it out with chèvre or any other light, creamy cheese. $9-11
France
Imported by Winebow

François Chidaine
MONTLOUIS Brut
Light- to medium-bodied. Very dry, crisp, and aromatic.
This sparkling Chenin Blanc from the Loire sports a fruity fragrance and a lemony, dry finish. It refreshes the mouth and cuts through oysters like a razor. $12-14
Loire, France
Imported by House of Fine Wines

Elio Perrone
MOSCATO D'ASTI
Light-bodied. Frothy, fruity, and lively, with a faint hidden richness.
This creamy-textured Moscato, with its strong taste and scent of

---

CAVA: THE SPARKLERS OF CATALONIA

The sparkling wine now called Cava ("cellar") originated in the Catalonian town of San Sadurni de Noy when José Raventos, head of the family firm that grew into the huge sparkling wine producer Codorníu, returned from a visit to France in 1872 and began making *méthode champenoise* wines. Almost all Cava, called Champagña until the early 1970s, is still grown in Catalonia and is made from the grapes Macabeo, Xarel-lo, Paradella, and sometimes a little Chardonnay.

A light and refreshing bargain Cava with a fruity, open personality is **Sumarroca Cava Brut "Reserva"** ($9-13), from Penèdes. It's citrusy right off the bat, with a touch of ginger and a clean, brisk finish. It's also a nice alternative to Fino Sherry when you're having tapas. *Imported by Frontier*

More serious is **Juve Y Camps Cava Brut Nature "Reserve de la Familia"** ($15-17), one of the new generation of handcrafted, estate-grown Cavas. ("Brut Nature" indicates a wine unsweetened by *dosage*.) Full of nutty complexity and crispy bubbles, it is dry, fairly forceful, and rather Champagne-like. This one makes a rich partner for grilled seafood, fried foods, nuts, and olives. *Imported by Bluegrass-Catalunya*

fresh apricots and spring flowers, is less than 6% alcohol, meaning it won't weigh you or your dinner down. Enjoy icy cold with fresh fruit, tarts, mousses, and crêpes. Also try the delicious pink **Bigaro** ($14-16), a strawberry-redolent blend of half Moscato and half Brachetto. $12-15 (500ml)
Piedmont, Italy
Imported by Vieux Vins

Avinyo
CAVA Brut
Light-bodied. Creamy fruit, crisp refreshment.
The label of this artisanal, boutique cava says in Catalan, "with the rigor of a work well crafted"—and justly so. A touch floral, a touch of lees, and a lovely food partner, it's a fitting companion for tapas, fried empanadas, and other Spanish specialties. $13-15
Penèdes, Spain
Imported by De Maison

Over $15

Eric Bordelet
SYDRE "Argelette"
Light- to medium-bodied. Sensuously creamy and fruity, quite dry, and just 4% alcohol.
This biodynamically grown sparkling apple cider comes from a former Paris wine steward who went home to his orchards. With its Champagne-like feel, it's about as elegant as cider gets. Think of it as something different to serve with cold cuts, farmhouse cheeses, ripe figs, and olives. **Bordelet's Poire "Authentique"** ($12-14) is a deep-gold pear cider that captures the essence of fresh pears. $16-18
Normandy, France
Imported by D. Polaner

Alain Renardat
VIN DU BUGEY CERDON
Light-bodied. Gently sweet, modest in alcohol, and just plain fun.
Here's a 100% sparkling Gamay, the grape of Beaujolais. Raspberry, strawberry, and jasmine trickle across your tongue in this fruity, frothy little bonbon. A winner after dinner with

strong triple-crème or blue cheeses, it's also lovely served predinner in Champagne flutes with a garnish of sliced strawberry.
$16-18
Bugey, France
Imported by Louis/Dressner

Gruet
BLANC DE NOIRS
Medium-bodied. A superior American bubbly with a rich, elegant character.
This 100% Pinot is grown in New Mexico at 4,000 feet above sea level by Laurent Gruet, formerly of the Paul Laurent house in Champagne. Its fruit is a fascinating mix of berries and lemons tempered by earthy, toasty complexity. Brighten up a dull evening with this conversation piece, whose willing partners include sushi, pâté, and croquettes or other fried appetizers.
$16-18
New Mexico

PROSECCO:
REFRESHMENT *IN EXCELSIS*

HE INCREASINGLY POPULAR Prosecco could be thought of as Champagne's more casual, yet quite elegant, Italian cousin. A generally dry, refreshing apéritif (*aperitivo* in Italian), it comes in both the *spumante* (fully sparkling) and *frizzante* (semi-sparkling) styles and is usually less expensive than Champagne.

It may be a surprise to many wine drinkers that Prosecco takes its name not from a place or a winemaking technique, but from a grape. All but five percent of production from this Veneto grape is of sparkling wine. The leading DOC is Prosecco di Conegliano–Valdobbiadene, west of the town of Conegliano. (Outside Italy, Prosecco is grown in Argentina, but to a very limited extent.)

Italy's largest Prosecco producer, Mionetto, specializes in the traditional style, making *frizzantes* with about half the sparkle of Champagne. **Mionetto Prosecco "Sergio"** ($10–12) is an appley and vivacious example that makes a wonderful warm weather wine. Serve it icy cold with antipasti, cold soups, or pasta primavera. *Imported by House of Burgundy*

More Champagne-like than most Proseccos (and, interestingly enough, the café wine of Venice and the traditional base for the Bellini cocktail) is **Nino Franco Prosecco de Valdobbiadene "Rustico"** ($14–16), which shows a bit more staying power than its peers. A pleasure by itself, it can also be enjoyed with fried appetizers and antipasti. **Franco's "Primo Franco"** ($19–21) is creamier, slightly sweeter, and sexy with a strawberry after dinner. *Both wines imported by Lauber*

The exceedingly dry and steely **Bisson Prosecco de Colli Trevigiano** ($13–15) is a quite distinctive version. Crisper and more lemony -than most Proseccos, it can handle shellfish and shrimp nicely but is still gentle enough to sip solo. *Imported by Rosenthal*

Ermete Medici
MALVASIA FRIZZANTE Secco "Daphne"
Light- to medium-bodied. Exotically scented and almost bone-dry.

The Malvasia grape expresses itself strongly here, with a pronounced bouquet of apricots and fresh flowers. How can a wine that smells so sweet finish so dry? It's a question worth pondering with an ice-cold bottle and some prosciutto with melon. $18-21

Emilia-Romagna, Italy
Imported by OmniWines

Foreau
VOUVRAY Brut
Medium- to full-bodied. A powerful Vouvray— but with bubbles!

Drier than most Brut Champagnes, this vivid, sparkling Chenin Blanc from the Loire is a wake-up call. Its tight, citrus peel nose belies a rich palate of baked apples and a complex yeasty character. A bit overwhelming on its own, it makes more sense with food. Seafood (especially crab cakes) brings out its fruit beautifully. $20-22

Loire, France
Imported by Rosenthal

Dr. Reuter
RIESLING SEKT Brut
Light-bodied. A splendid apéritif.

The crisp, citrusy varietal character of Riesling bursts out at you from the first sniff. Lighter than Champagne (and actually drier than many), this bubbly is very food-friendly—an exciting choice for smoked fish, entrée salads, and your most savory or vinegary appetizers. $20-22

Saar, Germany
Imported by Wines for Food

Schramsberg
BLANC DE BLANCS Brut
Medium-bodied. Elegantly balanced and pure, with a fine bead.

The most Champagne-like offering in California, with the finest bead (that is, smallest bubbles) in almost any *champenoise*-style wine, and nice, crackery flavors, with a bit of lees. Enjoy as an all-American apéritif at Thanksgiving or anytime with hors d'oeuvres, pâtés, and seafood salads. $20-25

California

FIND THAT WINE!

WHY IS IT that you often read of a wine that sounds enticing and different yet you hardly ever see on the shelves? The answer lies in the sheer number of wines out there—jillions of 'em. With the exception of releases from the largest domestic and international producers alike, the chances of finding what you want at your corner wineshop (or even the mega mart) are fair to slim at best.

To take things into your own hands, proceed as follows. First e-mail, phone, or visit your trusty local wine retailer, giving the winery's name, what it calls the wine, and, if you're looking for a certain vintage, the year. Your retailer can then order the wine from a wholesale distributor—who, if the wine is in stock, will usually deliver it to the shop the next day. (A hint: Placing orders with a shop's owner or general manager could increase your chances, since some clerks may not be well versed in special ordering.)

If the distributor has to order from the winery, you may have to wait two to six weeks for delivery.

At this point you could try the Internet. Many U.S. wineries represented in this book sell their wines online (they, plus the rest of the book's U.S. wineries, are listed on pages 224–227, complete with contact information). Then there are the wine search sites found on the Internet, several of which are listed on page 232. Advanced searches may require a sign-up fee, but an annual cost that works out to only about $2.50 a month may be well worth it. A caveat: Ordering online is complicated by direct shipping laws, as explained on page 228.

An alternative is to contact an importer, whose name you'll be lucky to get unless you're searching for a wine from this guide or another publication that specifies importers. How can they help? As often as not, an importer can give you the name of a distributor in your area who can then lead you to a local retailer. Some importers' Web sites provide find-a-wine information in state-by-state directories. If the importer in which you are interested does not provide such a list, a customer service representative reached by phone or e-mail should be able to give you the name of an area distributor.

A potential bonus: Once you've got your hands on a hard-to-locate wine, it just might taste all the sweeter. And what could be a better reward for your successful detective work?

CHAPTER SIX

Fortified and Dessert Wines

In many parts of the world, sipping Port, Madeira, Cream Sherry, or other sweetish fortified wines after dinner has long been de rigueur. But not all fortified wines are sweet, and not all sweet wines are fortified. Simply put, fortified wines have had distilled spirits added during winemaking to strengthen or "fortify" them, while sweet wines come from late-harvested grapes or have had sweet grape-must added. Whether you choose to serve them before, during, or after dinner depends entirely on which kind of wine you've chosen.

Fortified Wines

It has been proved time and again that necessity is the mother of invention, even in winedom. To see the aphorism borne out oenologically, look no further than fortified wine.

ROM THE TIME grapevines were first cultivated and their fruit was transformed into wine, keeping wine from spoiling was a struggle. Greeks extended its life a bit by storing it in amphorae (urns). Romans did the same using oaken barrels. Both civilizations sought to disguise spoilage by flavoring wines with honey, herbs, salt water, and even cheese (!). Exactly when stronger wines or spirits began to be added to wine to preserve it is lost to history, but it worked—and fortified wine was born.

History does record how the fortified wines Port and Madeira came to be. In the late 1600s English wine merchants in Portugal added a little brandy to the dark, astringent red wines they had discovered up the Douro River to ensure that they would arrive in London unspoiled. Eureka! Port. Around the same time, British sailors stopping at Madeira began to stabilize the wines they found there with cane sugar to help them survive the long sail back to England, and in the process unwittingly created Madeira (see "Madeira: The Happy Accident," page 208).

Modern-day wines are fortified in one of two ways. Adding grape spirit or other stronger alcohol **during fermentation,** before all the grape sugar has been converted to alcohol, kills the yeast and bacteria and results in longer-lived, higher-alcohol, sweeter wine. The earlier the alcohol is added, the sweeter the wine will be. Alcohol added **after fermentation** makes strong, dry wines, with Sherry and the drier Madeiras as two examples. Any sweetness comes from the pre-bottling addition of a sweetener, be it sugar or a mixture of grape juice and spirit.

This complicated vinification, usually coupled with long aging in cask and bottle, ultimately ups the price of fortified wines. (Vermouth is also fortified, but in the U.S., Cradle of the Cocktail, it long ago crossed the line from wine to mixer and apéritif.) Nevertheless, the lengthy life of a fortified wine helps offset the cost. That $60 bottle of Vintage Port doesn't look so pricey when it can improve over fifty years and complement a week's worth of dinners. And Madeira is practically immortal. The great unsung bargain is Sherry, which ranges from bone-dry to treacly-sweet and rarely exceeds forty dollars.

SHERRY

Americans may not realize it yet, but Sherry is the perfect apéritif. Its affinity for the snacks we love (pretzels, olives, chips), coupled with its wide range of styles and reasonable prices, would make it a runaway hit if it were marketed better. Its unique and fascinating solera fractional blending system alone makes it appealing. (See "The Solera," page 205.)

Sherry is made in wineries called bodegas at or near the ancient town of Jerez, in the Andalusia region of southern Spain. "Sherry" is the anglicized "Jerez," and "Xérès" is French. All three names appear on the bottle of all true Sherries—those from the three towns in the Jerez DO: Jerez de la Frontera, Sanlúcar de Barrameda, and Puerto de Santa María.

Running the gamut from very dry to very sweet, Sherries are of three types, with subtypes therein. The pale-colored **Fino–style Sherries** are the elegant **Manzanilla,** revered for its delicacy and salty tang, and **Fino**—tangily dry, faintly nutty, and refreshing. Both of these Sherries should be drunk very fresh and very cold. More complex is the aged, amber Fino called **Amontillado,** which is redolent of smoke and nuts and comes in very dry and slightly sweeter versions. All Fino–style Sherries owe their refinement to protective *flor,* the unique white crust that forms spontaneously on the wine as it develops in the barrel.

Oloroso–type Sherries are darker, fuller, and richer. Because of their higher alcohol content, they remain uninfluenced by *flor* as they age. A standard **Oloroso** is also quite dry, but the version called **Oloros Dulce** is sweet. **Palo Cortado** is a rare, spontaneously occurring type of Sherry that offers the floral delicacy of Amontillado plus the richness and depth of an Oloroso. The molasseslike **Pedro Ximénez** is made from the grape of the same name and is most often used as a dessert wine or to sweeten dry Sherries. **Cream Sherries** are Olorosos sweetened with much Pedro Ximénez, and their degree of sweetness and overall quality vary widely from producer to producer.

Under $12

Antonio Barbadillo
FINO SHERRY "Pale Dry"
Light-bodied. A piquant, bone-dry, pale, refreshing sherry.
Served chilled, this sherry makes the perfect apéritif. With its mouthwatering acidity and faint salty tang, it whets both the appetite and thirst.
$8-10
Jerez, Spain
Imported by Frontier

Antonio Barbadillo
AMONTILLADO SHERRY
"Medium Dry"
Light- to medium-bodied. Essentially dry, with a sweet-salty tang at the finish.
Amontillado Sherry is often used for cooking, but if you fill a *copita* with it and start sipping (*copita* is the name for the traditional small sherry glass), you'll find it bracing. The Barbadillo has typical mouthwatering character enhanced by nutty, smoky

aromas. It pairs well with all salty snacks and creamy chowders. $8-10

Jerez, Spain
Imported by Frontier

Antonio Barbadillo
OLOROSO SHERRY
"Full Dry"

Medium- to full-bodied. Dry it is, but to some tasters its richness seems sweet.

Here's a soul-satisfying Oloroso at an amazing price. As for flavor, just imagine drinking a bowl of chocolate-covered hazelnuts capped by a whiff of smoke. It works well after dinner with a creamy cheese or a handful of nuts. It's also not bad at buffets when sipped with thinly sliced Smithfield ham on biscuits. $8-10

Jerez, Spain
Imported by Frontier

Hidalgo
MANZANILLA SHERRY
"La Gitana"

Light-bodied. Light and fragrant, with a savory (some say salty) tanginess.

This exquisite dry Sherry has a palate of lemon, citron, and blanched almond. It's a charming partner for green olives, pasta with garlic and olive oil, and smoked fish. $10-13 (500ml)

Sanlúcar de Barrameda, Spain
Imported by Classical Wines

$12 to $25

Emilio Lustau
FINO SHERRY "Jarana"

Light- to medium-bodied. One of the richest, most aromatic, and jazziest Finos.

Pale straw in color, flowery, nutty, and *dry*, this Fino has exceptionally fresh character

and lively alcohol. Serve it chilled with stuffed olives, shrimp in garlic, smoked cheeses, and your favorite baked shellfish dishes. $14-17

Jerez, Spain
Imported by M. Skurnik

Toro Albala
DON PEDRO XIMÉNEZ
"Grande Reserve"

Full-bodied. Sweet and syruplike.

Vintages from the 1970s of the startling wine are floating around the market, so snap them up. A tidal wave of coffee, caramel, and pralines fruit floods the palate and recedes slowly to a mellow finish. Molten chocolate cake or pecan pie would excel. $23–25

Montilla-Moriles, Spain
Imported by Classical Wines from Spain

Emilio Lustau
AMONTILLADO SHERRY
"Escuadrilla"

Medium-bodied. Fragrant and complex but uncompromisingly dry—a connoisseur's style.

Some tasters will be wowed by this totally dry Sherry while others will be puzzled. Salty and tangy, it has earth, coffee, rye, and roasted-nut flavors jet-propelled by acidity. It's best sipped at room temperature with classic tapas: firm cheeses, cured Spanish ham, smoked seafood, and mushrooms sautéed in butter (preferably infused with a few drops of Sherry from the bottle). $20-22

Jerez, Spain
Imported by M. Skurnik

Emilio Lustau
PEDRO XIMÉNEZ "San Emilio"

Full-bodied. An opaque sherry that's lavishly sweet and syrupy.

Blended from stocks of very old wine, this showstopper coats the glass thickly and offers mouthfuls of coffee and molasses with

unapologetic zeal. It's a little intense to sip but great poured over a bowl of vanilla ice cream with walnuts, chocolate chunks, and raisins. If you're the daring sort, pour it over pancakes at Sunday brunch. $22-24
Jerez, Spain
Imported by M. Skurnik

Over $25

Emilio Lustau
PALO CORTADO SHERRY Almacenista "Vides 1/50"
Medium-bodied. Deep layers of spice and salt-air complexity propelled by succulent acidity.
The Almacenista line of Sherries is the pinnacle of Sherry production—the reserve wines of the Sherry stockholders themselves. Palo Cortado is the rarest style, an anomaly that occurs spontaneously in the cellars of the bodega and shares qualities of both Amontillado and Oloroso. Profoundly scented with coffee, roasted nuts, and aromas reminiscent of the sea, it can enhance smoked or grilled meats and seafood but provokes the imagination by itself. $32-35
Jerez, Spain
Imported by M. Skurnik

Antonio Barbadillo
PALO CORTADO SHERRY "Obispo Gascon"
Medium- to full-bodied. Incredibly complex and stimulating on the palate.
In this startling drink, succulent acidity balances the richness and caramelly sweetness, leaving you somewhere between refreshment and satiation. Flavors of butterscotch, toffee, and campfire smoke keep coming and linger. It works with foods as disparate as smoked hams and sausages, crème caramel, and a simple dish of smoked almonds. $34-36
Jerez, Spain
Imported by Frontier

Emilio Lustau
OLOROSO SHERRY Gran Reserva "Emperatriz Eugenia"
Medium- to full-bodied. Dry, powerful, and very complex.
In this Gran Reserva, the oldest wines in the solera span many decades. The bouquet smells like a coffee roastery and the texture is firm, juicy, and dense. Try this jewel with aged cheeses or after-dinner biscotti. $36-40
Jerez, Spain
Imported by M. Skurnik

THE SOLERA

A trace of the blend of any Sherry you sip could be as much as two centuries old, thanks to the solera, a unique system of fractional blending. To maintain the historical continuity of their Sherries, winemakers hold the vintages of many different years in rows of old American oak barrels stacked four or five high (the solera), with the oldest Sherries on the bottom. One or more times each year, 10 to 25 percent of the wine is taken out of the oldest barrel when Sherry is to be bottled and sent to market. This is replenished with an equal quantity from the next-oldest barrel, and these in turn from younger barrels. At the top, the solera is fed with the wine of the current year, which is known as the *añada*.

Resulting as it does from the continual blending of younger wines into older wines, Sherry isn't the product of any one year—the reason it never carries a vintage date.

PORT

True, honest-to-god Port, named for the town of Oporto, comes from the Douro region of northern Portugal. But whether made in Oporto, South Africa, or upstate New York, this brandy-fortified wine is high-alcohol, sweet, full, and practically made for postprandial enjoyment. (The after-dinner pairing of Port and an aromatic wedge of English blue-veined Stilton is a happy legacy of the colonial British Empire.)

So what is it, besides its place of origin, that makes the wine Port? The technique with which it is made. After the grapes have been crushed (a combination of native Portuguese grapes including Touriga Nacional, Tinta Roriz, and Tinta Cão), they are macerated in a tank for about a day. As fermentation begins and the grapes' sugars begin converting to alcohol, fermentation must soon be halted. This is accomplished by pouring the wine into a vat containing clear brandy, the alcohol of which kills the yeast and thus slows fermentation to almost nil. The result is a sweet wine with about 10% residual sugar and up to 20% alcohol.

It takes a long time for Ports to reach full maturity, with the best Vintage Ports left to age for decades. Difference in aging time largely explains the many permutations of the wine, as defined in "A Port Primer," page 207.

Note that all of the Ports recommended here are from Portugal—the idea being that once you've tasted the real thing, you'll have a standard by which to judge those made elsewhere.

Quinta do Infantado
PORT "Estate Reserve"
Medium-bodied.
Moderately sweet, savory, and exquisitely balanced.
This Portuguese-owned estate, of which there aren't many, makes wine the old-fashioned way—and yes, that means stomping on the grapes with bare feet. The Estate Reserve is a deep ruby-colored Port with tawny highlights, dominated by fruit but accented with nutmeg, cinnamon, and sandalwood.
The **10 Year Tawny** ($35-40) is winey, complex, and distinctively dry for its type. Sip either Port with gingerbread or cookies.
$18-20
Douro, Portugal
Imported by Louis/Dressner

Quinta do Noval
TAWNY PORT 20 Year
Medium- to full-bodied.
Sensuous, generously smooth, and with sweet, lasting flavor.
Imagine a handful of caramel-covered pralines melting slowly into a warm, soothing pool in your mouth. Now extend that sensation for ten minutes or so—about the length of this Port's finish. A great after-dinner sipper from one of the most revered Port houses. $50-55
Douro, Portugal
Imported by Wm. Grant

Warre's
VINTAGE PORT
Full-bodied. A heady, broad style that evolves slowly.
This is first-rate Port from a three-hundred-year-old house at the

top of its game. While the '85 is losing its baby fat and evolving into a spicy, succulent, clove- and currant-scented behemoth, '94 and '97 remain muted and tannic. Warre's are serious, deep, and mysterious wines, so while you're waiting for them, drink the **Late Bottled Vintage 1992** ($24-26), a rich black elixir redolent of blueberries, black cherries, and bittersweet chocolate. $65-90
Douro, Portugal
Imported by Vineyard Brands

Smith Woodhouse
VINTAGE PORT
Full-bodied. Powerful, drier style of Port with a deep, smoky character.
This rich, vastly underrated Vintage Port is loaded with

SMITH WOODHOUSE
VINTAGE PORTO

black currant, pipe tobacco, and caramel flavors; look for the '85, a perfect cigar Port. The single-*quinta* **Madalena** ($33-36) seems more opaque and monolithic than the regular vintage and needs time (and some rich cheese) to tame it; look for the '99. The **Late Bottled Vintage Port** ($24-28), which is bottled unfiltered and is aged several years in wood and bottle before release, is sweet, dense, and altogether extraordinary; look for the '92. $65-100
Douro, Portugal
Imported by Premium Ports

Dow's
VINTAGE PORT
Full-bodied. Richly layered, and often quite tannic when young.
Owned by the Symington family, whose Scottish ancestor moved to Oporto in 1882 and founded a Port-producing dynasty, Dow

A PORT PRIMER

Tawny Port. Vintage Port. Ruby Port. What's the difference between these and the other designations you see on Port labels? From most expensive to least, here are the various styles.

Vintage Ports are wines from a single year's harvest that are blended and bottled after aging two or three years in wood. The customer is expected to cellar them and age them to maturity—often a ten-year-or-more wait. Only a few years in each decade are "declared" a vintage by each house, though in practice certain vintages (like 2000, 1997, and 1994) are universally declared. Vintage Port accounts for only about one percent of all ports sold. **Late-bottled Vintage Ports** (LVB), dated on their labels but aged a few years in wood and a few more in bottle, are designed to be drinkable on release. **Aged Tawny Ports** are blends of Ports barrel-aged six or more years so that they develop nutty, brown sugar flavors and silky texture. Less expensive versions have no indication of barrel age on the label, suggesting they're under ten years old. The best examples include ten-, twenty-, thirty-, and forty-year Tawnies, referring to the average amount of time spent in wood. The fruity **Ruby Port**, aged for two to three years, is the least complex because it goes almost straight to market after bottling.

Two other Port-related translations: A *quinta* (Portuguese for "farm") is a vineyard site or estate. A **single-*quinta* Port** is blended from grapes grown in the same vineyard.

makes what is considered a comparatively dry style of Vintage Port. Very powerful, fragrant, and saturated with blackberries and cocoa-dusted cherries, it pairs heartily with bread pudding and blue cheeses. Look for '94, '97, and '00 vintages. The rare **Crusted Port** ($22-25) is blended from multiple vintages, left unfiltered, and matured in the bottle before release. The vintage **Quinta do Bonfim** ($38-40) is a single-*quinta* opaque Port with a licoricey, pungent earthiness. $75-85

Douro, Portugal
Imported by Winebow

Taylor Fladgate
VINTAGE PORT
Full-bodied. Hugely flavorful and fragrant—hedonistic!
Considered by many the best producer, Taylor turns out Ports that are warm, sweet, smooth, and deep. Crammed with black currants and blueberries when young, this wine ages beautifully, developing a wealth of spices and secondary flavors. If food is a must, limit it to a handful of almonds. Look for 2000, '97, '94, and the bewitching '83. $95-200 (more for older vintages)

Douro, Portugal
Imported by Kobrand

MADEIRA: THE HAPPY ACCIDENT

The great fortified wine was accidentally "invented" by the English. En route to the colonies, British ships would stop at the south Atlantic island of Madeira and stock up on white wine made from native grapes. Sailors would then fortify the wine with alcohol distilled from cane sugar to help it survive the journey. Tropical temperatures and months of gentle rocking in a ship's hold wrought a miraculous transformation. Rather than being ruined, the cooked, oxidized, shaken wine was found to be the mellowest, nuttiest, most complex beverage imaginable.

Madeira winemakers soon learned to duplicate the conditions of ocean voyages, creating an important export both for Portugal and the English. Madeira was, in fact, the most popular alcoholic beverage in the American colonies during the Revolutionary War Era.

Modern Madeira is mostly made from five grapes. Red Tinta Negra Mole makes inexpensive blends; the four whites make the noble wines: Sercial, Verdelho, Bual and Malmsey, in ascending order of sweetness. **Justino Madeira "Rainwater"** ($10–12) is a light blend—modestly sweet and nutty, very mouthwatering, and enticing with soups and firm cheeses. (*Imported by Monsieur Henri*) The richer **Broadbent Madeira 5–Year "Reserve"** ($18–20) is redolent of roasted nuts, peaches, and orange oil; it makes a versatile after–dinner drink with dates and ripe, aged cheeses. (*Imported by F. Wildman*). **Blandy's Malmsey Madeira 15 Year** ($30–35) (500ml) is a cornucopia of dried fruits and treacle—a great partner for sweet cakes and pastries. (*Imported by Premium Port*).

Unfortunately, almost no vintage Madeiras are made anymore. Limited stocks are sold, however, through The Rare Wine Company. One triumphant example is **Verdelho d'Oliveiras 1912** ($275+), an alluringly dark, spicy wine that in some ways still seems young.

One of the beauties of Madeira is that you can open a bottle and pour from it for months without worrying about spoilage. The longer you leave it open, the better it gets!

VINS DOUX NATUREL

Though *vin doux naturel* means "naturally sweet wine," the sweetness of these wines actually comes from the process called *mutage*—the addition of spirit halfway through fermentation to halt the conversion of grape sugar to alcohol. Brought forth are very strong, very grapey wines with at least 14% alcohol—not fortified in the usual sense, but close enough.

The high-sugar Muscat and Grenache (white and red, respectively) are the usual grapes, and white *vins doux naturels* are generally sweeter and less alcoholic than the reds. The most famous is Muscat de Beaumes de Venise. If you haven't tried it, you're in luck. The example we recommend is amazingly inexpensive for a dessert wine—a good thing, since you'll probably be coming back for more.

Domaine Beaumalric
MUSCAT DE BEAUMES DE VENISE
Medium-bodied. Deeply
perfumed and pleasant.
Here's the other side of the Port/
Sherry coin. Grapey, flowery,
tender, this Beaumes de Venise
offers one of
the gentlest
palates in the
dessert wine
kingdom,
hiding its alcohol skillfully under
fresh fruit and sweetness. Chill it
and pair with a light pudding,
panna cotta, or fresh fruit. $14-16
Rhône, France
Imported by R. Kacher

Domaine Bressy Masson
RASTEAU Vin Doux Naturel
Full-bodied. Very sweet and
satiny on the palate.
This hearty organic version of a
Grenache *vin doux naturel* has
flavors and aromas of black fruit,
milk chocolate, and spiciness
underpinned by a little leathery
rusticity. Serve it after dinner with
blue cheese or dark chocolate-
covered nuts.
$15-17
Rhône, France
Imported by
Jeroboam

Mas Amiel
MAURY "Vintage"
Medium-bodied. Soft, suave,
and comforting.
Similar to tawny Port but more sundried in taste, this wine develops
flavors of dried apricots, orange
peel, and figs as it ages. Vintage
Maury is bottled young and aged a
year prior to release. Pair it with
milk-chocolate candies or fruitcake.
The **10 Ans d'Age Cuvée Speciale**
($28-30) is matured from June to
June (outdoors!) in seventy-liter
bonbonnes, or jars. Its creamy,
nutty complexity complements
blue cheeses. $18-20 (375ml)
Roussillon, France
Imported by North Berkeley

Domaine de la Casa Blanca
BANYULS
"Cuvée de la Saint Martin"
Medium-bodied. Sleek, spicy-
tasting, and highly complex.
This hails from the benchmark
producer of Banyuls, a wine
capable of real longevity. Awhirl
with raisin, maple, brown spice, and
coffee, it works *with* desserts
rather than overpowering them. It
is also one of the greatest cheese
wines in the world. $45-50
Roussillon, France
Imported by Vineyard
Brands/Robert Haas

DESSERT WINES

Many Americans, including plenty in the "red 'n' dry only" crowd, are taking a second look at dessert wines, traditionally seen as cloyingly sweet. That could be because of the marvelous, aromatic complexity that rewards wine drinkers who pay close attention. It could also be chalked up to the appearance of better wines and a better appreciation of them. The key to any sweet wine is *balance*. A well-made dessert wine seals the palate with sweetness as it refreshes it with lively acidity.

As strange as it may seem, many of the best dessert wines are in debt to a fungus. In its benevolent form botrytis (*Botrytis cinerea*) will infect grapes left on the vine late in the harvest and intensify their sugars and flavors by draining water from them through the grape skins. Because these grapes make such deeply sweet, long-lived wines, botrytis has gained the alternate name of noble rot (as it is called in these pages). Picking botrytized grapes is a painstaking process, which helps explain why most dessert wines are so expensive. Many of the legendary sweet wines of Germany and Sauternes are made from botrytized grapes, as are many dessert wines from California, Australia, and elsewhere.

The wines on these pages give you a chance to become acquainted with wines that could become standards on your list: Muscat (Moscato in Italy, Moscatel in Spain), one of the oldest (and grapiest) grapes in the world; Tokay, the Hungarian grape that yields some of the best (and priciest) dessert wines; and the ambrosial Auslese and Eiswein (ice wine) Rieslings. Even without a sweet tooth, a wine lover can hardly fail to appreciate the surprising side of some of the most interesting wines to emerge on the scene.

Under $20

Domaine de la Maletie
MONBAZILLAC
Medium-bodied. Quite sweet but also tangy, supple, and easy to enjoy.
If Sauternes is Bordeaux's fair-haired darling, Monbazillac is the forgotten stepchild. The good news is that the wines are similarly made, with Monbazillac often as delicious and much less costly. This example, crafted from tenderly ripe, late-harvest Sémillon, is like a liquified caramel apple. It drinks wonderfully on release with pastry and custards. $13-15
Bergerac, France
Imported by Monsieur Touton

La Sera
MALVASIA DI CASORZO
Light-bodied. A frothy, fruity, chillable red with only 5.5% alcohol.
Made from Malvasia Rosso, one of Italy's classic dessert grapes, this strawberry-scented red has a pleasantly astringent snap. Great for picnics, antipasti, spicy fare, or dark-chocolate mousse. $13-15
Piedmont, Italy
Imported by Matt Brothers

Union des Producteurs
CLAIRETTE DE DIE "Lou Lou"
Light-bodied. Frothy, creamy, and joyously fruity.
Made from 80% Muscat and 20% Clairette Blanc (a high-acid, low-

alcohol grape), this unique *pétillant* (frothy) specialty of the Rhône is just 5.5% alcohol and fresh as a late summer peach. It's a cool after-dinner match for cakes, trifle, or biscotti. $13-15
Rhône, France
Imported by Wines for Food

Ochoa
MOSCATEL DULCE
Light-bodied. A pale, lightly sweet Muscat of silken delicacy.
A lively cascade of peaches, tangerines, and white honey. Sound good? Try it with a fruit tart and you'll swoon. $15-18 (375ml)
Navarra, Spain
Imported by Frontier

Ca' del Solo
FREISA Frizzante
Light-bodied. A sweet, sassy, frothy essence of red berries with only 5% alcohol.
Soft bubbles, the fragrance of strawberries, and just enough sweetness make this a carefree after-dinner treat with berries in cream or peach cobbler. $16-18
Monterey, California

Selaks
ICE WINE
Light- to medium-bodied. Sweet-tart and enlivening on the palate.
Lime and honeysuckle spring from this tangy, sweet nectar, an interesting South Seas take on Eiswein. Made from varying blends of Riesling and Gewürz, it's a great match for crème caramel or flan. $16-18 (375ml)
Marlborough, New Zealand
Imported by American Estates

Concadoro
VIN SANTO "Cerasi"
Medium-bodied. Satiny and very nicely concentrated.
The "holy wine" of Tuscany is made from the concentrated essence of sun-dried grapes and aged in special small oak barrels called *caratelli*. This heady example, redolent of caramel and candied almonds, is a plunge into pleasure with a rich baklava, nut pastry, or biscotti. $16-18 (500ml)
Tuscany
Imported by J. Given

Domaine de l'Ancienne Cure
MONBAZILLAC
Light- to medium-bodied. A rich, honeyed character that suggests a Sauternes.
This late-harvest Sémillon is grown upstream from Sauternes and is similar in style to that region's famous wines: honeyed, soft, caramel-scented, and pleasantly tangy. It's a reasonably priced, reasonably sweet white for biscotti, cakes, and apple tarts. $18-20 (375ml)
Bergerac, France
Imported by Bayfield

Domaine Bourillon-Dorleans
VOUVRAY Demi-Sec
"La Coulée d'Argent"
Medium-bodied. Half-savory, half-sweet, it's drinkable during or after a meal.
The Demi-Sec on the label implies a wine with noticeable

sweetness, but bracing acidity keeps this one in perfect balance as a food partner. Flavors of fresh cream, apple, and caramelized lemon virtually quiver the palate.

THE OLDEST WINE IN THE WORLD

Guess where the oldest registered, individually labeled wine in the world comes from? Rome? Greece? Close. It's Cyprus.

The wine is Commandaria, dating to the Crusades and the Grand Commandery of the Knights of St. John of Jerusalem, a feudal holding on the island. Its vineyards produced the wine that would bear its name.

Reasonably priced **Keo Commandaria St. John** ($8–12), made from sun-dried white Xynisteri and red Mavro grapes, is redolent of dried apricots, pralines, and caramel. Sweet and tasty, it's an ideal match for baklava or sheep's milk cheese drizzled with honey. *Imported by Athenée*

Think sweetly rich dishes like sweet-and-sour fish or a pork roast stuffed with apricots. For dessert, go for something a little less sweet—say, lemon cookies or panettone. $18-20
Loire, France
Imported by M. Skurnik

Rivetti
MOSCATO D'ASTI
"La Spinetta"
Light-bodied. *Frizzante*, creamy and delightfully sweet.
Here's a frothy and aromatic semi-sparkling white from the hills near Asti in Italy's Piedmont region. Its low alcohol and billowing aromas of peach and melon make it a delightful picnic partner or a fine after-dinner drink with fresh fruit. On self-indulgent Sunday mornings it's a decadent treat with smoked whitefish and bagels with cream cheese. $18-20
Piedmont, Italy
Imported by M. Skurnik

$20 to $40

Bonny Doon
MUSCAT "Vin de Glacière"
Medium-bodied. Very sweet.
Vintner Randall Grahm's quirky take on Eiswein, Vin de Glacière ("wine of the icebox") captures the essence of frozen,

late-harvested grapes. Plump, peachy, and practically perfect, it's a pretty partner for poached pears and plum cakes. $20-22 (375ml)
California

Vasse Felix
NOBLE RIESLING
Medium-bodied. A flamboyant "stickie" from Australia.
Sourced from the Forest Hill vineyard in the remote state of Western Australia, this rich Riesling combines sultry, earthy, sun-ripened fruit with a nice lemon crème acidity. Like many sweet Rieslings, it owes its honeyed character to noble rot. Serve with apricot or peach tarts, grilled fruit, or pumpkin pie. $20-22
Western Australia
Imported by Old Bridge Cellars

Château Raymond-Lafon
SAUTERNES
Medium-bodied. A model of grace and balance, and a very fine cellar candidate.
In 1972 Pierre Meslier, the manager of Château d'Yquem, purchased the neighboring estate of Raymond-Lafon. The wine he now makes there is a gem. Honeyed and caramelly in its youth, it's supported by a bit of lemony acidity. Pair it with light desserts like pound cake or

meringues. It also goes well with foie gras. $20-22
Bordeaux
Imported by Bayfield

Saucelito Canyon
LATE HARVEST ZINFANDEL
Full-bodied. Intensely flavorful and concentrated with smooth texture.
This winery turns out great Zin practically every vintage from carefully tended hundred-year-old rootstock planted near San Luis Obispo. The LH is a mind-boggling mix of raspberry, chocolate, and plum compote. It's great with blue cheeses or a pear poached in red wine. $22-24 (375ml)
Arroyo Grande, California

Gutiérrez de la Vega
ALICANTE MUSCAT
"Casta Diva"
Medium- to full-bodied. Strong, musky, slick, and very sweet.
Imagine a mouthful of honey, marmalade, and dried apricot purée swirled together in a smooth elixir. Now think of enjoying it with bananas flambé or any rich, caramelized dessert. Decadent and exciting! $25-30
Alicante, Spain
Imported by Classical Wines

Chateau Pierre Bise
COTEAUX DU LAYON
BEAULIEU "L'Anclaie"
Medium-bodied. Creamy yet lively on the palate, with a long and juicy finish.
The flavor of apple dominates in this smooth, sensuous Chenin Blanc, accented by clover honey and a nice leafy "greenness." Fantastic with apple pie! It's

also an original choice for foie gras. $25-30 (375ml)
Loire, France
Imported by Louis/Dressner

Olivares
DULCE MONASTRELL
Full-bodied. A luscious, purple, powerful dessert wine.
Pruney, very sweet, and intensely concentrated, this wine made from the grape Monastrell (a.k.a. Mourvèdre) tastes like a pan-seared reduction of red wine sweetened with chocolate and lavender. Serve it with Spanish blue cheeses like Cabrales and Idiazabal, dried plums or prunes, or a dark-chocolate cake with blueberries. $25-35 (500ml)
Alicante, Spain
Imported by Rare Wine

Selbach–Oster
RIESLING Auslese
"Zeltinger Himmelreich"
Medium-bodied.
Great finesse and length.
This is vintner Johannes Selbach's best, with its zingy, peachy palate and a solid slate foundation. These wines get very diesely for the first five or six years of cellaring, then settle down and become smooth and pleasing. When it's ready, enjoy with cheeses or custards. $28-30
Mosel, Germany
Imported by M. Skurnik/Terry Theise

Domaine Baumard
COTEAUX DU LAYON
"Cuvée Le Paon"
Medium-bodied. Plump and creamy but not too sweet.
In this wine the vibrant Chenin Blanc flavors of spiced apple and banana and the delicate scents of minerals are nicely amplified by sweetness. *Paon* means

ICE WINES

*S*OME DESSERT WINES get their sweetness from grapes that were botrytized with noble rot (as defined on page 210), but in other cases the same concentration of sugar and acidity is brought about when grapes freeze on the vine. These Eisweins (Anglicized from the German to "ice wines") date only from the early 1960s, when the first Eisweins vintage in Germany was released. Four decades later they gain steam with each passing year in spite of their high cost. (Less expensive ice wines, all of them made outside Germany, can be found on pages 211 and 212.)

The frozen grapes for Eisweins are picked and pressed immediately so that most of the water in the grapes separates out as ice. The sweet, concentrated juice left over (grape juice has a lower freezing point than water) is the basis of Eisweins.

An affordable example of this chilly delicacy, **Fitz–Ritter Riesling Eiswein "Durkheimer Hochbenn"** ($50–55 for 500ml), is opulently sweet and vibrant when young and becomes more plush as it matures. Its pineapple, mango, and other tropical flavors are given a freshening lift from buzzing, limelike acidity. It's a gorgeous partner for key lime pie. *Imported by Chapin Cellars*

One of the raciest Eisweins is **Karlsmuhle Riesling Eiswein "Lorenzhofer"** ($85–100 for 375ml). Bursting with fresh ginger, lemon blossoms, key limes, and coriander, it pulls off a fantastic balancing act of ripe fruit and delicacy. Serve it with a grilled pear and slivers of a salty blue cheese. If the cost of this jewel is prohibitive, drink the exquisite **Karlsmuhle Riesling Auslese "Lorenzhofer"** at half the price. *Imported by M. Skurnik/Terry Theise*

Dr. F. Weins–Prum Riesling Eiswein "Bernkasteler Johannis-brunnchen" ($100–125) is a bountifully rich example from Mosel. Flavors hit the palate with clarity and force—tropical fruit, lemon custard, wet stones, and sugar-glazed flowers are just a few of many. Cellar this one or serve it with fruity desserts and creamy pastries. Finally, for those who prefer absolute power and vigor (and for whom price is no object), there is no better wine we know than the **Robert Weil Riesling Eiswein "Kiedrich Grafenberg"** ($300–400). High levels of residual sugars and acid allow this wine to age beautifully when it is properly cellared. *Imported by Cellars International/Rudi Wiest*

peacock—as in a peacock's tail of flavors fanning out on your palate. It's fruit-saturated and appealing when young, though some fans like to cellar it. Serve at a holiday party with apple tart or pound cake with lemon crème frosting. $33-35
Loire, France
Imported by Monsieur Touton

Von Buhl
RIESLING Auslese GoldKap "Forster Ungeheuer"
Medium-bodied. Mind-bendingly ripe and honeyed.
Enjoy a ladling of clover honey, berries, and broiled peaches in the abundantly fruit-saturated style this producer is known for. The bracing acidity that keeps it from cloying also keeps it alive in the cellar for thirty (even forty) years. It's a treat with a dish of candied fruits, pineapple cake, or no food whatsoever. $34-36 (375ml)
Pfalz, Germany
Cellars International/Rudi Wiest

Von Hovel
RIESLING Auslese "Oberemmeler Hutte"
Light- to medium-bodied. An exceedingly delicate Riesling with distinctive freshness.
Baron Eberhard von Kunow typically produces winsome Rieslings—like this glassy, pure Auslese cascading with minerals, green apples, and wildflowers. The Hutte vineyard is pebbly and steep, a source for refined sweet wines occasionally honeyed by noble rot. Sip it after dinner with pastry or madeleines. $34-38 (375ml)
Saar, Germany
Imported by Cellars International/Rudi Wiest

Tommaso Bussola
RECIOTO DELLA VALPOLICELLA "bg"
Full-bodied. A deeply sweet, thick, sensuous red of extravagant proportions.
From one of Italy's most revered producers comes this Recioto, a wine whose grapes have been specially selected and partially dried to concentrate their flavors. The result is Portlike but not as alcoholic; winelike but more raisiny; liqueurlike but more complex; and a perfect after-dinner pleasure. Try it with a fresh hunk of Parmigiano-Reggiano or chocolate biscotti. The rarer, pricier "tb" ($90-100) is pursued by collectors. $35-40
Veneto, Italy
Imported by Rare Wine

Over $40

Fritz Haag
RIESLING Auslese "Brauneberger Juffer-Sonnenuhr"
Medium-bodied. Certainly sweet, but the acidity wakes up your palate.
Herb-kissed limes and lemons, ginger, vanilla, and an elusive saltiness from minerality persist on the palate of this Auslese. In warm, wet years, noble rot adds a honeyed and almost woodsy element. Cellar this wine and wait for a most auspicious occasion before serving it. $45-50
Mosel, Germany
Imported by Cellars International

H. Donnhoff
RIESLING Auslese "Niederhauser Hermannshohle"
Light- to medium-bodied. Great clarity and purity of flavor.
This wine astonishes in every vintage. Suggestions of

tangerines, peaches, tea leaves, and rain-wet pebbles waft from each sip. It's a long-term cellar candidate (20+ years) and a sublime match for fresh foie gras or the sticky black sesame buns of Szechuan cuisine. $45-60 (375ml)
Nahe, Germany
Imported by M. Skurnik/Terry Theise

Domaine Zind-Humbrecht
RIESLING Vendange Tardive "Brand"
Full-bodied. Rich in everything—sugar, alcohol, and sheer force of flavor.
This masterful late-harvest Riesling is a powerhouse from ancient vines. Redolent of caramel, broiled peaches, and lemon drops, it is sweet but not overly so, and its deep earthiness rebounds on the finish. It is traditional with seared slices of foie gras (especially with a fruit element) or the pungent Alsatian Münster, a cheese intimidating to lesser wines. $50-55
Alsace, France
Imported by Kermit Lynch

C. von Schubert
RIESLING Auslese "Maximin Grünhauser Abtsberg"
Medium-bodied. Practically glowing with fruit when young, then swiftly turning savory and subtle in later years.
Baron Carl von Schuber's Auslese, from selected bunches of late-ripened, botrytized grapes, boasts dozens of exotic fruit notes and a minerally aroma that reflects the *terroir*. As the wine ages, it drops much of its sweetness and becomes a

sipping wine, albeit very complex and smooth. Vanilla cream cakes or trifle would be a fun pairing if the wine is young; after more bottle age, sip it solo. $50-60
Ruwer, Germany
Imported by Valckenberg

Bodegas Oremus
TOKAJI ASZU "5 Puttonyos"
Medium- to full-bodied. Sweet and completely mouthfilling.
The legendary dessert wine of Hungary, Tokaji (the "*j*" is silent) is crafted from indigenous grapes, mainly Furmint and Harslevelu. *Puttonyos* are basketfuls of dried, late-harvested grapes added to the base wine to increase its sweetness (six *puttonyos* is the maximum). Its concentrated core of dried peach, apricot, and nut fondant will develop for decades in the cellar. Serve it on its own or with biscotti, rich cakes, cobblers, or even foie gras. $55-60 (500ml)
Hungary
Imported by M. Skurnik

J. J. Christoffel Erben
RIESLING Auslese "Ürziger Würzgarten"
Light- to medium-bodied. Enticing sweetness balanced by shimmeringly fresh acidity.
Hans Leo Christoffel releases several Ausleses every year, labeling different cuvées with one, two, or three stars. Though subtly different, all serve as vehicles for the slate, honey, and pungent florality of the Würzgarten ("spice garden"). Wines this delicate and contemplation-worthy are best tasted by themselves rather than with food. $68-70
Mosel, Germany
Imported by M. Skurnik/ Terry Theise

STORING WINE

MOST WINE LOVERS don't waste too much energy worrying about wine storage, nor should they. At the same time, they'd do well to acquaint themselves with the basics.

Luckily, learning how to store a wine properly to make sure it maintains or reaches optimum drinkability doesn't require a class or seminar. All it takes is noting a few facts: First, wine deteriorates when it's exposed to sunlight or gets "too hot," meaning a temperature over 77°F or so. Second, wines meant to be stored for a year or more should be kept in a place with reasonable humidity; otherwise, the cork could dry out, shrink, and let air seep in. Third, if wine gets cold enough to freeze, it will expand and force the cork to pop out.

The type of wine is another consideration. Most white wines and inexpensive to moderately priced reds are meant to be drunk right away, and won't suffer from being stood on a counter for a few days. If you wait longer before enjoying your latest purchase, give some thought as to how to store it; this is essential if you have a certain red you want to keep for a longer period of time.

How important is it to store the bottle horizontally or angled rather than standing up? For short-term storage (anything under a couple of months), not very. Long-term storage is another matter: Horizontal is the answer, since the cork needs to be kept moist so it won't shrink and let in oxygen—the reason wine racks were invented.

"Cellaring"

The word "cellaring" may call to mind an Irish lord poking around in the castle's musty depths, but it's simply wine lingo for long-term storage. Your "cellar" could be anything from a kitchen cupboard to the floor of a closet to a spare dresser drawer. The temperature (ideally around 65°F) is your primary consideration. Also make sure the bottles won't be disturbed: Vibrations or anything else that shakes a wine up even slightly can throw off the precious balance of its elements.

Leftover Wine

The party's over, so what do you do with that half-bottle of Chablis or Bordeaux you're loath to pour down the drain? First, be aware that the fuller-bodied the wine, the longer it lasts. To keep oxygen out of leftover wine, plastic levered stoppers, rubber stoppers (often part of a vacuum kit), or a chrome, rubber-lined winestopper with a handle are preferable to shoving the cork back in. For an anti-oxidation double whammy, store the stoppered wine in the fridge, which will prolong its drinkability. Generally speaking, reds should stay drinkable for up to four days, whites for two to three days.

Another tip: The more air space there is in a leftover wine, the faster the wine will oxidize. Pouring it into a smaller screw-top container—say, a club-soda or tonic-water bottle from a six-pack—could mean an extra day or two of drinkability.

GLOSSARY

abundant *See* generous.

acidity The acid content of a wine (largely tartaric acid, which occurs naturally in grapes). Acidity makes wine "juicy" in the mouth—imperative in white wines. Acidity also allows certain white wines to cellar well.

AOC Abbreviation for *Appellation d'Origine Contrôlée* ("protected place of origin"), the French system that sets standards for three categories of wine. In order of quality, the categories are *Vins d'Apellation d'Origine Contrôlée* (AOC); *Vins Délimités de Qualité Supérieure* (VDQS); and *Vins de Pays* (country wines).

appellation The name of the place from which a wine originates, determined by a country's laws and often a part of the wine's name. *See also* AOC, DO, DOC, DOCG.

astringent Describes the puckering effect that tannins or acids in wine have on the mouth. Not necessarily a pejorative term.

balance The relative proportions of a wine's structural elements, such as alcohol, residual sugar, acid, fruit, and tannin. In a well-balanced wine, no one component stands out.

barnyard(y) An aroma that is the quintessence of Burgundy, and positive in connotation. Characterized by the aroma of stables, including loam and damp hay.

barrel-aged Used to describe wines (usually white) that have spent time in wood barrels after fermentation. The wines receive oxygen through the barrels, turning them darker, softer, and frequently sweeter. *See also* oak.

barrel-fermented Describes wines fermented in wood barrels, most often of oak. The result is a richer wine, often sweeter and higher in alcohol.

barrique A small new oak barrel (225 liters, or nearly 60 gallons) used for aging and storing wine. Originally a Bordeaux design, now in global use.

big Describes wines that are especially full or intense. *See also* full; intense.

biodynamism System of organic grape growing and winemaking based on the holistic principles of Austrian philosopher Rudolph Steiner. Known as *biodynamie* in France, it combines principles of astronomy and homeopathy with total avoidance of conventional fertilizers, herbicides, or pesticides in the vineyard.

blend A wine made from the juice of different grape varieties or the wines of different vineyards, regions, or vintages.

blush wine A wine made pink when the skins of black grapes are left to briefly soak in the fermenting must.

body Impression of a wine's weight in the mouth—light, medium, or full.

botrytis *See* noble rot.

bouquet Aromas of a wine. Also called nose.

bready *See* yeasty.

bright Describes a wine whose aroma or flavor, is vividly perceived.

buttery A term used to describe wines—usually whites that have undergone malolactic fermentation— that 1) taste like butter from the resulting diacetyl compounds or 2) feel "buttery-smooth" from the softening of acidity.

carbonic maceration A fermentation method in which bunches of whole grapes are placed in a closed tank so that the weight of the top bunches crushes those at the bottom.

Fermentation then takes place inside each grape of the top bunches, leading to extremely fruity wines such as those of Beaujolais. Also called whole-berry fermentation.

character The personality or overall impression a wine makes on the taster—"serious," "fun," "insipid," etc.

château The French word for castle, most commonly referring to estates in Bordeaux. Despite the translation, a château can be a single small building.

chewy Mouthfeel term for a wine so rich and concentrated that it creates the impression of chewiness; often applied to highly tannic wines.

clos French term for a vineyard surrounded by a wall.

compact Describes wines that are not "big" but give the impression of intensity. *See also* big, intense.

complex, complexity Describes a wine with several aromas and flavors; often a product of maturation in the bottle.

concentration The perceived or actual density of a wine.

co-op Short for cooperative. A consortium of growers who pool their resources to produce a single wine or brand of wines.

crackling Describes wine with a light sparkle.

crisp Said of a wine (usually young), with pleasant tartness; opposite of soft.

cru French for both "growth" and "vineyard," used to designate a vineyard often classified as high-quality. Grand Cru ("great growth") is the highest designation in Burgundy, Alsace, and Champagne. Premier Cru ("first growth") is the highest in Bordeaux.

cuvée A special bottling made separately from an estate's regular wine.

depth Attributed to full-bodied wines with multiple layers of flavor. *See also* intensity, complexity.

descriptor(s) The word(s) used to describe the flavors or aromas of a wine, usually comparative. Typical nouns include herbs, berries, flowers, or generalized references to orchard fruits (apples, pears, quince) or brown spices (cloves, nutmeg, cinnamon). Often-used adjectives include buttery, citrusy, cedary, plummy, etc. Some descriptors, like weedy or musty, are considered pejorative. *See also* earthy, floral, fruity, minerally, woody.

DO Abbreviation for *Denominación de Origen*, the Spanish equivalent of France's AOC.

DOC Abbreviation for Spain's *Denominación de Origen Calificada*, the highest classification; Portuguese *Denominaçao de Origen Contralad;* or Italian *Denominazione di Origine Controllata*, all the equivalent of France's AOC.

DOCG Abbreviation for *Denominazione di Origine Controllata e Garantita*, Italy's highest classification.

domaine The French word for a wine-making estate (especially in Burgundy, the Loire, and Alsace) that owns one vineyard or parts of many.

dry Describes a wine in which all or most of the sugars have been converted to alcohol during fermentation. Little or no sweetness is perceived. A dry wine with a slight touch of sweetness is variously described as off-dry, medium-dry, or semi-dry.

earthy, earthiness Describes a nice flavor or aroma evocative of the soil. *See also* terroir.

elegant, elegance Most often used to describe a well-balanced, high-quality wine with evident finesse.

estate The physical holdings of a winery, including all facilities.

estate–bottled In America this term refers to a wine that has been grown at vineyards the winery owns and vinified and bottled at the winery itself. Other countries' definitions are looser.

fat Said of wine that is fruit-saturated and weighty on the palate, but not necessarily tannic.

fermentation The complex process by which yeasts devour the sugars in grape juice, producing the by-products ethyl alcohol and carbon dioxide.

filtering The process by which winemakers remove unwanted solid matter from their wines prior to bottling. This is often accomplished with layers of porous fabric or cardboard. Controversy has arisen over whether this partially strips the finished wine of flavors.

fining The clarification of wine by removing its volatile or unstable molecules. The traditional clarifying agent, egg white, is now often replaced with minerals, clays, or proteins.

finish In simplest terms, the aftertaste of a wine; more technically, the impression of flavor and texture that remains after a wine has been swallowed or spit.

firm An impression of solidity or "chewable" texture in a wine, caused by structural elements such as tannin or acidity. *See also* chewy.

first growth *See* cru.

flabby Said of a wine that lacks adequate acidity.

floral, flowery Describes a wine with aromas of nonspecific flowers.

frizzante Italian for lightly sparkling. Often applied to Prosecco, Lambrusco, and Moscato wines.

fruity Describes a wine whose primary aroma or flavor is that of fresh fruit. Typical fruity wines include Beaujolais (Gamay), Riesling, Muscat, Zinfandel, and Barbera among others.

full Describes the body of a wine with an abundance of extract, alcohol, and/or tannin; a texture that seems to fill up the mouth. *See also* body.

generous Said of wines with characteristics that are full-flavored in the mouth or are expressive enough to be easily perceived. Synonyms include abundant and giving.

giving *See* generous.

Grand Cru *See* cru.

harmonious An old-fashioned term, more in use in Europe today, that describes a wine of particularly appealing balance. *See also* balance.

intense, intensity Describes a wine with a strong character, one that cannot be ignored. Not a pejorative, although often perceived as so by consumers.

late harvest (abbr. LH) Applied to wines made from very ripe grapes picked late in the growing season. Usually very sweet, late harvest wines are often used as dessert wines.

lees The spent matter left over from fermentation, including dead yeast cells, skins, and other grape fragments. Wines aged on their lees are often richer in flavor and texture.

length The amount of time a wine's flavor remains in the mouth after it has been spit or swallowed. *See also* finish.

light Describes the body of a wine that feels delicate or airy in the mouth.

Not a pejorative "light" is sometimes a great compliment, since wine can feel light yet offer abundant flavor. Light wines with little flavor are critiqued as thin. *See also* thin.

lively Said of a wine that is tingly on the tongue, whether because of acidity or carbonation.

luxurious Describes particularly lush, flavorful wines, usually with soft mouthfeel.

malolactic fermentation The secondary fermentation, often artificially induced, that converts naturally occurring malic acid (the acid in apples) into lactic acid (the acid in milk), giving wine a creamy mouthfeel.

medium–dry *See* dry.

medium–sweet Often used to describe dessert–grade and fortified wines, including Sherry and Madeira, whose sugars remain in balance.

minerally, mineral, minerality An aromatic suggestion of stones, wet rocks, or flint. Many tasters recognize it as the smell of a clean sidewalk just after a rain. A source of complexity, particularly in white wine. *See also* terroir.

mouthfeel The combined sensation of all aspects of a wine on the tongue, gums, and palate—one of the most important criteria by which a wine's quality is judged. *See also* texture.

must The fermenting juice, skins, seeds, pulp, etc. of grapes.

négotiants French for "merchant." A person or firm that purchases fruit or finished wine, then blends, bottles, and ships it under his or her own label. Those who work with the growers and take an artisanal approach are known colloquially as *petit négotiants*.

noble rot A beneficial fungus (*Botrytis cinerea*), the mold of which penetrates grape skins and saps water from the juice. The concentration of sugar, flavor, and acid in the grapes results in very sweet, complex wines.

nonvintage A wine blended from grapes that were picked in more than one year. Also the largest category of Champagne.

nose *See* bouquet.

oak The wood from which most wine barrels are made, varying in provenance. American white oak, from the eastern U.S., is used for many California Zinfandels and Australian and Spanish wines, while more expensive French oak (from designated forests such as Limousin, Nevers, and Tronçais) is used for Bordeaux, Burgundy, and many prestigious wines from around the world. Oak barrels also vary in age, with **new oak** imparting strong flavors and tannins and **old oak** (previously used) imparting none. Some unfinished barrels are given a "toast" or "char" over fires that partly burn their interiors, thus caramelizing the sugars in the wood; a heavily charred barrel imparts strong, sweet, or smoky flavors to the wine. Not all oak influence comes from barrels: Cost-conscious wineries may buy oak chips in nylon sacks (the chips come in light, medium, or heavy char), which they dip like giant tea bags into fermenting or aging wines to impart the desired oaky flavor—very typical of Californian and Australian wines costing less than $10. Less scrupulous wineries add oakiness with powders, essences, and artificial flavorings.

off–dry *See* dry.

Oenology The study or science of wines and winemaking. Also spelled enology.

palate Literally the soft, fleshy surfaces at the top and bottom of the mouth. In wine parlance the palate has come to mean 1) the physical tasting platform of the mouth—as in, "That wine feels great on the palate" and 2) the natural ability of the taster to judge the quality of wines as in, ("He's got a very sophisticated palate.")

petit négotiant See négociant.

phylloxera Plant–eating louse native to North America that migrated and devastated European vineyards in the nineteenth century, then rebounded in American vineyards at the end of the twentieth. Planting in sandy soils or grafting vines onto genetically resistant rootstock have thus far been the only defense against this persistent pest, which burrows in the soil and feeds on the roots of vine plants.

plush Describes wine that is texturally luxurious on the tongue.

Premier Cru *See* cru.

release A wine that is commercially available from a winery, or the official offering of that wine for sale.

reserve Supposedly the best (or better) cuvée from a winery, "reserved" for special customers or the winemakers themselves. In practice, use of the term usually describes a wine that has spent more time in oak, for better or worse. Reserve wines are more expensive than a winery's regular offerings.

rich Said of wine with particularly pronounced flavor, texture, or both.

round Describes a wine that feels smooth and ample in the mouth, lacking sharpness or "edges."

Schloss The German word for castle, similar to *château* in France.

second label A wine priced lower, bottled separately, and given a different name and label than a winery's regular offerings.

silky Refers either to a wine's mouthfeel or the quality of its tannins.

Suggests a seductive softness reminiscent of the feel of spun silk.

single–vineyard A wine whose grapes were grown in one vineyard, often named on its label. *See also* cru.

smooth Describes a wine that glides easily and pleasingly over the palate.

soft A mouthfeel term used to describe a wine whose acidity and/or tannins are minimal. Can imply "gentle" in a positive context or "insipid" in a negative one. *See also* crisp.

spritzy A wine with either lively sparkle or the high acidity that creates a sparkling impression.

spumante A catch–all term for Italian wines that sparkle.

structure, structural components The combination of all a wine's physical elements that constitute its mouthfeel: acidity, sugar, alcohol, extract, tannin (if any), oak (if any), etc. A poorly structured wine is one exhibiting an imbalance in these elements; a well–structured or "well–crafted" one is balanced—and, by implication, likely to age well.

supple Describes a wine that simply feels good in the mouth, offering ample fruit and a gentle enough structure that it can be enjoyed at its current state of development.

sur lie The French term for a wine aged on its lees. *See also* lees.

sweetness The perceived sensation of sugar in a wine—not to be confused with actual sugar content. A wine with less sugar and low acidity can actually taste sweeter than a wine with a bit more sugar but much higher acidity; it's all in the balance. Sweetness, which implies ripeness, is inherently good. A technically dry red, like a red Zinfandel, can have fruit so ripe–tasting that it seems "sweet," and saying that such a wine has "beautiful sweetness" is high praise.

tannin(s) A complex group of chemical compounds found in tree bark, tea, and the skins of many fruits, including grapes. They play a major role in the aging of wine—particularly red wines, the pigmented tannins of which impart color and sensory qualities. In the mouth, astringent (drying) tannins taste slightly bitter and cause a puckering sensation.

terroir A French term that encompasses the climatic, geographic, geologic, and environmental aspects of a vineyard. A wine that reflects the character of the place from which it comes is said to be *terroir*-driven or expressive of its *terroir*. Some wine writers use the term, for which there is no English equivalent, as a synonym for earthy or minerally.

texture An alternate word for mouthfeel.

thin Pejorative term describing wines that lack concentration or flavor.

tight Describes a wine whose tannins need time to settle down, meaning it is too young to enjoy. Synonyms include closed, mute, and dumb.

unfiltered *See* filtering.

unfined *See* fining.

unripe, underripe Said of a wine whose grapes were picked before they were fully ripe and thus usually have more acidity and less character.

varietal Term for a wine named after the dominant grape variety from which it is made. An adjective, it is commonly misused as a noun.

vegetal Describes a family of flavors reminiscent of green vegetables. The term is often used as a synonym for unripe.

vendage tardive French for "late harvest." An official label designation in Alsace. Sometimes appears in plural form.

vin de pays French for "wine from the country." A category of the French appellation system, it is also a catchall term for inexpensive French wines. *See also* AOC.

vin doux naturel French for "naturally sweet wines." The sweetness, however, comes from the fortifying process called *mutage*—the addition of spirit halfway through fermentation to halt the conversion of grape sugar to alcohol. The resulting wine is semi-, rather than fully, fortified.

vinification The process of winemaking.

vintage The year in which the grapes for a wine were picked. Vintage wines tend to be more highly regarded than nonvintage wines.

viticulture The growing of grapes for the purpose of winemaking.

weight *See* body.

weingut German for "winery."

whole-berry fermentation A nontechnical term for carbonic maceration. *See also* carbonic maceration.

woody A term, usually pejorative, for wines whose oak flavors are particularly evident.

yeasty Describes wines with pungent, floral aromatics derived from time spent on their lees; bready is a common synonym.

THE U.S. WINERIES

Some of the wineries whose wines were chosen for this book maintain Web sites that leave no stone unturned, providing contact information, retail store locations, and sometimes selling their wines online. (Note: Browsing wineries' Web sites is also a fun diversion, giving you a glimpse of the personal side of winemaking.) You can get in touch with some other wineries only by phone—or better still, a prearranged visit should you happen to be in their neck of the woods.

California

ALBAN VINEYARDS
http://www.albanvineyards.com

ALEXANDER VALLEY VINEYARDS
http://www.carterhouse.com/atlas/
    wineries/alexval.html

AU BON CLIMAT WINERY
http://www.aubonclimat.com

AVILA WINERY
http://www.avilawine.com

BAREFOOT CELLARS
http://www.barefootwine.com

BARNWOOD VINEYARDS
http://www.barnwoodwine.com

BARON HERZOG WINERY
http://www.baronherzog.com

BELEVEDERE VINEYARDS AND WINERY
http://www.belvederewinery.com

BENSON FERRY VINEYARDS
http://www.bensonferry.com

BERNARDUS WINERY AND VINEYARD
http://www.bernardus.com

BLACKSTONE WINERY
http://www.blackstonewinery.com/
    0.0.0_flash.html

BLOCKHEADIA WINERY
http://www.blockheadia.com/

BOGLE VINEYARDS
http://www.boglewinery.com

BONNY DOON VINEYARD
http://www.bonnydoonvineyard.com

BOUCHAINE VINEYARDS
http://www.bouchaine.com

CA' DEL SOLO WINES
See Bonny Doon Vineyard

CALERA VINEYARDS
http://www.calerawine.com/vineyards

CAPAY VALLEY VINEYARDS
http://www.capayvalleyvineyards.com

CAPIAUX CELLARS
http://www.capiauxcellars.com

CARNEROS CREEK WINERY
http://www.carneros-creek.com

CARTLIDGE & BROWNE WINERY
http://www.cartlidgebrowne.com

CASTLE ROCK WINERY
http://www.castlerockwinery.com

CAYMUS VINEYARDS
http://www.caymus.com

CLAY STATION VINEYARDS
http://www.delicato.com/cs_vineyard/
    history.asp

CLINE CELLARS
http://www.clinecellars.com/

CLOS DU BOIS WINERY
http://www.closdubois.com/home.
asp

CLOS LA CHANCE WINERY
http://www.closlachance.com/
frameset.asp

CLOS MIMI WINERY
http://www.closmimi.com

CLOS PEGASE WINERY
http://www.clospegase.com

COSENTINO WINERY
http://www.cosentinowinery.com

COTURRI NATURAL WINES
http://www.coturriwinery.com/
main.html

DARIOUSH WINERY
http://www.darioush.com/
index2.html

DAVID BRUCE WINERY
http://www.davidbrucewinery.com
/history4.htm

DE LOACH VINEYARDS
http://www.deloachvineyards.com

DUCKHORN WINE COMPANY
http://www.duckhorn.com

EASTON WINERY
http://www.terrerougewines.com

EDMEADES WINERY
http://www.edmeades.com

EDMONDS ST. JOHN WINERY
http://www.edmundsstjohn.com

FESS PARKER WINERY AND
VINEYARD
http://www.fessparker.com/html/
winery.html

FIFE VINEYARDS
http://www.fifevineyards.com

FORMAN VINEYARDS
http://www.foremanvineyard.com

FOXEN VINEYARDS
(805) 937-4251

GARY FARRELL VINEYARDS
AND WINERY
http://www.garyfarrell.com

GIRARD WINERY
http://www.girardwinery.com

GRGICH HILLS CELLAR
http://www.grgich.com/index.html

GRUET WINERY
http://www.gruetwinery.com

HAGAFEN CELLARS
http://www.hagafen.com

HAVENS WINE CELLARS
http://www.havenswine.com

HEITZ CELLARS
http://www.heitzcellar.com

JORY WINERY
http://www.jorywinery.com

JOSEPH PHELPS VINEYARDS
http://www.jpvwines.com

LANE TANNER WINERY
http://www.lanetanner.com

MCMANIS FAMILY VINEYARD
http://www.mcmanisfamily
vineyards.com/

MACROSTIE WINERY
AND VINEYARDS
http://www.macrostiewinery.com

MARIETTA CELLARS
http://www.mariettacellars.com

MARTINE'S WINES
http://www.mwines.com

MIDNIGHT CELLARS
http://www.midnightcellars.com

MIETZ CELLARS
http://www.mietzcellars.com

MONTERRA WINERY
http://www.monterrawine.com

MOSS BRIDGE WINERY
http://www.mossbridgewinery.com

MOUNT EDEN VINEYARDS
http://www.mounteden.com

MURPHY-GOODE ESTATE WINERY
http://murphygoodewinery.com

NEWTON VINEYARD
http://www.clicquotinc.com/
    newton/index.asp

OJAI VINEYARD, THE
http://www.ojaivineyard.com

PAGOR/ROLLING HILLS
VINEYARDS
805-484-8100

PHILLIPE-LORRAINE VINEYARDS
707-963-0121

RAMSAY WINES
http://www.kentrasmussenwinery.
    com/wines/ramsay_wines.html

RANCHO ZABACO WINERY
http://www.ranchozabaco.com/
    home.html

RENWOOD WINERY
http://www.renwood.com/
    ourwines.cfm

R. H. PHILLIPS WINERY
http://www.rhphillips.com

SAUCELITO CANYON VINEYARD
AND WINERY
http://www.saucelitocanyon.com

SCHRAMSBERG VINEYARDS
http://www.schramsberg.com

SEGHESIO FAMILY VINEYARDS
http://www.seghesio.com

SHENANDOAH VINEYARDS
http://www.sobonwine.com

SHOOTING STAR
See Steele Wines

SPELLETICH CELLARS WINERY
http://www.spellwine.com

SPRING MOUNTAIN VINEYARD
http://www.springmtn.com

STEELE WINES
http://www.steelewines.com

SUMMERS WINERY AND VINEYARDS
http://www.summerswinery.com

TALBOTT VINEYARDS
http://www.talbottvineyards.com

TOAD HOLLOW VINEYARDS
http://www.toadhollow.com

VINUM CELLARS
http://www.vinumcellars.com/flash/
    vc_main.html

WATERSTONE
Z Wine Company
707-253-2511

WYATT WINES
http://www.polanerselections.com

Connecticut
SHARPE HILL VINEYARD
http://www.sharpehill.com

New Mexico
GRUET WINERY
http://www.gruetwinery.com

New York State
DR. KONSTANTIN FRANK'S VINIFERA
WINE CELLARS
http://drfrankwines.com

GALLUCCIO FAMILY WINERY
http://www.gallucciowineries.com

MILLBROOK VINEYARDS
AND WINERY
http://www.millbrookwine.com

PAUMANOK VINEYARDS
http://www.paumanok.com

PELLEGRINI VINEYARDS
http://pellegrinivineyards.com

RED NEWT CELLARS
http://www.rednewt.com/site/
    index.html

SCHNEIDER VINEYARDS
http://www.schneidervineyards.
    com/A_001.html

WARWICK VALLEY WINERY
http://www.wvwinery.com

Oregon

ADELSHEIM VINEYARD
http://www.adelsheim.com/
    consumer/index.html

ARGYLE WINERY
http://www.argylewinery.com

CRISTOM VINEYARDS
http://www.cristomwines.com

DOMAINE DROUHIN
http://www.domainedrouhin.com

EOLA HILLS WINE CELLARS
http://www.eolahillswinery.com

LANGE ESTATE WINERY &
VINEYARDS
http://www.langewinery.com/
    aboutus.htm
l
PATRICIA GREEN CELLARS
503-554-0821
winery@patriciagreencellars.com

O'REILLY WINERY
http://www.northwest-wine.com/
    oreillys-winery.html

WILLAKENZIE ESTATE WINERY
http://www.avalonwine.com/
    Willakenzie-Estate-Winery.htm

WILLAMETTE VALLEY VINEYARDS
http://www.wvv.com

Texas

PHEASANT RIDGE WINERY
www.pheasantridgewinery.com

Washington

L'ECOLE NO. 41
www.lecole.com/thewinery.htm

PEPPER BRIDGE
www.pepperbridge.com

POWERS WINERY
www.badgermtnvineyard.com

WOODWARD CANYON WINERY
www.woodwardcanyon.com

IMPORTERS OF FOREIGN WINES

Wines can have multiple importers on a national level, so the importer we specify for a featured wine may or may not be the source for it in your area. Also, importers change constantly as contracts and relationships change. Thus, if you go wine hunting, the contact information we provide here may be your final call or your first of several. At least you'll be on the track to finding the wine you seek.

Note: The level of information found on an importer's Web site varies. Most provide a phone number, some list wine retailers by state, and others make it possible for you to purchase a wine online. Importers without Web sites can be reached by phone or e-mail.

AV IMPORTS
http://www.avimports.com

ABARBANEL
http://www.kosher-wine.com

ALAIN JUNGUENET SELECTION
908-654-6173; junguenet@aol.com

AMERICAN ESTATE WINES
908-273-5060;
wines@eamericanestates.com

AMERICAN WINE DISTRIBUTORS
415-775-2656

ARTISAN WINES
800-847-2780; arttwine@snet.net

ATHENÉE
www.atheneeimporters.com

BARON FRANÇOIS LTD.
http://www.baronfrancois.com

BAYFIELD IMPORTING LTD.
718-091910; natebayfield@aol.com

BILLINGTON IMPORTS/
CHAPIN CELLARS
http://www.billingtonwines.com

BLUEGRASS-CATALUNYA
INTERNATIONAL
www.bluegrasscatalunya.com

BROADBENT SELECTIONS
http://www.broadbent-wines.com

CADET WINES LTD
http://www.cadetwines.com

CAPE CLASSICS
http://www.capeclassics.com

CELLARS INTERNATIONAL
http://www.germanwine.net

CHAPIN CELLARS
See Billington Imports/Chapin Cellars

CLASSICAL WINES
http://www.classicalwines.com

CLICQUOT, INC.
http://www.clicquotinc.com

COMMONWEALTH WINES & SPIRITS
http://www.commwine.com/
    index2.html

DALLA TERRA
http://www.dallaterra.com

DAVID BOWLER WINE
212-807-1680;
amanda@bowlerwine.com

DE MAISON SELECTIONS
http://www.demaisonselections.com

DIAGEO CHATEAU & ESTATE WINES
http://www.aboutwines.com

DISTINCT EXPRESSIONS, INC.
http://www.distinctexpressions.
  com

DOMAINE SELECT WINE ESTATES
http://www.domaineselect.com/
  home/Home1.html

DREYFUS, ASHBY & COMPANY
http://www.dreyfusashby.com

DUFORT & COMPANY
888-455-8466;
bgroper@dufortandcompany.com

EBER BROTHERS
WINE & LIQUOR
800-999-2903

EMPSON USA
703-684-0900

ENOTEC IMPORTS
http://www.enotec.net

EPIC WINES
http://www.epic-wines.com

EPICUREAN WINES
http://www.epicureanwines.com

EUROPEAN CELLARS DIRECT
http://www.europeancellars.com

EVATON INC.
http://www.evaton.net

F & F FINE WINES
INTERNATIONAL
http://www.fwiwines.net/
  main.htm

FREDERICK WILDMAN &
SONS, LTD.
http://www.frederickwildman.com

FRENCH PRESTIGE WINES, INC.
415 296-7798

FRUIT OF THE VINE
212-828-1500; hofw@nyc.rr.com

FRONTIER WINES
973-328-4500;
wineimport@optonline.net

GRAND CRU IMPORTS
http://www.grandcruimports.com/

GRAND VINTAGE
609-688-8488;
grandvintage@earthlink.net

THE GRATEFUL PALATE
888-472-5283;
info@gratefulpalate.com

HOUSE OF BURGUNDY
914-937-6330

HOUSE OF FINE WINES
212-828-1500;
hofw@nyc.rr.com

INTERNATIONAL GOURMET
http//:intlgourmet.com

JANDELL SELECTIONS
516-364-9889;
bsavitsky@jandell.com

JEROBOAM WINES
http://www.jeroboamwines.com

JOHN GIVEN WINES
http://www.jgwines.com

KERMIT LYNCH
510-524-1524; klwmjt@aol.com

KOBRAND CORPORATION
212-490-9300
jlisa@kobrand.com

LANGDON SHIVERICK IMPORTS
http://www.shiverick.com

LAUBER IMPORTS, LTD.
http://www.lauberimports.com

LORENZO SCARPONE
villaitaliawines.com

LOUIS/DRESSNER SELECTIONS
http://www.louisdressner.com

MARC DE GRAZIA SELECTIONS
http://marcdegrazia.com

MARIE BRIZARD
http://www.mariebrizardusa.com

MARTIN SCOTT WINES LTD.
Sheila Esposito; 516-327-0808;
sesposito@martinscottwines.net

MATT BROTHERS & CO, INC.
www.mattbrothers.com

METROPOLIS
212-581-2051; invinoveritas@cs.com

MICHAEL SKURNIK WINES, LTD.
http://www.skurnikwines.com

MIONETTO USA, INC.
http://www.mionettousa.com

MONSIEUR HENRI
http://www.monsieurhenri.com

MONSIEUR TOUTON
212-2550674;
guillaume@mtouton.com

OLD BRIDGE CELLARS
http://www.oldbridgecellars.com

NÉGOCIANTS USA
http://www.negociantsusa.com

NEW CASTLE IMPORTS
http://newcastleimports.com

OMNIWINES
http://www.omniwines.com

OPICI IMPORT COMPANY
http://www.opici.com

ORGANIC VINTAGES
http://organicvintages.com

PALM BAY IMPORTS
http://www.palmbayimports.com

PANEBIANCO
http://www.panebiancollc.com/uk/
    catalogue/trentino.asp

PARLIAMENT WINE COMPANY
http://parliamentwineco.com

PASTERNAK WINE IMPORTS
http://www.pasternakwine.com

PATERNO WINES INTERNATIONAL
http://www.paternowines.com

PEERLESS IMPORTERS INC.
http://www.peerimp.com

R.H. PHILLIPS-HOGUE
http://www.vincorusa.com

PINNACLE IMPORTS
205-945-6003

PLEASANT IMPORTERS, INC.
718-842-7201; pleasant-
    importers@verizon.net

POLANER SELECTIONS
http://www.polanerselections.com

PREMIER WINE AND SPIRITS
http://www.pwsny.com

PREMIUM PORT WINES INC
http://www.premiumport.com

RAVENSVALE IMPORTS
203-552-9275;
ravensvale@aol.com

RÉMY AMERIQUE
212-399-4200

ROBERT KATCHER SELECTIONS
202-832-9083

ROBERTO COHEN WINES
AND CHAMPAGNE
516-869-9170

ROSENTHAL WINE MERCHANT
http://www.madrose.com

ROYAL WINE CORPORATION
http://royalwines.com

SDG SELECTIONS
800-462-2100

SELECTED ESTATES OF EUROPE
http://www.selectedestates.com

SIGNATURE WINES INC.
503-730-7655

SOUTHCORP WINES/THE
AMERICAS
http://www.devils-lair.com/

SOUTHERN STARZ INC.
http://southernstarz.com

SOUTHERN WINE & SPIRITS
http://www.southernwine.com/

SPAIN WINE COLLECTION INC.
845-268-2622

SUPREME WINES
http://www.supremewines.net

SUSSEX WINE MERCHANTS
856-608-9644

T. EDWARD WINES LTD.
http://tedwardwines.com

TEMPRANILLO INC.
914-576-9190; vinos.antonio@att.net

TGIC
www.wineofakind.com

TRI-VIN
www.tri-vin.com

UNIQCO
256-534-6758; fio@ro.com

P. J. VALCKENBERG
http://www.valckenberg.com

VERDONI IMPORTS
http://www.verdoniimports.com

VIAS IMPORTS LTD.
http://www.viaswine.com

VIEUX VINS
http://www.rarewineco.com

VILLAGE WINES
212-866-4266;
anitavw@earthlink.net

VINAFERA
800-615-5170

VIN DIVINO
http://www.vindivino.com

VINEYARD BRANDS
http://www.vineyardbrands.com

VOS SELECTIONS
http://www.vosselections.com

WEYGANDT/METZLER
IMPORTING, LTD.
http://www.weygandtmetzler.com

WILLIAM GRANT
http://www.grantusa.com

WILSON DANIELS LTD.
www.wilsondaniels.com

WINEBOW
http://www.winebow.com

WINE SYMPHONY
212-226-8283;
andrewbell@bellwines.com

WINES FOR FOOD
http://winesforfood.com

WINES WE ARE IMPORTERS
888-680-8244

WINGARA WINE GROUP
http://www.wingara.com.au

WORLD WIDE WINES
646-322-4253;
info@wwwine.net

ONLINE SUPPLIERS

When it comes to ordering wines online, direct-to-consumer shipping laws differ from state to state, often making it difficult to obtain the wine you want. Most suppliers specify to which states they can legally ship, but the issue isn't always cut-and-dried; some may choose to ship to your state, while others will not. For this reason, you'll want to cast your net wide, starting with the suppliers listed here.

To stay up to date on federal and state direct-shipping legislation, two Web sites that should tell you all you need to know are Direct Wine Shipments (http://www.wineinstitute.org/shipwine) and Free the Grapes (http://www.freethegrapes.org).

67 WINE
http://67wine.com

B-21
www.b-21.com

BEVMO.COM
www.bevmo.com

BROWN DERBY.COM
www.brownderby.com

K & L WINE MERCHANTS
www.klwines.com

MacARTHUR BEVERAGES
www.bassins.com

MORRELL
http://store.morrellwine.com

PREMIER CRU
www.premiercru.net

THE RARE WINE COMPANY
www.rarewineco.com

SAM'S WINES AND SPIRITS
www.samswine.com

SHERRY LEHMAN WINE & SPIRITS
www.sherry-lehmann.com

WINE.COM
www.wine.com

WINE ACCESS.COM
www.wineaccess.com

WINE EXCHANGE
www.winex.com

WINE LIBRARY.COM
http://winelibrary.com

WINE-SEARCHER.COM
www.wine-searcher.com

ZACHYS WINE ONLINE
www.zachys.com

COUNTRY AND REGION INDEX

If you're partial to wines from certain countries or specific growing regions (Bordeaux, for example), this index shows you where the wines recommended in this book come from. Don't be flummoxed by some of the regional breakdowns, which are often determined by law. For example, wines sourced from various appellations of California are designated merely as California, not Napa, Sonoma, or any other well-defined region. Likewise, the designation South Eastern Australia indicates not one of that country's states but transcends state boundaries, just as the French designation Southwestern France is not as geographically tidy as Bordeaux or the Rhône. Wines made from grapes sourced from different places are listed under the heading "no appellation specified."

Argentina

Mendoza
Altos Las Hormigas Malbec 99
Giaquinta Malbec 99
Mayol Bonarda 99
Morichetti Malbec 104
Navarro Correas Malbec 90

Tulum
Graffigna Malbec 93
Graffigna Pinot Grigio 139

Australia

New South Wales
HUNTER VALLEY
Cockfighter's Ghost Chardonnay 121
Heritage Road Merlot 39
Heritage Road Shiraz 68
McGuigan Brothers Merlot 38

South Australia
BAROSSA VALLEY
Charles Melton Nine Popes 36

CLARE VALLEY
Tim Adams Cabernet Sauvignon 21

COONAWARRA
Katnook Estate Merlot 43
Penley Estate Cabernet Sauvignon 23
Penley Estate Merlot 43

LANGHORNE CREEK
Bleasdale Cabernet Sauvignon 20
Bleasdale Shiraz 71
Bremerton Shiraz 74
Lake Breeze Bernoota 73

McLAREN VALE
Gatekeeper Shiraz 73
Rockbare Chardonnay 120
Shottesbrooke Shiraz 72

RENMARK
Argove's Pinot Noir 51

NO APPELLATION SPECIFIED
Australian Domaine Wines Petite Verdot 107
Hardy's Chardonnay 119

South Eastern Australia
Alice White Shiraz 68
McGuigan Brothers Shiraz 68
Marquis Philips Shiraz 71
Miranda Shiraz 68
Teal Lake Petit-Verdot 96
Teal Lake Shiraz 69

Tasmania
Piper's Brook Pinot Noir 53

Victoria
GOULBURN VALLEY
Plunkett Shiraz 71

GRAMPIANS
Best's Wines Cabernet Sauvignon 22

Savoie
Franck Peillot Mondeuse 105
Franck Peillot Roussette de Bugey
184
Jean-Paul Trocadero Blanc de
Blancs Brut 196
Pierre Boniface Vin de Savoie 173

Southwest France
Château Boucassé Madiran 112
Château La Caminade Cahors 98
Château Montus Madiran 113
Cosse Maisonneuve Cahors 98
Domaine de la Chanade Côtes du
Tarn 89
Domaine de la Chanade Loin de
L'Oeil 167
Domaine de Lagrezette Cahors 106
Domaine Mouréou Madiran 98
Elian Daros Côtes du Marmandais
104

Germany

Baden
Blankenhorn Spätburgunder 51
Hugelheim Gewürztraminer 135
Joachim Heger Pinot Gris Trocken
142
Von Franckenstein Gewürztraminer
Kabinett 135

Franken
Michael Frohlich Müller-Thurgau 171

Mittelrhein
Ratzenberger Riesling Spätlese
Trocken 149

Mosel
C. von Schubert Riesling 148
C. von Schubert Riesling
Spätlese 148
C. von Schubert Riesling Kabinett
148
Dr. F. Weins-Prüm Riesling Eiswein
214
Dr. F. Weins-Prüm Riesling
Halbtrocken 145
Dr. F. Weins-Prüm Riesling Kabinett
145
Dr. F. Weins-Prüm Riesling Spätlese
145
Dr. Loosen Riesling 145
Dr. M. Prüm Riesling 145

Egon Müller Riesling Kabinett
151
Franzen Elbling Dry 173
Freiherr von Schleinitz Riesling
Spätlese 151
Fritz Haag Riesling Auslese 215
J. J. Christoffel Erben Riesling
Auslese 150, 216
J. J. Christoffel Erben Riesling
Kabinett 150
J. J. Christoffel Erben Riesling
Spätlese 150
J. J. Prüm Rielsing Kabinett 153
J. J. Prüm Riesling Spätlese 153
Joh. Haart Riesling Kabinett 146
Max Ferdinand Richter Riesling 144
Max Ferdinand Richter Riesling
Kabinett 144
Max Ferdinand Richter Riesling
Spätlese 144
Monchhof Riesling 147
Monchhof Riesling Spätlese 147
Meulenhof Riesling Kabinett 147
Meulenhof Riesling Erdener
Treppchen Spätlese 147
Reinhold Haart Riesling Kabinett 150
Selbach-Oster Riesling Auslese 213
Willi Haag Riesling Spätlese 151
Willi Schaefer Riesling 148

Nahe
Dr. Ganz Blauer Portugieser Rosé
115
H. Donnhoff Riesling Auslese 215
H. Donnhoff Rielsing Kabinett 151
H. Donnhoff Riesling Spätlese 151
Kruger-Rumpf Riesling Spätlese 150
Schafer-Frohlich Riesling Spätlese
152
Schafer-Frohlich Riesling
Halbtrocken 152

Pfalz
Blankenhorn Gutedel Trocken 168
Dr. Bürklin-Wolf Riesling 153
Fitz-Ritter Chardonnay Spätlese
Trocken 122
Fitz-Ritter Gewürztraminer Spätlese
135
Fitz-Ritter Riesling Eiswein 214
Kurt Darting Muskateller Kabinett
177
Kurt Darting Riesling Kabinett 147
Kurt Darting Scheurebe Spätlese
183

Lebanon

Madeira

Mexico

New Zealand

Portugal

South Africa

Spain

WINES FOR FOOD

Wondering what sort of wine will go well with your porterhouse steak tonight? Or even a take-out pizza? This handy wines-for-food index provides some answers (though by no means the only ones) to the question wine lovers ask on many nights: "What am I drinking with this?" From the thousand-plus wines in this book, we offer our picks for everything from barbecue to blue cheese, pork loin to paella. If you can't find the exact wine we recommend in your local store, just ask your merchant for the next best thing—at least you'll be on the right track, and you might even make a great discovery.

Note: When the food categories in this index are as simple as chicken and steak, the assumption is that the dish will be fairly plain. If the dish is highly seasoned or sauced, refer to the categories that seem to be the best fit—Curries, say, or Sweet 'n' Saucy barbecue. In those cases, it's the preparation that guides the match, not the main ingredient.

ANTIPASTI
Monte del Fra Bardolino "Sorelle" 94
Nino Franco Processo de
    Vadobbiandene "Rustico" 198
Scarbolo Tocai Fruilano 172

BARBECUE, DRY RUBBED
Girard Petite Sirah 109
Tim Adams Cabernet Sauvignon 21

BARBECUE, SWEET 'N' SAUCY
Coturri Zinfandel "Workingman's"
    83
Marquis Philips Shiraz 71
McGuigan Brothers Shiraz
    "Black Label" 68
Summers Charbono "Villa Andriana"
    108

BARBECUE, VINEGARY
Coturri Albarello 105
Franz Künstler Riesling "Estate"
    149

CASSEROLES/GRATINS
François d'Allaines Montigny 125
Monte Schiavo Lacrima 191
Schloss Gobelsburg Riesling 146
Villa Russiz Superiore Sauvignon
    Blanc 163

CAVIAR
Pierre Gimonnet & Fils Blanc de
    Blancs Brut 1er Cru 192
Laurent-Perrier Champagne
    "Cuvée Ultra-Brut" 191

THE VERSATILE ROAST CHICKEN
If there's a food more wine-friendly than roast chicken, we don't know of it. Like wine, its styles run from one pleasant extreme to the other. From fatty, crusty rotisserie chickens to slow-baked, delicate poussins (baby chickens) to fiery, Peruvian *pollo a la Brasa*, there's a bird for every taste—and practically every wine in this book. Use your intuition. Pair rich reds like Syrah and Grenache with saucy, bold-flavored chicken; serve crisp, herby whites with delicate, herbed hens; try rich, smooth wines—white or red—with Mom's oven-stuffers. When in doubt, use the *tabula rasa* of a plain, baked chicken to show off the subtleties of any mature, complex, or otherwise precious bottling you have tucked away. You'll never be disappointed.

CHICKEN, FRIED
Marietta Cellars Old Vine Red 98
Ramsay Pinot Noir 52

CHICKEN, SAUTÉED/BRAISED/POACHED
Capay Valley Viognier 178
Domaine du Clos du Fief Juliénas 29
Philippe Raimbault Sancerre "Apud Sariacum" 162
Selaks Sauvignon Blanc 159

CHEESE, BLUE
Benson Ferry Zinfandel 82
Domaine de la Sansonnière Anjou "La Lune" 133
Dow's Vintage Port 207
Edmeades Zinfandel "Alden Ranch" 84
Karlsmühle Riesling Eiswein "Lorenzhofer" 214
Olivares Dulce Monastrell 213
Quinta do Noval Tawny Port 20 Year 206
Zenato Ripassa di Valpolicella 109

CHEESE, HARD/SEMI-FIRM
Domaine d'Andézon Côtes du Rhône 70
Emilio Lustau Oloroso Sherry Gran Reserva "Emperatriz Eugenia" 205
Forman Cabernet Sauvignon 23
Justino Madeira "Rainwater" 208
Pesquera Ribera del Duero "Condado de Haza" 80

CHEESE, SOFT/SEMI-SOFT
Château Bastian Bordeaux 18
Domaine de Fontenille Côtes du Luberon 33
Palacios Remondo Rioja "Placet" 180
Zenato Lugana "San Benedetto" 176

CHEESE, SMOKED
Château de Trignon Côtes du Rhône 33
Domaine Mouréou Madiran 98
Emilio Lustau Fino Sherry "Jarana" 204

CHILI
Aveleda Estremadura 92
Ochoa Garnacha Rosado 114

COLD CUTS AND SANDWICHES
Château Aiguilloux Corbières 90
Didier Fornerol Côte de Nuits-Villages 54
Domaine de Cassagnoles Côtes de Gascogne 167
Domaine du Roncée Chinon 13
Graffigna Malbec "Seleccion Especial" 93
Max Ferdinand Richter Riesling "Estate" 144

CURRIES
Château de la Guimonière Rosé d'Anjou 114
J. J. Martin Beaujolais-Villages 28
J. J. Prüm Riesling Kabinett "Gracher Himmelreich" 153
Liegenfeld Ottonella 174

DESSERTS, CAKE/PASTRY
Concadoro Vin Santo "Cerasi" 211
Madeira Malmsey 15 Year 208
Quinta do Infantado Tawny Port 10 Year 206
Union des Producteurs Clairette de Die "Lou Lou" 210

DESSERTS, CHOCOLATE
Emilo Lustau Pedro Ximénez "San Emilio" 204
Mas Amiel Maury "Vintage" 209

DESSERTS, FRUIT-BASED
Rivetti Moscato D'Asti "La Spinetta" 212
Saucelito Canyon Late Harvest Zinfandel 213
Von Buhl Riesling Auslese GoldKap 215

DUCK
Château Boucassé Madiran "Vielles Vignes" 112
Coturri Syrah "Workingman's" 71
Domaine le Sang des Cailloux Vacqueyras 36
Marietta Cellars Petite Sirah 107
Robert Weil Riesling Spatlëse "Kiedriche Grafenberg" 152

THREE GO–WITH–EVERYTHING REDS

For the sake of convenience, here are three reds that, from our experience, just seem to please everybody and go with almost any food you put on the table—no mean feat! They hail from France, Italy, and California, and all of them are reasonably priced, costing less than $20. **Château Aiguilloux Corbières** ($7–9) from the Languedoc region, is described on page 90; **La Tunella Cabernet Franc** ($12–14) on page 13; and **Au Bon Climat Pinot Noir** ($18–20) on page 54. If you're a foodie who has yet to buy wine by the case, now is your time to start.

FOIE GRAS
Château Pierre Bise Côteaux du
    Layon Beaulieu "L'Anclaie" 213
Château Raymond-Lafon Sauternes
    212
Domaine Albert Mann
    Gewürztraminer Gran Cru
    "Furstentum" 137
(See also Pâtés and Terrines)

FONDUE
Domaine Les Grands Bois Côtes du
    Rhône "Cuvée Gabrielle" 33
Pierre Boniface Roussette 173

GAME
Allegrini Amarone della Valpolicella
    11
Domaine Bressy-Masson Rasteau
    "Cuvée Paul Émile" 33
Domaine Henri Gouges Nuits-St.
    Georges 1er Cru 59
Domaine l'Aiguelière Montpeyroux
    71
Fattoria Le Pupille Morellino di
    Scansano 64
Muri-Gries Lagrein Dunkel 104
Phillippe Alliet Chinon
    "Vielles Vignes" 16

GAME BIRDS
Bollinger Champagne Brut 193
Domaine François Lamarche
    Vosne-Romanée 1er Cru 59
François Buffet Volnay 1er Cru 58
Tommaso Bussola Valpolicella
    Classico "bg" 103

GRILLS, FISH
Au Bon Climat Pinot Noir 54
As Laxas Albariño 181
Keller Riesling Kabinett
    "Florsheim-Dalsheim" 149

Saucelito Canyon Zinfandel 84
Zerbrina Sangiovese di Romagna
    "Ceregio" 63

GRILLS, MEAT
Cantina Zaccagnini Montepulciano
    d'Abruzzo 102
Château Mourgues du Gres Costières
    de Nimes Rosé 115
Emilio Lustau Palo Cortado Sherry
    Almacenista "Vides 1/50" 205
Pagor Cabernet Sauvignon 19
Palacios Remondo Rioja
    "La Vendimmia" 79

GRILLS, VEGETABLE
Clos Roche Blanche Touraine Rouge
    "Cabernet" 14
Koura Bay Sauvignon Blanc 162
Ransom Pinot Noir 53
Villa Giada Barbera d'Asti "Suri Russ" 95

HAM
Domaine Bart Marsannay Rosé 115
Domaine Trimbach Gewürztraminer
    135
Emilio Lustau Amontillado Sherry
    "Escuadrilla" 204
François Raquillet Mercurey
    "Vielles Vignes" 55
Franz Küntsler Riesling Kabinett
    "Hockheimer Reichestal" 149

HOT 'N' SPICY FOODS
Château de Montfort Vouvray 129
Isabelle et Bruno Perraud Beaujolais-
    Villages 28
Josef Leitz Riesling 146
Kurt Darting Riesling Kabinett
    "Dürkheimer Michelsberg" 147
Kurt Darting Scheurbe Spätlese
    "Dürkheimer Spielberg" 183
Moss Bridge Zinfandel 82

LAMB
Brancott Vineyards Sauvignon
Blanc "Reserve" 161
Bodegas Castano Yecla Rosé 115
Château Gruaud Larose St. Julien
24
Château Haut-Brion Graves 26
Domaine Mosse Anjou Rouge 20
Giuseppe Mascarello Barolo
"Montprivato" 49
Phillipe-Lorraine Cabernet
Sauvignon 21
Yannick Amirault Bourgueil
"Quartiers" 16

**LASAGNE AND OTHER
BAKED PASTAS**
Baroncini Morellino di Scansano
"Le Mandorlae" 62
Ca' dei Frati Lugana "I Frati" 179
D'Angelo Aglianico del Vulture 104
Foradori Teroldego Rotaliano 106
Giuseppe Mascarello Barbera
d'Alba "Santo Stefano di Perno"
110
Pecchenino Dolcetto di Dogliani
"San Luigi" 106

**LIVER, SWEETBREADS, AND
OTHER ORGAN MEATS**
Dr. Bürklin-Wolf Riesling "Gaisbohl"
153
Gary Farrell Pinot Noir
"Russian River" 56
Tommaso Bussola Valpolicella
Classico "bg" 103

MUSHROOM DISHES
Castello di Bossi Chianti Classico
66
Domaine Duffour Vin de Pays des
Côtes de Gascognes 168
La Vis Lagrein "I Baldazzini" 101
Marziano & Enrico Abbona
Nebbiolo d'Alba 47
Schiopetto Tocai Friulano 187

**OMELETS, QUICHES,
AND FRITTATAS**
Domaine du Pavillon Côte
Roannaise 28
Domaine Jean Touzot Mâcon-
Villages 119
Domaine Saint Vincent Saumur-
Champigny 13

PAELLA AND JAMBALAYA
Bodegas Pucho Bierzo 96
Pagor Tempranillo 80
Vilarico-Cambados Albariño 168

**PASTA WITH BUTTER OR
WHITE SAUCE**
Château Lamothe de Haux
Bordeaux Blanc 157
Gini Soave Classico 179
San Rustico Valpolicella 103
Tiefenbrunner Müller-Thurgau 187

PASTA WITH RED SAUCE
Badia a Coltibuono Chianti
"Cetamura" 62
Gallino Barbera d'Alba 91
Le Terrazze Rosso Conero 105

PÂTÉS AND TERRINES
Domaine Olivier Dumaine Crozes-
Hermitage 72
Hervé Sigaut Chambolle-Musigny
51
Kir-Yianni Akakies Rosé 115
(See also Foie Gras)

PIZZA BIANCO (TOMATOLESS)
Marco Felluga Pinot Grigio 141
Sessa Lacryma Christi Bianco Del
Vesuvio 176

PIZZA, PLAIN OR VEGETARIAN
Mionetto Cabernet Franc 13
Renzo Masi Chianti Rufina 62
Villa Diana Sangiovese 62

PIZZA WITH MEAT
Cataldo Nero d'Avola 89
Gianni Gagliardo Dolcetto d'Alba
105
Miranda Shiraz "Firefly" 68
Warwick Valley Winery Black Dirt
Red 94

PORK
Avide Cerasuolo di Vittoria 97
Karthäuserhof Riesling Spätlese
"Eitelsbacher
Karthäuserhofberg" 150
Kruger-Rumpf Riesling Spätlese
"Munsterer Dautenpflanzer" 150
Ramblilla Tempranillo 78
Seghesio Zinfandel "Sonoma" 83
Vinicola del Priorat Onix Priorat 32

THREE GO–WITH–EVERYTHING WHITES

A Vouvray from France, a Sauvignon Blanc from New Zealand, and a Riesling from an ancient German vineyard are so versatile with food that it's almost impossible to go wrong with these three. Each also rates sidebar treatment in this book. Check out **Château de Montfort Vouvray** ($8–10) on page 129, **Vavasour Sauvignon Blanc "Dashwood"** ($12–14), on page 158, and **C. von Schubert Riesling "Maximin Grünhauser"** ($16–18), on page 148. Then settle into a comfy chair and start browsing your cookbooks.

**POT ROASTS/
SLOW-COOKED MEATS**
Domaine de la Pousse d'Or Volnay
    1er Cru "Clos des 60 Ouvrées"
    60
La Vis Lagrein "I Baldazzini" 101
Valdinara Nebbiolo d'Alba 47

RIBS, SHORT
Clos l'Église Pomerol 45
Domaine Jean-Luc Joillot
    Pommard "Les Noizons" 58
Domaine Louis Cheze St. Joseph
    "Cuvée Ro-Ree" 72
Viñedos Agapito Rico Carchelo 92

SALADS, CHICKEN/SEAFOOD
Domaine Peyrilhe Picpoul de Pinet
    175
Joachim Flick Pinot Gris 139
Martin Codax Albariño 168
Monchhof Riesling "Estate" 147
Rockbare Chardonnay 120

SALADS, GREEN
Château de Chesnaie Muscadet
    169
Jacky et Fabrice Gasnier Chinon
    "Les Graves" 13
William Cole Sauvignon Blanc 156

SAUSAGE
Bisci Verdicchio Matelica 170
Cosse Maisonneuve Cahors
    "Les Laquets" 98
Giuseppe Mascarello Dolcetto 103
Henry of Pelham Baco Noir 93
Lucien Albrecht Gewürztraminer
    136
Villa Fanelli Primitivo 89

SHELLFISH, COOKED
Domaine Bourillon-Dorléans
    Vouvray Sec Vielles Vignes
    "La Coulée d'Argent" 131
Didier Fornerol Aligoté 180
Foreau Vouvray Brut 199
Stoneleigh Sauvignon Blanc 158

SHELLFISH, RAW
Domaine de la Pepière Muscadet
    "Clos des Briordas" 174
François Chidaine Montlouis Brut
    196
Guy Larmandier Champagne
    Côtes des Blancs Brut 1er Cru
    192
Stephan Reuter Riesling Dry 145
Txomin Etxariz Txakolina de
    Gataria 181

STEAK, FATTY
Château Lynch Bages Pauillac 25
Morichetti Malbec 104
Penley Estate Cabernet
    Sauvignon 23
Valdipiatti Vino Nobile di
    Montepulciano 65

STEAK, LEAN
Barnwood Cabernet Sauvignon
    20
Château Grand Pey Lescours St.
    Émilion Grand Cru 42
Château Pichon Longueville
    Comtesse de Lalande Pauillac
    26
Ercole Velenosi Rosso Piceno
    "Roggio del Filare" 112

STEWS, FISH
Les Lauzeraies Tavel Rosé 114
Moncaro Esino Bianco "Terrazzo" 169

STEWS, RED MEAT
Caves Alianca Alentejo "Alabastroc 92
Domaine de la Terre Rouge Zinfandel "Easton" 82
Domaine Tempier Bandol "Classique" 112
Guilhem Durand Syrah "Vielles Vignes" 69

STIR FRY
C. Von Schubert Riesling "Maximin Grünhauser" 148
Joachim Flick Riesling 145

SUSHI AND CEVICHE
H. Donnhoff Riesling Kabinett "Norheimer Delchen" 151
Johannes Ohlig Riesling Trocken "Nikki" 144
Vissoux Beaujolais "La Chermette" 28

TAPAS
Antonio Barbadillo Amontillado Sherry "Medium Dry" 203
Avinyo Cava Brut 197
Coop. del Masroig Montsant 97
Tilenus Bierzo Roble 103

TARTS AND PIES, SAVORY
Château des Tours Brouilly 30
Domaine Schofitt Chasselas "Vielles Vignes" 185
Goisot Sauvignon de St. Bris 159
Martin Zahn Gewürztraminer 135

TURKEY
Blockheadia Winery Zinfandel "Blockheadia Ringnosii" 82
Bouchaine Pinot Noir "Buchli Station" 52

VEAL
Caparzo Rosso di Montalcino 64
Domaine Le Mas de Collines Gigandas 34
Domaine Schoffitt Gewürztraminer "Harth" 136
Gunderloch Riesling Kabinett "Jean-Baptiste" 148

VEGETABLES, LEAF AND GREEN
Blanco Nieva Sauvignon Blanc 157
Frederic Mabileau St. Nicolas de Bourgueil 13
Marotti Campi Verdicchio dei Castelli di Jesi "Luzano" 175
Villa Maria Sauvignon Blanc 159

VEGETABLES, ROOT
Arnaldo-Caprai Montefalco Rosso 109
Domaine Saint Antonin Faugères 96
Kurt Darting Muskateller Kabinett "Durkheimer Steinberg" 177
Ratzenberger Riesling Spätlese Trocken "Steeger St. Jost" 149

VEGETABLES, WINTER AND SQUASHES
Coturri Merlot "Workingman's" 41
Domaine Chaume-Arnaud Vinosobres 34
François Chidaine Montlouis "Clos Habert" 131

INDEX

F

Fanti
  Brunello, 65
  Rosso di Montalcino, 65
Farnese
  Montepulciano d'Abruzzo, 89
  Sangiovese Daunia, 62
Fattoria Le Pupille Morellino di
  Scansano, 64
Fausto Gemme Gavi di Gavi, 179
Fefinanes Albariño, 183
Felline Primitivo di Manduria, 99
Fernand Girard Sancerre, 162
Fernand & Laurent Pillot Chassagne
  Montrachet, 126
Ferngrove
  Chardonnay, 120
  Shiraz, 69
Ferrando Cavanese Rosso, 47
Fess Parker Frontier Red, 69
Fife Vineyards Max Cuvée, 74
fining, 44, 70, 220
Fino-style Sherry, 203
  Emilio Lustau, 204
Fitz-Ritter
  Chardonnay, 122
  Riesling Eiswein, 214
Foradori Teroldego Rotaliano, 106
Foreau
  Vouvray Brut, 199
  Vouvray Demi-Sec, 133
  Vouvray Sec, 133
Forman Cabernet Sauvignon, 23
fortified wines, 201, 202–209
  Port, 206–208
  Sherry, 203–205
  vin doux naturel, 209
Foxen Chardonnay, 125
Framingham Sauvignon Blanc, 160
Francesco Boschis Dolcetto di
  Dogliani, 100
Franck Peillot
  Mondeuse, 105
  Roussette de Bugey, 184
François Buffet Volnay 1st Cru,
  58–59
François Cazin
  Cheverny, 157
  Cour-Cheverny, 183
François Chidaine Montlouis, 131,
  196
François d'Allaines Montagny, 125
François Montand Blanc de Blancs,
  195

François Pinon Vouvray, 130
François Raquillet Mercurey, 55
Frank and Jean-François Bailly
  Sancerre, 161
Franzen Elbling Dry, 173
Franz Künstler Riesling Kabinett, 149
Franz Prager Riesling Federspiel, 151
Frascati Casale Marchese, 169
Frederic Mabileau St. Nicolas de
  Bourgueil, 13–14
Freiherr von Schleinitz Riesling
  Spätlese, 151
Fritz Haag Riesling Auslese, 215
Fritz Salomon Grüner Veltliner, 177
frizzante, 195, 220
Fuedo Monaci
  Primitivo, 92
  Salice Salentino, 90

G

Gallino Barbera d'Alba, 91
Galuccio Gristina Chardonnay, 119
Gamay, 27–30
garrigue, 96
Gary Farrell
  Bien Nacido Chardonnay, 127
  Chardonnay, 126
  Pinot Noir, 56
Gatekeeper Shiraz, 73
Gatinois Champagne, 194
Gavi
  Broglia, 181
  Fausto Gemme, 179
  Stefano Massone, 175
  La Zerba, 181
Geografico Vernaccia di San
  Gimignano, 172
Georg Breuer Riesling, 150–151
Gerard Mugneret Bourgogne, 55–56
German wine labels, 144
Gewürztraminer, 134–137
La Ghersa Monferrato, 100
Gianni Gagliardo Dolcetto d'Alba, 105
Giaquinta Malbec, 99
Gini Soave Classico, 179
Giovanni Struzziero Greco di Tufo,
  178
Girard
  Petite Sirah, 109–110
  Sauvignon Blanc, 161
Giuseppe Mascarello
  Barbera d'Alba, 110–111
  Barolo, 49
  Dolcetto, 103
  Freisa, 101

BIBLIOGRAPHY

Brook, Stephen. *The Wines of Germany.* London: Mitchell Beasley (Octopus Publishing Group), 2003

Clarke, Oz. *Oz Clarke's New Encyclopedia of Wine.* New York: Harcourt, 2003

Diel, Armin, and Joel Payne. *German Wine Guide.* New York: Abbeville Press, 1999

Gluckstern, Willie. *The Wine Avenger.* New York: Simon & Schuster, 1998

Hazan, Victor. *Italian Wine.* New York: Alfred A. Knopf, 1982

Herbst, Ron and Sharon Tyler Herbst. *The New Wine Lover's Companion.* New York: Barron's, 2003

Jefford, Andrew. *Wine Tastes, Wine Styles.* London: Ryland, Peters & Small, 2000

Johnnes, Daniel. *Daniel Johnnes's Top 200 Wines.* New York: Penguin Books, 1996

Johnson, Hugh. *Hugh Johnson's Pocket Wine Book 2004.* London: Mitchell Beasley (Octopus Publishing Group), 2003

Johnson, Hugh. *The World Atlas of Wine (4th Edition).* New York: Simon & Schuster, 1994

Joseph, Robert. *French Wines.* New York: DK Publishing, 1999

MacNeil, Karen. *The Wine Bible.* New York: Workman Publishing Company, Inc., 2001

Morrell, Peter. *I'm In the Wine Store, Now What?* New York: Silver Lining Books, 2002

Osborne, Lawrence. *The Accidental Connoisseur.* New York: North Point Press, 2004

Robinson, Janis. *The Oxford Companion to Wine.* New York: Oxford University Press, 1999

Root, Waverly. *The Food of France.* New York: Vintage Books, 1992

Root, Waverly. *The Food of Italy.* New York: Vintage Books, 1992

Wilson, James. *Terroir.* San Francisco: The Wine Appreciation Guild, 1999

Zraly, Kevin: *Windows on the World Complete Wine Course.* New York: Sterling Publishing Company, Inc., 2000

http://www.erobertparker.com

http://www.wineloverspage.com/site

http://www.wine-searcher.com

http://www.winespectator.com

ACKNOWLEDGMENTS

The Ultimate Wine Lover's Guide was born of the work of many. Foremost thanks are due to the intrepid staff (past and present) of Nancy's Wines for Food: Ben Crumlich (Nancy's first manager and designer), Peter, Wayne, Max, Johnny, Stephen, Mark, Tom, Ben F., Steve O., Steve K., Kent, Katy, Jeannine, Louise, Leah, Beth, and the entire crew. Thanks, too, to Willie Gluckstern, who filled the store with wine, taught us how to taste, and wrote the manifesto. And special thanks to Jason Spingarn (aka "The Tongue"), whose infallible palate and integrity have made him a New York wine–world legend.

Kudos to Peter Morrell and Fern Grant, who helped us onto the road, and to Emanuel Berk, Nate Archibald, and Stewart Randall, who smoothed the way. The authors would also like to thank those who were always ready with answers, not to mention labels: Shirley Alpert, Abigail Boyd, Tim Buzinski, François Chirumburro, Sheila Esposito, John Evans, Jane Delaney, Sheila Doherty, Teresa Giavannoni, Sarah Kalliney, Stephanie Kane, Kerry Madigan, Barbara Mansell, Kim Mata, Amanda Miller, Simone Olen, Jillian Rein, Judy Sandland, Antonio Santofimia, Shawna Shandrick, Lisa Skurnik, and Cecile Vielle.

We are also grateful for the practical advice offered by Marsha and Sam Horowitz, John Brusco, and, not least, Tom Foster, whose limitless passion for wine is nothing less than inspirational.

PHOTO CREDITS